The Art Nouveau Book in Britain

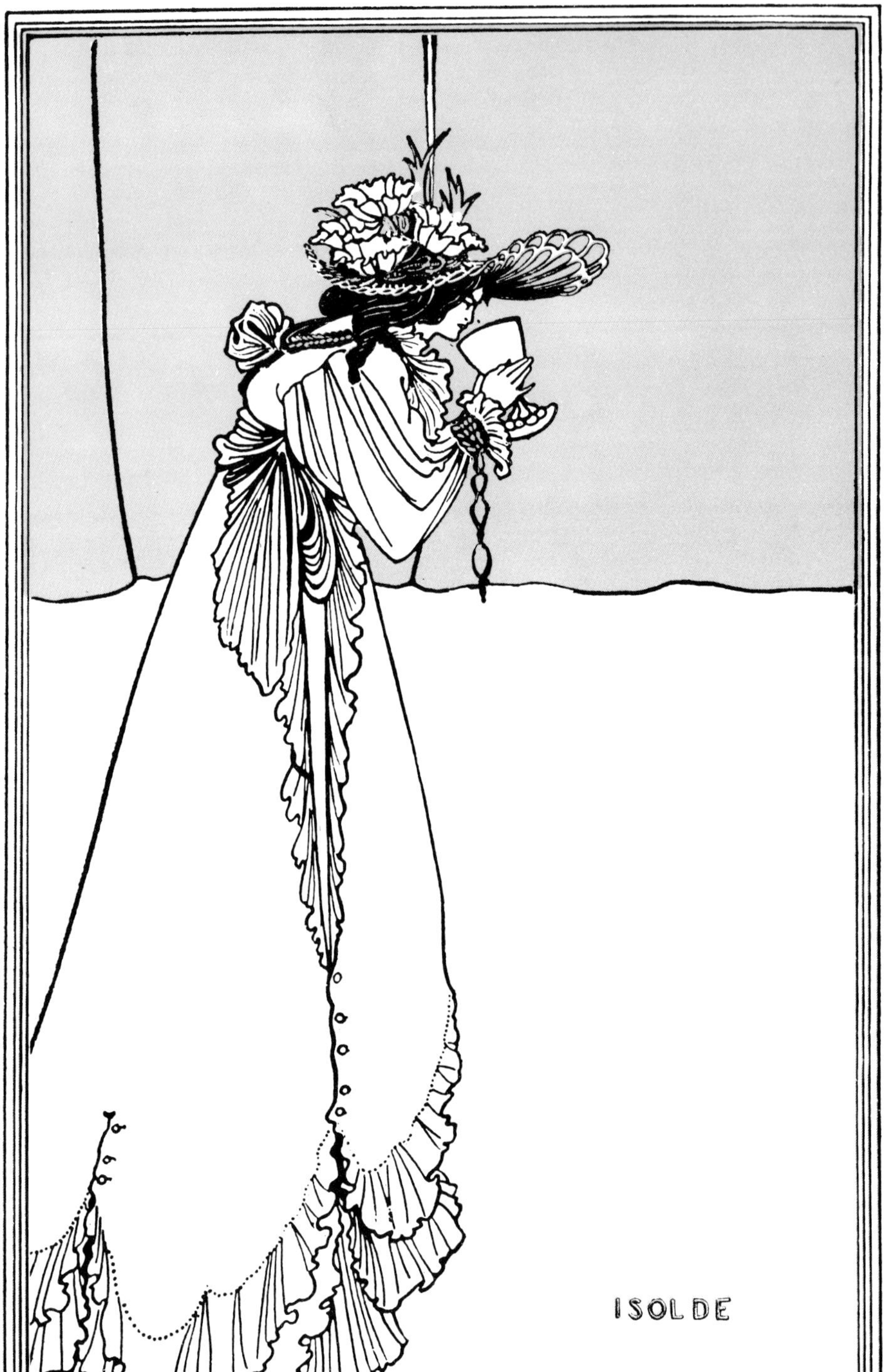

Frontispiece: Aubrey Beardsley's 'Isolde' (1895)

The Art Nouveau Book in Britain

John Russell Taylor

Paul Harris Publishing
Edinburgh

First edition published 1966 by Methuen & Co Ltd, London
This edition first published in Great Britain 1979 by Paul Harris Publishing, 25 London Street, Edinburgh 3

ISBN 090 4505 85 5

Printed and bound in Great Britain by the Scolar Press, Ilkley, West Yorkshire.

Contents

Many people have helped me during the years I have been studying art nouveau. The most long-suffering has been Mr Roderick Gradidge, to whom I owe a particular debt of gratitude for a constant interchange of ideas and for his readiness to tolerate and where possible moderate my more unreasonable prejudices. Others I would like to thank for talking or writing to me and answering my importunate questions with unfailing speed and courtesy are Mr and Mrs Anthony Ballantine, Mr Brian Brooke, Mr Timothy d'Arch Smith, Mr Douglas A. Foulis, Professor Thomas Howarth, Mr Gordon F. Huntley, Mrs Katharine Cameron Kay, Mr Ruari McLean, Professor Nikolaus Pevsner, Sir John Rothenstein, Mrs Mary Newbery Sturrock, Mr Frank Tashlin, Miss Merle Taylor, Mr Alan Wheeler.

Grateful acknowledgement is made to the William Morris Gallery, Walthamstow, for illustrations on pages 29 and 35.

Illustrations

Preface

This book, which first appeared in 1966, is inevitably in certain respects a period piece, and it has been felt best to leave it as such, without major revisions. Now I would, of course, write it quite differently, not so much because I have had any radical changes of opinion, but because the world has changed so much meanwhile. The revival of interest in art nouveau which was being predicted in 1966 has long since come about. Artists whose careers were shrouded in mystery have now been extensively documented; books which were neglected on the shilling trays of booksellers (it was a time when such things still existed) have now ascended to dizzying heights; an artist like Jessie M. King, virtually unknown in 1966, has become one of the most expensive and sought-after of her period, and was in 1977 the occasion of a Sotheby's sale seriously described as "one of the most important studio sales of the century".

All of these things make a difference. But curiously enough I do not feel that they invalidate this book's facts and its attitude towards them. No one, anyway, has yet tried to cover the same ground in one book, and I hope therefore that, if only as a simple introduction to a complicated field of study, it does remain of use.

A few misprints and small errors have been silently corrected, and the chance has been taken to improve the quality of many of the illustrations. I should perhaps mention, in addition, that several examples of the "lost" Mackmurdo chair on page 34 have since turned up: two are in the William Morris Gallery, Walthamstow, and one in the Victoria and Albert Museum. And I was too hasty in suggesting (page 61) that Blackmore's comments on Bradley's illustrations to his *Fringilla* had not survived: in 1896 he wrote in typical combative style to one of his publishers "To me it appears impossible that any *sane* person can help laughing at the baby scrawls called 'illustrations'; and as for the borderings, there is more grace and fancy in the marginal paper of my water-closet."

John Russell Taylor
July 1979

Introduction

First, a couple of problems.

To begin with, the little matter of what standards should be applied to art nouveau. A few years ago art nouveau was not known by name to most averagely cultivated people, though its products, in so far as they were not lumped under the general head of 'Victoriana', were likely to be regarded as hideous even by those trained by Mr Betjeman to regard the Victorian as amusing, nostalgic and even, sometimes, beautiful. During 1964, however, the term 'art nouveau' gained such general currency that it even made a headline in the *Daily Mirror*; everybody knows that art nouveau is culturally O.K., even if they are not quite sure what it is. The result of this, naturally, is that people are for or against art nouveau without, often, having much notion of what the proper grounds for judgment should be. In 1964 a commercial gallery held what was said, no doubt correctly, to be the first comprehensive retrospective exhibition of art nouveau in London. It was a mixed bag, with Burne-Joneses and Brangwyns and Carrières rubbing shoulders with Mucha and Frances MacNair and Jessie M. King, but the major part of the exhibition consisted of mass-produced metal-work and miscellaneous cheap (in their day, that is) objets d'art. The radio Critics, and quite a number of other people who might have been expected to know better, proceeded to discuss this conglomeration of more or less pleasing oddments as though they were fully representative of art nouveau, as though one could in fact reach a sensible conclusion about art nouveau from them – which is much as though one were to discuss the aesthetic qualities of Victorian art on the basis of a selection of antimacassars, papier-maché trays and cases of stuffed birds, with a couple of minor Pre-Raphaelites thrown in for good measure. Needless to say, those who said, very properly, that many of the things shown in the exhibition were hideous, coarse and quite lacking in aesthetic value often believed that in saying this they were dismissing art nouveau entire, and were as often assured by others that they were only being square for not appreciating what tremendous fun it all was – that art nouveau was amusing and/or significant just because it was all so nasty. Well, undeniably this 'fun' side of art nouveau does exist, and even some of the good, tough, individual art nouveau – that which is not merely a commercial dilution or exaggeration – may be a little difficult to adjust to. But the sort of art nouveau which is interesting only because it is fun, and fun only because it is bad, can well look after itself; its present prices in bric-à-brac shops demonstrate that. Therefore everything I write about in this book I have chosen because it seems to me good, or interesting, or at least importantly symptomatic of something or other. It is above all the elegance of art nouveau rather than its extravagance that interests me, and as this seems to be an aspect which has hitherto received much less attention that it merits, I have attempted in this book to make some small move towards repairing the omission. The second problem is intimately connected with the first: it is the relationship between British (which is to say English and Scottish) art nouveau and the various Continental styles. It is tempting to be categorical and say simply that if the British variety is art nouveau then Continental isn't, or vice versa. This of course is silly: at the time they all inclined to think they belonged to the same movement, or at least to the same wave of reaction; they exhibited together; they influenced one another in varying degrees. But the fact remains that there are radical differences. To generalise wildly but not altogether unfairly, British art nouveau is a reaction in favour of spareness and simplicity after the intricacy of what has gone before, while Continental art nouveau is a further elaboration. Continental art nouveau is largely based on the much-discussed sinuous line, the bulging, bulbous, wilfully irregular shape, while British art nouveau is more a matter of flat or slightly curved surfaces, straight or slightly curved lines. British art nouveau is concerned primarily with the arrangement of empty spaces, Continental with their filling. ❧ Perhaps the reason for this may be sought in the primacy of British architecture during this period. In Britain architecture was the art nouveau par excellence, and it was British architecture which took the lead in Europe for the first time in five hundred years. All through the history of British art nouveau, from the Century Guild to the end of the Glasgow school, architects play a prominent part, directly or indirectly: in our particular field, book design, for example, a number of influential figures, such as Herbert P. Horne and C. R. Ashbee, were also practising architects, while many of the rest – Mackmurdo, Beardsley, Talwin Morris, Anning Bell – worked at some period of their career in an architect's office. Hence architectural principles of construction, a certain tendency to build designs on a firm framework, however freely the details might be organized within it, are apparent in British art nouveau right from the start, and remain constant. Continental art nouveau, on the other hand, tends until its very latest phase to throw away the framework, to avoid as far as possible any hint of 'construction', regarding it, as N. F. Simpson would say, as 'breaking faith with chaos'. In Continental art nouveau – the architecture of Gaudi, the decorations of Horta, the glass of Lalique, the graphics of Mucha – the sinuous lines run free, and their manipulators glory in their freedom from any restricting given notion of overall design, any norm from which to deviate. Continental art nouveau is a reaction against form itself, while British art nouveau is a search for essential form by the stripping-away of inessentials. In this, of course, the end of the nineteenth century was merely repeating the pattern in the arts established on many previous occasions. At the end of the middle ages, British gothic developed into the severe and rectilinear Perpendicular style, at the same time that on the Continent Decorated gothic became progressively wilder and freer, more florid and more neglectful of what exactly the decoration was supposed to be decorating. In the eighteenth century the more extravagant flights of Rococo on the Continent are matched in Britain by a revival of strict Palladianism. The British tendency has always been to draw back from decadence by a return to geometrical severity and simplicity, and if Continental art nouveau, like Continental late-gothic styles or Rococo, can be seen as in certain respects a decadent style, British art nouveau is more a reformation, carried out at times, especially on its Arts and Crafts fringes, with almost crusading fervour.

Well, then. This book is mainly about British art nouveau. First, because in the field of book design, illustration and production British work is far more abundant, lively, beautiful, long-lived and generally influential than Continental, which proved to be on the whole a brief fad taking the form as often as not of a few decorative extravagances grafted on to an otherwise perfectly conventional book. Second, because up to now British art nouveau has been considered almost entirely from the angle of Continental art nouveau (since most books on art nouveau have been written by Continental or American writers) and what did not fit conveniently into this view of the period has been brushed over or disregarded. And lastly because British art nouveau, because of the characteristics suggested above, is the variety which is most evidently a beginning, least easily mistaken for a dead end. A work of art can be properly judged only by what it is, not by what it does or does not lead to. However, where a student's intentions are historical as well as critical, what his subject leads on to must have a certain interest for him, even if it is not central to his judgment of the thing itself.

The Beginnings

When a new style emerges in the arts and is generally accepted as revolutionary, the first task of the art historian is usually to explain that nothing comes from nothing, and to work out exactly where it did come from: what processes of refinement, elaboration, continuation and reaction shaped it, what influences worked in what way to produce it, and so on. Such considerations, of course, are always to a certain extent suppositious, and the conclusions drawn from them can be proved wrong (an artist cannot have been influenced by someone or something he was demonstrably unacquainted with, for instance) but never really *proved* right, since even the artist himself cannot be a reliable authority on what actually did influence him: at best he can tell us what might have. Relevance, anyway, is bound to be to some extent in the eye of the beholder: what he judges relevant depends, after all, very much on the way he sees the original phenomenon. So, since I see the essential characteristics of British art nouveau as being somewhat different from those postulated by most writers for art nouveau at large, it is likely that I shall find different things relevant to its evolution, or the same thing relevant in different ways. The most favoured starting-point in considerations of the development of art nouveau is the illustrative work of William Blake (1757-1827). And it is as good a place as any to begin, since his relevance to certain

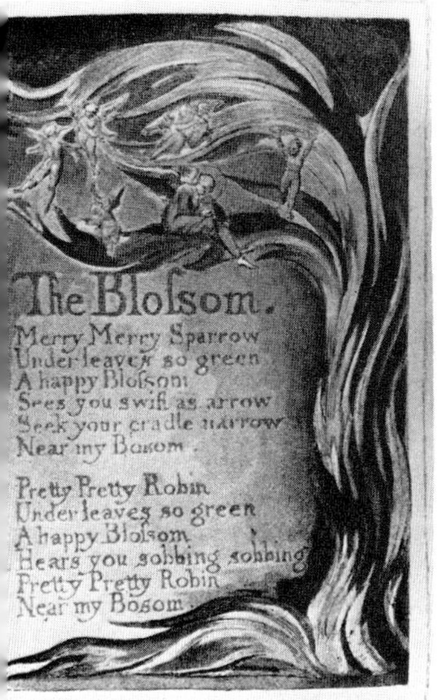

William Blake: 'The Blossom', a page from *Songs of Innocence* (1789) approx. 8½ × 5 in.

strains of art nouveau, and the origin in his art of certain recurrent images and motifs, is undeniable. But here we come up against the first stumbling-block. The most prominent of the art nouveau characteristics to be found in Blake is that sinuous, scintillating, whiplash line which is so typical of Continental art nouveau until the latest, 'decadent' phase, but is hardly a leading motif in British art nouveau at all. As early as *Songs of Innocence* (1789), the first of the books produced by Blake in his own highly individual process of illumination, the free, flowing, sinuous forms are pervasive: strange, sub-aqueous plant-forms twist and struggle around the lines of text or frame little scenes; flowers flicker into flame, or flames curl like tendrils up and around the page. It is a fluid universe, in which everything flows into everything else. Needless to say, even Blake's practice is not 'original' in the sense that it sprang unaided from his own head; he believed that he drew from visions, like the boy who thought and then drew lines round his thinks, but scholars have come in to supply analogues and influences, from the Decorated gothic traceries among which he spent much of his apprenticeship as an engraver to the rococo pattern-books familiar in his youth. However, this need not concern us: the point is that in Blake these elements were fused together in a new way, that what was latent in these previous styles became the leading characteristic of Blake's early style and remained a constant factor right through to his latest works, such as the watercolour drawings in illustration of Dante's *Inferno*. It was the earliest works, particularly the *Songs of Innocence* and *Songs of Experience* (1794) with which they were later combined, which first attracted attention to Blake again, after a period of neglect, in the mid nineteenth century. In the 1850s Alexander Gilchrist, a professional biographer, became interested in Blake as a subject for a biography – largely, according to the *Dictionary of National Biography*, because his enthusiasm was fired by seeing Blake's engravings for *The Book of Job* – and had written about two-thirds of it at the time of his death in 1861. The rest was completed by his widow, with the friendly aid of Dante Gabriel and his brother William Michael Rossetti, for publication in 1863; a further revised edition appeared in 1880. Thus Dante Gabriel Rossetti (1828-82) became involved in the study of Blake – the supplementary chapter dealing critically with Blake's art is entirely his work – and the stage was set for the reintegration of Blake into the British tradition of design. ❦ It is unfortunate that in his writing on Blake's graphic work Rossetti deals almost exclusively with his colour sense, his 'most original and prismatic system of colour' which 'must be viewed as being, more decidedly than the system of any other painter, the forerunner of a style of execution now characterizing a whole new section of the English school . . .'[1] There is little about Blake's forms; though Rossetti does describe Blake's 'fair tongues and threads of liquid flame' in *The Song of Los* (1795) and attributes to Blake 'a kind of Shakespearian sympathy with all forms of life and growth'[2], the nearest he comes to a direct account of the use to which Blake puts natural shapes and forms is in his suggestion that in Blake's designs 'we are somehow shown, in figurative yet not wholly unreal shapes and lines, the mingling of organic substances, the gradual development and perpetual transfusion of life'.[3] ❦ Rossetti's interest in Blake dates back at least as far as 1847, when he was already acquainted with the *Songs of Innocence* and acquired from Samuel Palmer's brother the volume of autograph poems, notes and drawings by Blake now known as the Rossetti Manuscript. At first it seems to have been primarily a literary interest, and one of his principal contributions to Gilchrist's *Life* was editing the text of a selection of Blake's poems. Even in 1880, when his interest in Blake was rekindled by Mrs Gilchrist's request that he should revise his contributions to the *Life* for a new edition, his main reaction was to say that 'Shakespeare, Shelley and Blake are the three greatest names – intrinsically – in English poetry'.[4] It is natural, however, that he should have been interested too in the ensemble of Blake's work, since as a painter-poet himself he was in a favourable position to appreciate the problems of an earlier artist bent on combining, indeed fusing, the two functions. And it is notable that he came to write enthusiastically about Blake's use of colour in the illuminated books just at the time (the early 1860s) when his own pictorial style was veering away from the paler, more attenuated idiom of his properly Pre-Raphaelite work towards the richer, more full-bodied style of his later paintings. No doubt his changing outlook had something to do with his vocal appreciation of Blake's colour, but it also seems possible that his intensive study of Blake's graphic work at this period may have had some effect in making his treatment of form more fluid, rounded and sensuous, as well as persuading him to use such Blakean motifs as the human frieze in *How Sir Galahad, Sir Bors and Sir Percival Were Fed with the Sancgreal; But Sir Percival's Sister Died By the Way* (1864). Whereas his Pre-Raphaelite style has a certain spikiness and rigidity, with every shape sharply defined and differentiated, his later work has precisely the new feeling of 'the mingling of organic substances, the gradual development and perpetual transfusion of life'. In this sense at least there are strong elements of latent or proto-art nouveau in Rossetti's later and these days less regarded pictorial style. There are others too. Not only in the playing, widely remarked upon, with what we now regard as art-nouveau motifs in his early paintings – lilies, props with sinuously irregular patterns and so on, two of the most striking of which, in the *Annunciation* and the *Childhood of the Virgin Mary*, are precisely the details Yeats, perhaps significantly, hit on for comment in his essay 'Symbolism in Painting' of 1897[5] – but in his whole attitude to the management of pictorial space. Nicolette Gray has noted in her illuminating book *Rossetti, Dante and Ourselves* that it is a constant, almost obsessive, characteristic of

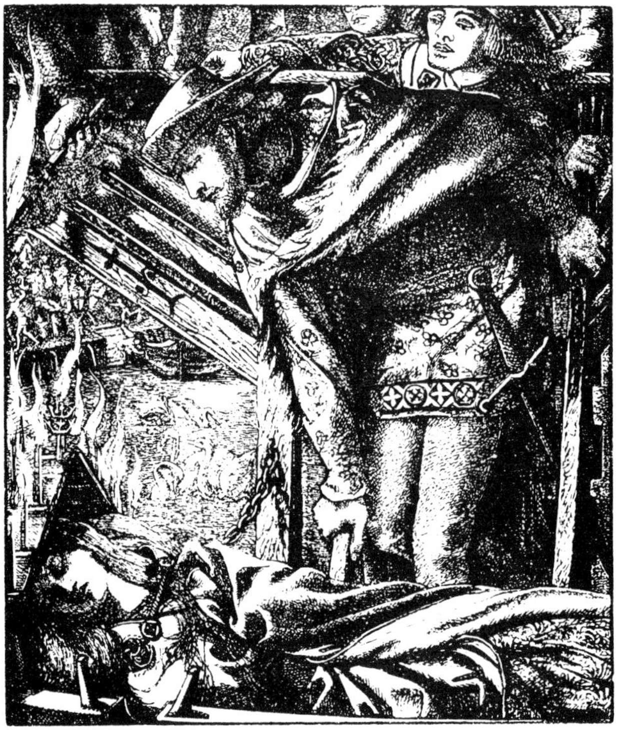

Dante Gabriel Rossetti: Illustration for 'The Lady of Shalott', from the Moxon Illustrated Tennyson (1857)

Rossetti's early work (and it remains true even in his later, more expansive phase) that 'with very few exceptions the setting to the figures is an enclosed space, in many cases so confined that there is no room for them to stand upright. In the majority of designs the setting is a small room, in others the space is enclosed by a curtain, a high hedge, dense foliage, or an architectural arrangement of walls or steps. The effect is a sense of airlessness . . .' Is not this equally true of most high art nouveau design: the airlessness, the claustrophobic elaboration and confinement of the space represented, the delight in involved patterning within this artificially limited but often quite intricately articulated field of vision?

Certainly it can be found again and again in Continental art nouveau – in the paintings of Fernand Khnopff and Jan Toorop, in the detailing of Gaudi's architecture or the decorative glass of Lalique and Gallé – and it can to some extent be found in British art nouveau: in the illustrations of Laurence Housman and the earlier work of Charles Ricketts. But in general it seems to be something which British art had got out of its system before art nouveau proper had really developed: much of British art nouveau, from its earliest manifestations, can best be regarded as a reaction against all this – the later work of Rossetti, the elaborately patterned paintings of Burne-Jones or the tapestries and stained glass of Morris and Co. – in favour of spareness, elegance and simplicity. Mention of Burne-Jones leads us on to a possible different and hitherto little regarded line of influence deriving ultimately from Blake. It was part of Rossetti's proseletysing zeal to bring his enthusiasms to the attention of his younger friends and admirers. One such was Edward Burne-Jones (1833-98), who was introduced by Rossetti to Blake's work in his twenties and towards the end of his life grumbled to Sebastian Evans that the introduction had not come even earlier.[6] Curiously enough, what had most effect on Burne-Jones was not the tense involutions of Blake's flowing line or the sumptuousness of his colouring, but the strange, boneless, disembodied character of most of Blake's human figures, especially the limply draped female figures. For in Blake there is this odd contrast between the darting, writhing flame-plants and the graceful, languid, uninvolved figures which live among them. Blake is capable of dynamic figures as well, but what seems to have drawn Burne-Jones to him was his more tranquil, frieze-like figure compositions, in which the coiled spring is for the time being relaxed (it is recorded that when Burne-Jones told Sebastian Evans he wished he had been shown Blake's vision of Behemoth in his teens, Evans

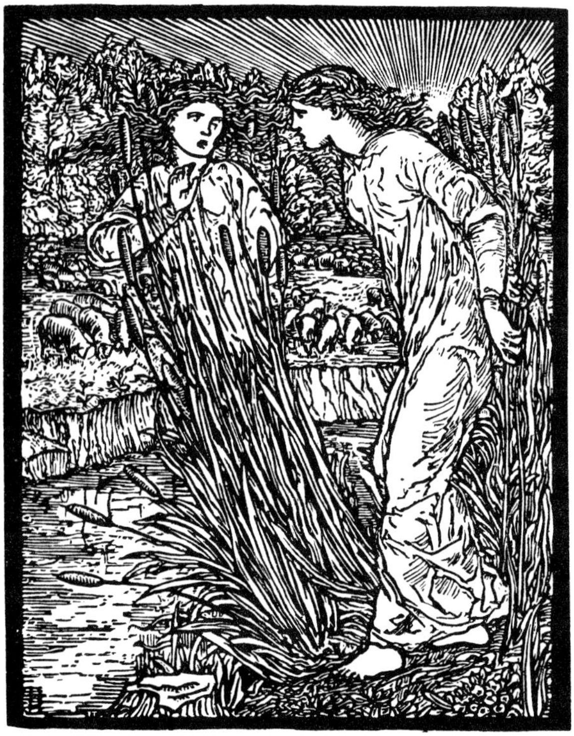

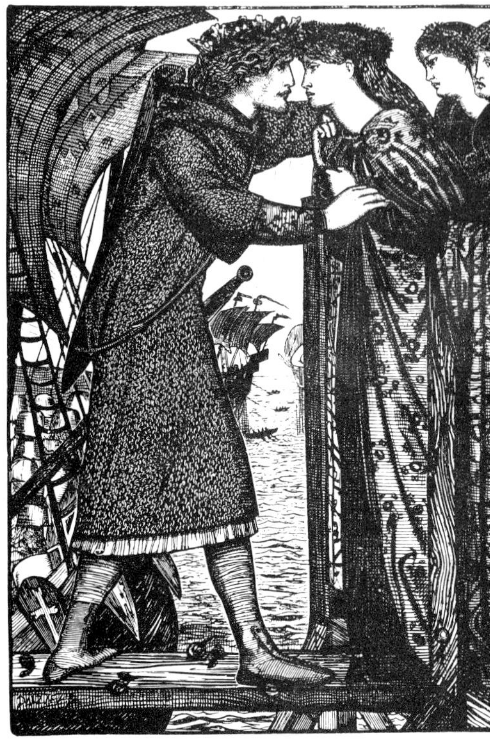

Edward Burne-Jones: 'Syrinx and Psyche', for a projected edition of *The Earthly Paradise*: engraved by William Morris, 1866

Edward Burne-Jones: 'Sigurd' from *Good Words* (1862). Compare the very different rendering given to this design by the Dalziel Brothers and to 'Syrinx and Psyche' by Morris

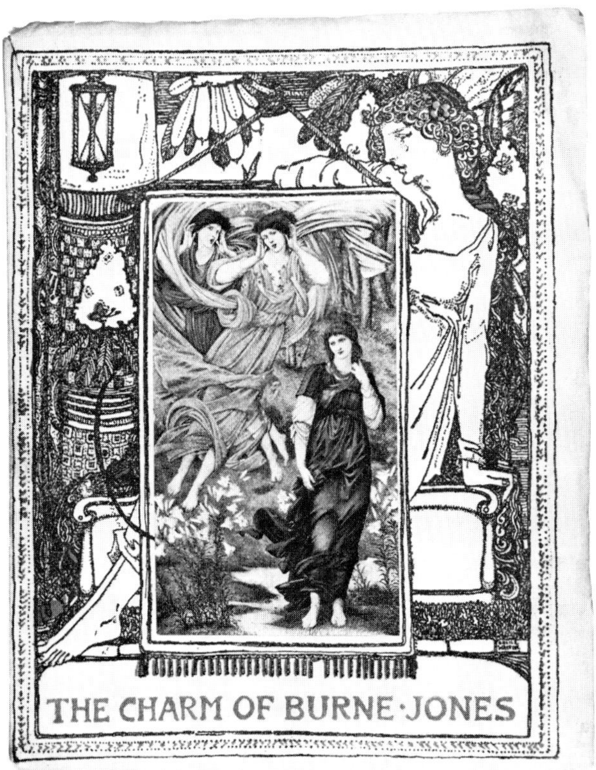

'Sponsa de Libano' by Edward Burne-Jones. Incorporated into the Beardsleyesque cover design by Cecile Walton for S. L. Bensusan's booklet on the artist (Jack, 1911) 6 × $5\frac{5}{8}$ in.

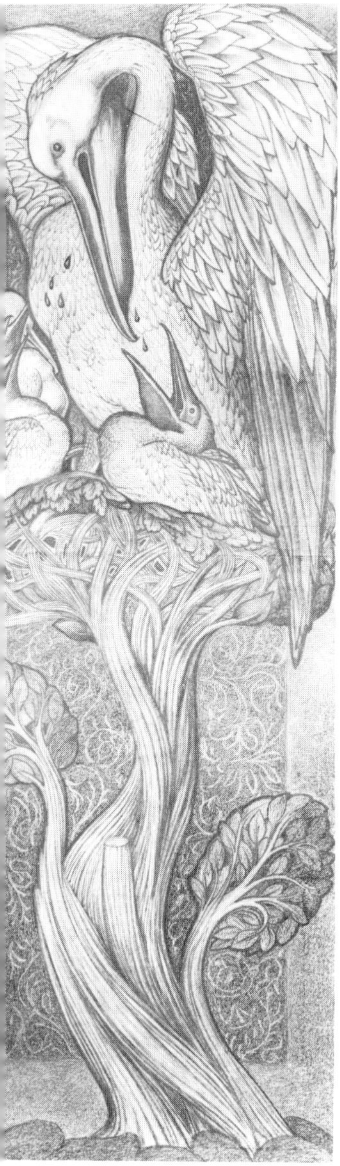

'The Pelican'. Design for stained glass by Edward Burne-Jones (*c* 1880)

replied 'My dear, you would have been carried off in convulsions'[7]). The direct influence of the smooth, easy, almost suave side of Blake's art on Burne-Jones can be seen in a number of confrontations between works of the two artists, and it is this side of Blake which through Burne-Jones and combined with other influences, of which more in a moment, contributed most to British art nouveau: the inert, purely conventional filling up of space in Burne-Jones's designs, particularly the most widely disseminated of them, the tapestries and stained glass, was dropped or reacted against, as was the similar tendency in Rossetti's later work, but the pale, weightless, insubstantial figures with which Burne-Jones, in the wake of Blake, peopled his elaborate settings survived as a potent, if unacknowledged, influence right through British art nouveau.

Next in the train of sources and influences come two curiously intertwined, the Japanese and the Dutch. Interest in Japanese art began in Britain in the early 1860s. The first shop in Western Europe to stock Japanese porcelain and prints was opened in the Rue de Rivoli in 1862, where it was eagerly patronized by artists, among them Whistler. Whistler brought some blue-and-white china and Japanese prints back to London, and rapidly inspired a number of his friends and acquaintances, prominent among them Rossetti, with an avid interest in them; Rossetti and others then began buying Japanese wares from the oriental warehouse of Farmer and Rogers, which was managed by Lasenby Liberty, later founder of the famous and, in the history of art nouveau, inescapable Liberty's store in Regent Street. As early as 1863 one can find John Leighton lecturing on Japanese art at the Royal Institution and even such a conservative critic as Francis Turner Palgrave, compiler of *The Golden Treasury*, recommending in the *Saturday Review*[8] the study of Japanese art for its pleasing irregularity and elegant simplicity, since 'the pomps of Louis Quatorze and the vanities of Louis Quinze . . . are happily out of date; whilst Italian and Gothic decorations are, at present, practically confined to a few wealthy experimentalists'.[9] The most immediate result of this was a vogue for blue-and-white china – not only Japanese, but Dutch delft wares as well; anything, in fact, provided it was blue-and-white. More to our purpose, though, are the longer-term effects of the conventions of Japanese figurative art on painting and illustration. These were partly direct, from the study of original Japanese prints and paintings, but more tellingly they were indirect, through the paintings of James McNeill Whistler (1834-1903) and his designs for the Peacock Room (1876-77) in the London house of the art patron Frederick Richard Leyland. (Leyland's taste, incidentally, was a remarkable amalgam of various trends of the time: he collected Rossettis, Botticellis and blue-and-white china, had his house designed by Norman Shaw in a characteristic 'Queen Anne' style, and his tomb by Burne-Jones in what can only be called art-nouveau Celtic.) Whistler not only developed in his Peacock Room a whole repertoire of decorative motifs – and a way of placing them uncompromisingly in empty spaces – which were assiduously seized upon and developed by later artists, most evidently Beardsley in his *Salome* designs, but in his paintings he moved on rapidly from aping Japanese models and cluttering his canvases with Japanese props to a deeper understanding of the aesthetic of Japanese art, so that his best paintings of the later 1860s and 1870s are distinguished by boldly asymmetrical compositions, extremely elegant, simplified silhouettes, and above all the rendering of pictorial space as a collection of flat planes superimposed on one another. Admittedly in his work this convention is put to the service of an Impressionist approach to scenery and atmosphere, but all the same his paintings provide a formula which could be used and developed and modified even by artists

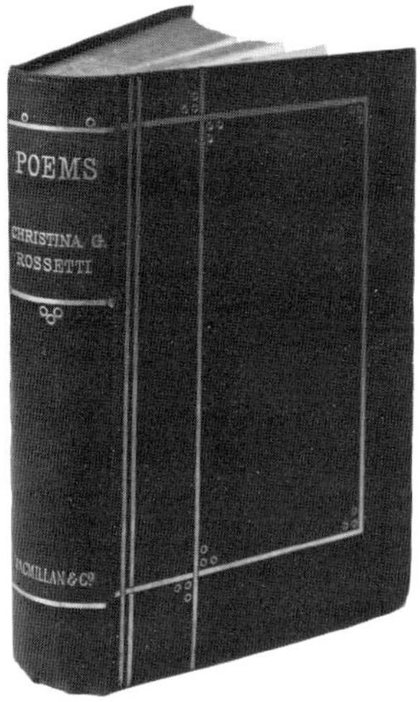

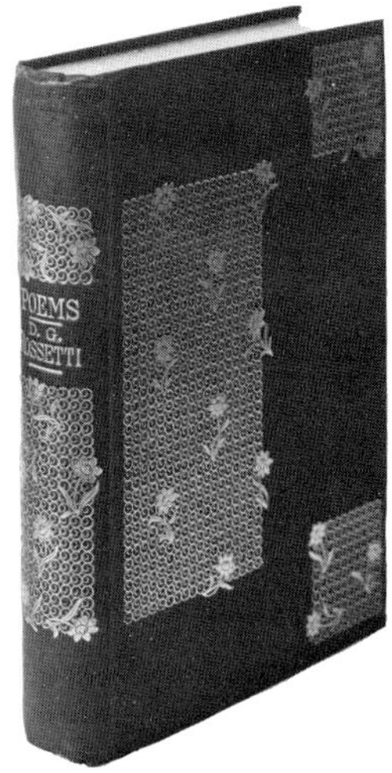

Bindings by Dante Gabriel Rossetti for the *Poems* of Christina Rossetti (first used 1861) $7\frac{1}{8} \times 4\frac{5}{8}$ in. and his own *Poems* (1881) $7\frac{7}{8} \times 5$ in.

who were quite out of sympathy with Impressionism and its aims. In the 1860s the Japanese influence touched all sorts of unlikely people: Rossetti in his designs for book-bindings, Burne-Jones in some surprisingly uncluttered decorations. But, as mentioned, it nearly always went hand in hand with a less noticed but in the long run equally telling influence, the Dutch. A combination of blue-and-white Japanese china and blue-and-white Dutch seems natural enough, but other obvious instances, like Leyland's Norman Shaw house with Whistler/Japanese decor or Murray Marks's Oxford Street shop with a Queen Anne-Dutch shop-front by Norman Shaw designed to display Marks's blue-and-white Japanese porcelain wares, seem to us decidedly odd, and it is curious to discover that Norman Shaw's early associate William Eden Nesfield, who designed the two earliest examples of the 'Queen Anne' style made famous by Shaw, lodges in Regent's Park (1864) and Kew Gardens (1866), was also noted as one of the earliest enthusiasts for Japanese art in Britain, and one of the first to use Japanese motifs in his interiors. Evidently there must be some connection which was clear at the time, but has somehow become obscured for us. I believe that the reason Japanese art and eighteenth-century Dutch architecture had such an appeal to the same people at the same time resides in the fact that they both have qualities characteristic of British, though not of Continental, art nouveau from the first, and therefore chimed very well with the prevailing mood: for the fussiness and over-elaboration of much art and architecture of the time they substituted simplicity, directness and clear, uncluttered lines, with areas of elaborate decoration set off by plain, flat surfaces. Moreover, they both tend to be composed asymmetrically, favour exaggeratedly high, narrow shapes, and formal definition by straight or very slightly curved lines, which to tastes already sated with the maddening symmetry of Victorian wall-papers and fabrics (even Morris fabrics and wallpapers, while representing a stage in the reaction to mid-Victorian tastes, were generally heavily patterned and overallish in effect and often, though not always, as symmetrical as their predecessors), the irrepressible curves and bulges of Victorian furniture, and the claustrophobically elaborate, significance-packed compositions of most mid-Victorian painting, must have come as a tonic indeed. ❧ There are of course other influences to be borne in mind. Greek motifs were often mingled and confused with Japanese. The principles of a number of mid-Victorian industrial designers like Owen Jones and Christopher Dresser, busy rationalizing and conventionalizing designs derived from plant-forms – for educational purposes as much as anything – threw up some extraordinary shapes which later, less high-principled designers took up and exploited for their decorative values alone. The architectural drawing, which was enjoying its golden age in the last quarter of the nineteenth century, and particularly the perspectiveless elevation, also contributed to the technique of illustrators and designers – it is noteworthy how many of them worked at some period of their career in architects' offices. New interest in Egyptian art and in the illustrations of early printed books all helped to upset strictly scientific notions of perspective and the organization of pictorial space. Even the Celtic began to intrude; Celtic motifs featured in Owen Jones's *Grammar of Ornament* as far back as 1856, but they were not widely used until later, in the 1890s, and then one has to be on one's guard, as references to 'Celtic' influence in the work of designers around this time[10] more usually refer to a vague and largely fictitious literary vision of the Celtic twilight than to any use of actual Celtic motifs. But it is time to look at the first real fusion of these various disparate ideas and influences into something recognisably art nouveau: the work of the Century Guild. ❧ The Century Guild was a group founded

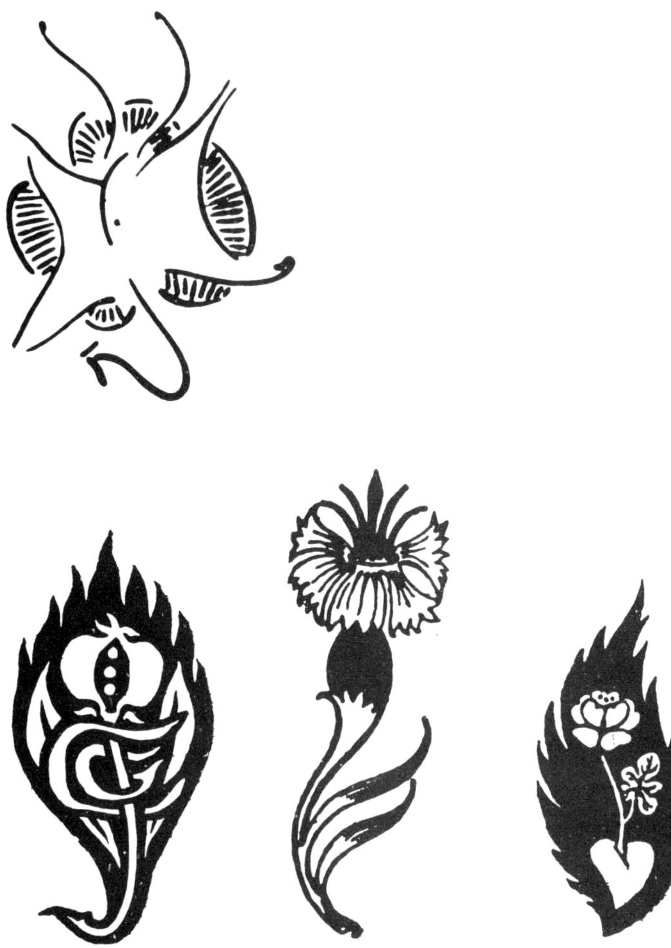

A Shape of the period:

(i) James McNeill Whistler's Butterfly Signature

(ii) Arthur Heygate Mackmurdo's device for the Century Guild

(iii) C. R. Ashbee's device for the Guild of Handicraft

(iv) Charles Ricketts' device for *The Ballad of Reading Gaol* (Smithers, 1898)

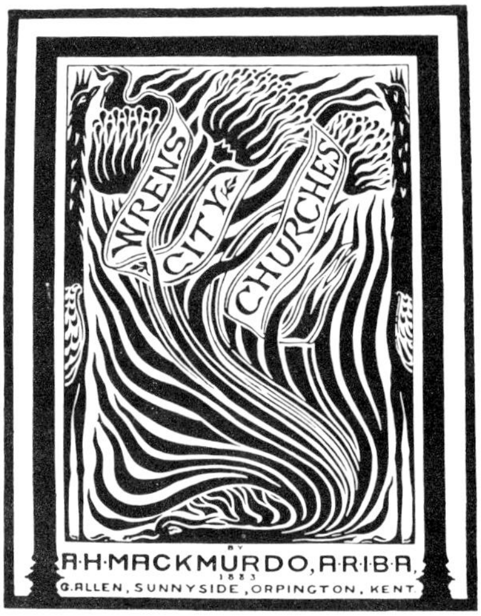

Arthur Heygate Mackmurdo: title page to *Wren's City Churches* (1883) large-paper version: $11\frac{1}{2} \times 8\frac{3}{4}$ in.

in 1882 by Arthur Heygate Mackmurdo (1851 - 1942) as a workshop, on somewhat Morrisian lines, 'to render all branches of art the sphere no longer of the tradesmen but of the artist'. It, or rather its members, worked in all sorts of media: painting, woodwork, metalwork, glass, ceramics, restoration and even on occasion building; they also published a magazine to put over their ideas, *The Hobby Horse*. Mackmurdo himself was an important figure, both for what he actually did and for the influence he wielded and the people he knew. After leaving Oxford he went into the architect J. Brooks's office, and soon became friendly with Norman Shaw and with Philip Webb, designer of Morris's Red House. He knew Whistler and Wilde, and many painters, poets, architects and critics of the 1880s and 1890s (Alan M. Fern[11] even suggests that Whistler's butterfly signature may have had a formative influence on Mackmurdo's 1884 monogram for the Century Guild). He also designed what are generally recognised as the first pieces of full, conscious art nouveau: the chair of 1881 (now lost, but known from a photograph in *The Studio*) and the title-page to his book *Wren's City Churches* (1883). These, it will be noticed, both offer a strange collocation: the chair is a very stolid, conservative, almost Queen Anne construction, except for its back, which is evidently high art nouveau, all swirling, free curves

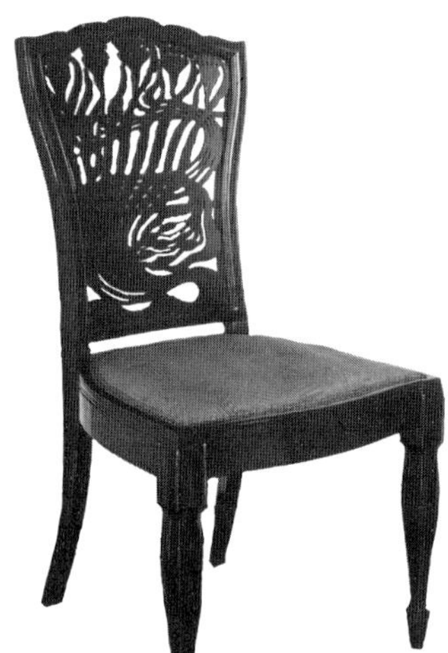

Arthur Heygate Mackmurdo: Chair (1881)

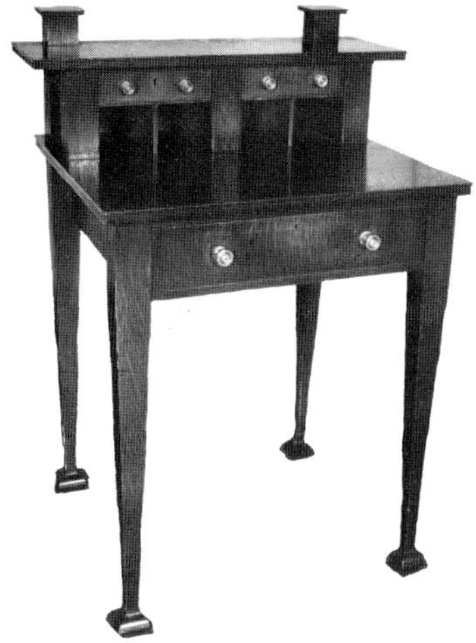

Arthur Heygate Mackmurdo:
Writing Desk (1886)

and flaming flowers *à la* Blake; similarly the title-page, though in terms of design it is all of a piece, sits very oddly, we cannot help thinking, on a book about Wren of all people. But a moment's consideration shows that this is precisely the point: both works have in them, juxtaposed as it were, the elements of British art nouveau; now all that is needed is to fuse them, the free asymmetrical curves from Blake and the spare elegance of the House of Orange style (for it was always, needless to say, the cool domestic Wren more than the baroque Wren which appealed most to art nouveau sensibilities). The mistake is to consider only so much of these two works as it suits one to consider; and admittedly the chair back without its chair and the title-page apart from its book fit very well somewhere in the line from Blake to Horta. But if one does this one misses the vital fact that British art nouveau did not develop at all along the lines the back and the title-page suggest: this is, if you like, high art nouveau already, but Mackmurdo himself very rapidly developed beyond it, and as early as 1886, when he designed the classically simple, elegant writing-desk now in the William Morris Gallery at Walthamstow, he had already reached what Continental writers classify as 'late art nouveau' – and that before the movement had even begun elsewhere! So the Century Guild and its artists – Mackmurdo himself, Heywood

Sumner, Herbert Horne, William de Morgan, Selwyn Image, Frederick Shields and others, all of whom considered book illustration and design within their province, even if it was the central interest of none – are already at the threshold of art nouveau proper. And with the Century Guild's magazine, *The Hobby Horse*, we have the first of the many magazines of the arts which flourished from the mid-1880s to the 1900s to put over the ideas and familiarize the styles of most of British art nouveau's chief exponents. But before we come to consider in more detail exactly what all this presaged in the specific field of book-design, it is necessary to go back a few years and examine the situation of the printed book in the years before the new movement was born.

The Victorian Book

The sudden tremendous flowering of British printing, illustration, binding and indeed all the arts of the book in the 1890s has tended until quite recently to blind us to much that was admirable in the previous half-century. Little by little, though, the pendulum of taste has swung back, and one by one the masters of the Victorian book have been reinstated. The first, both to appear and to reappear, has been the publisher William Pickering (1796-1854), whose finely printed, soberly but elegantly designed books began to come out in the early 1820s, had their admirers continuously thereafter and were significantly revalued by Sir Geoffrey Keynes as early as 1924. The keynote of Pickering's books, many of them printed by Charles Whittingham at the Chiswick Press, was directness, simplicity and readability. He published a number of superbly coloured art-books, notably those of Henry Shaw, but most of his books were, and were intended to be, popular: reasonably inexpensive editions of the classics (the best-known being the 'Aldine Poets' series), plain or simply decorated prayer-books, ordinary new works by authors of the day. What distinguished them was seldom spectacular art-work of any sort (though Mary Byfield's woodcut borders and decorations in such books as the *Queen Elizabeth's Prayer Book* of 1853 constitute a partial exception to this), but the general grace and seem-

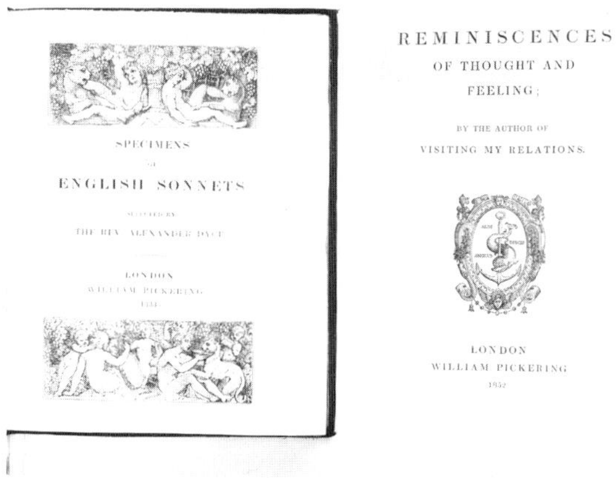

Two Pickering title-pages: *Thought and Feeling* $6\frac{7}{8} \times 4\frac{3}{8}$ in., *Sonnets* $5\frac{1}{2} \times 4\frac{1}{4}$ in.

liness of the overall design, the uncluttered title-pages, kept to a minimum of necessary information, and the careful choice of types (Caslon was favoured by Pickering from the early 1840s on for title-pages, and sometimes for whole books) with a weight and body which both made for easy legibility and helped to give the books colour and sparkle, with dense, strongly black blacks precisely placed in areas of pronouncedly white white. Pickering's taste was a highly personal one, and though the success of many of his books in terms of sales encouraged the appearance of various series from other publishers based on the 'Aldine Poets' model, few if any had the intelligence or the taste to emulate either the stylishness of the presentation or for that matter the scholarship of the contents. Even, it must be admitted, some of Pickering's own later productions fell below his own high standard, especially when not printed by Whittingham: the second edition of Bailey's *Festus* (1845), for example, is printed by Whittingham and a model of functional beauty in book-production; the third edition (1848), printed by R. Allen, Nottingham, has a fine title-page but nothing else to distinguish its cramped and gloomy text-pages from those of hundreds of other styleless books published at the time. Still, Pickering at his best had provided a model: Whittingham had perhaps learnt from him, but had anyway devised for the Chiswick Press a distinctive and distinguished printing style which continued, when required, to serve other publishers throughout the century (significantly, it was the Chiswick Press which printed the Century Guild's *Hobby Horse* in 1884), and one or two other publishers or peripatetic book designers continued to keep in mind Pickering's ideal of a book designed throughout and overall -- indeed, of a book designed at all rather than permitted, like Topsy, just to grow. ❧ One of these publisher-designers, and perhaps the most interesting in our particular perspective, was Joseph Cundall (1818-95). Cundall is one of the great figures behind the scenes in Victorian publishing: his career, even after the devoted research of Mr Ruari McLean in his *Victorian Book Design* and elsewhere, remains obscure, and many of the books one would incline on internal evidence to attribute to him offer no external evidence that he had a hand in them. However, even if we confine our attention to those books which were published by him or are signed with his monogram as designer, it is immediately clear that he is a key figure in the nascent awareness of the nineteenth century that illustrated books as well as simple pieces of plain printing should be designed as a whole. Apart from the series of splendid coloured books on antiquarian subjects he published for the artist-scholar Henry Shaw, Pickering rarely ventured into the field of illustration, as distinct from decoration, and so did not have to face the special problems involved in achieving a precise and proper relationship between illustration-content and text-content or illustration-style and the printing-style of the text. ❧ As a matter of fact, these were questions little considered even in the mid-Victorian heyday of the illustrated gift-book. The Dalziel Brothers, for example, the best known of mid-Victorian book devisers (i.e. editors, effectively publishers, generally printers, at their own Camden Press, and always engravers of illustrations) because of their association

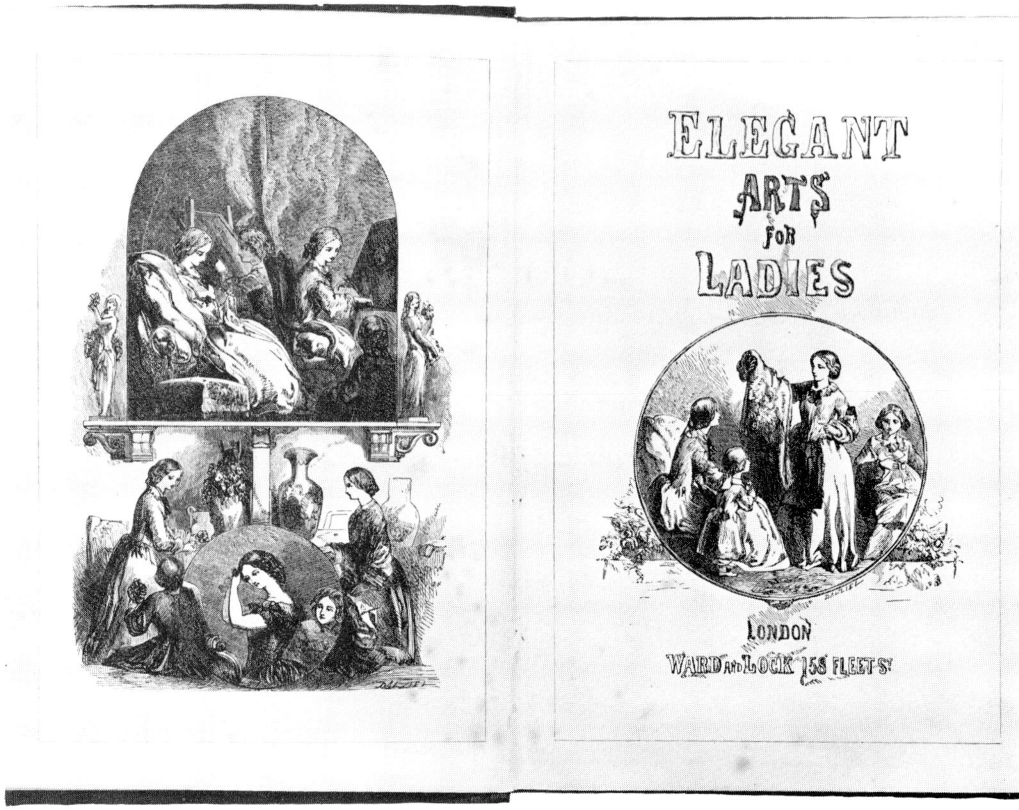

Dalziel Brothers:
Title-opening for
Elegant Arts for Ladies
(Ward and Lock, 1856) 7 × 4¾ in.

with most of the greatest illustrators of the 1860s, the so-called golden age of English illustration, were to all appearances very little concerned with the overall design of books: the typography of the volumes in which much of the finest illustrative work of Millais, Tenniel, Boyd Houghton, Pinwell, Arthur Hughes, Richard Doyle, Frederick Walker, J. W. North and others first appeared is undistinguished in the extreme, and the illustrations are mostly just dumped on the page, with little or no attempt to relate each illustration to its place in the text, or the various parts of the book to some coherent notion of the whole. Indeed, virtually the only attempts, Cundall apart, to design books as a whole were the illuminated gift books, in which the illustrations became the prime concern, with the text – usually of necessity brief: the Parables, the Sermon on the Mount, a single poem or a series of poetic snippets and mottoes – fitted into an intricately chromolithographed whole. Some of these books, especially when designed by Owen Jones or Henry Noel Humphreys, achieve a highly wrought eloquence and even, especially with the latter artist, considerable delicacy of detail; equally, many of them are hideous enough to tax the patience of even the most ardent appreciator of Victorian bric-à-brac. Either way, they are essentially books to be looked at rather than read, decorative objects to be left lying round (the bindings of some make it physically impossible to put them on a shelf), but on the outer margin of book publication as we normally know it today. Joseph Cundall's books, on the other hand, are very much books to be read, books for use. He began his career as a publisher of children's books, and they are among the most desirable ever produced. But his most notable contributions to the nineteenth century book were the splendid series of illustrated volumes he designed during the 1850s. Like the contemporary illuminated volumes and the later Dalziel books, they were produced to help satisfy the apparently insatiable appetite of the Victorians for gift books. But unlike the majority of the illuminated volumes they were intended to be read as well as merely looked at, and unlike the average product of the Dalziels they were planned as a pleasing whole, with text and illustrations designed to complement each other. Cundall worked with various illustrators – he had a particularly fruitful association with Birket Foster, both in black-and-white and in colour, thanks to the brilliant colour-printing of Edward Evans – and seems to have been, as few other gift-book editors were, a man of some literary knowledge and taste. But the real significance of his work lies in its intimate relation of printing-style and illustration, and his remarkable feeling for the right way words and pictures should be combined on one page. In particular, his choice of types was almost infallible: instead of the spindly Modern faces favoured for most books at the time, which were usually far too light to permit a proper balance of text and elaborate illustration, he continued and developed Pickering's experiments with Caslon and Old Style, heavier types with more body to match and set off the illustrations and decorations of the book. ❧ In all this he anticipated much which was to become the common ideal of the art nouveau book thirty or forty years later, and such volumes as his *Songs, Madrigals and Sonnets* (1849); *Sabbath Bells* (1856) and *The Poems of Oliver Goldsmith* (1859), both with

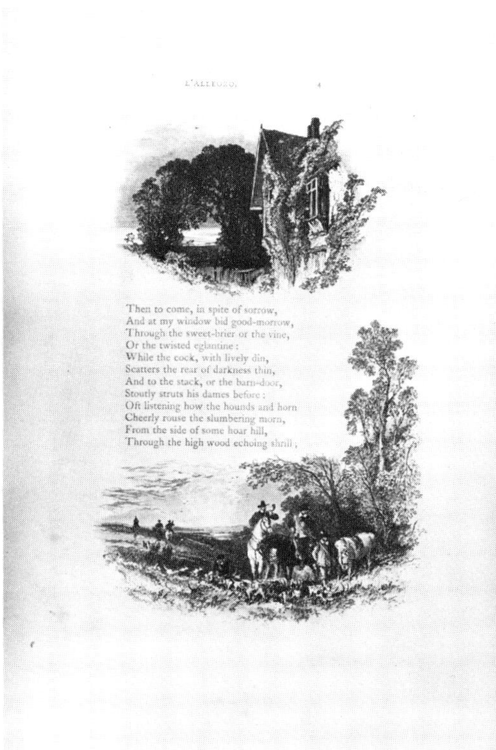

Then to come, in spite of sorrow,
And at my window bid good-morrow,
Through the sweet-brier or the vine,
Or the twisted eglantine;
While the cock, with lively din,
Scatters the rear of darkness thin,
And to the stack, or the barn-door,
Stoutly struts his dames before:
Oft listening how the hounds and horn
Cheerly rouse the slumbering morn,
From the side of some hoar hill,
Through the high wood echoing shrill;

Milton's L'Allegro and Il Penseroso (D. Bogue, 1855) Illustrated by Birket Foster, designed probably by Joseph Cundall. Typography in red $10\frac{1}{2} \times 7$ in.

coloured illustrations by Birket Foster; and *L'Allegro and Il Penseroso* (1855), printed in red with etched illustrations by Birket Foster, which, if not Cundall's own work, must at least have been produced under his strong influence, remain among the most beautiful Victorian books, a pleasure to read as well as to leaf through. And yet, oddly enough, Cundall remained almost unknown as a name in the history of book design and illustration, even during the 1890s and 1900s when the subject was inescapable and innumerable books and essays on it were published. Henry B. Wheatley's introduction to the catalogue of the Modern Illustration exhibition at the Victoria and Albert in 1901 pays a brief tribute to Cundall; otherwise the only reference I can find to him at this period is in the book on Birket Foster by his son H. M. Cundall published in 1906; after which outburst of filial piety there was nothing until Mr McLean's rediscovery of him in the 1960s. Did he, nevertheless, have an influence on the shape of books to come? Impossible to say with any certainty; but it seems unlikely that some of the great book illustrators and designers of the 1890s were not at least dimly aware of his books – especially considering that Morris and Burne-Jones were in later years friends of Birket Foster and visitors to his home. However, this is all rather in the realm of speculation. More to the point, and worth looking at before we reach the art nouveau book proper, is the interest – and this time an easily demonstrable interest – taken by a number of the book-artists of the 1890s in the illustrators of the 1860s. In 1897 appeared *English Illustration: 'The Sixties'*, an exhaustive, exhausting and profusely illustrated work by Gleeson White, friend and enthusiastic supporter of Shannon and Ricketts, sometime designer, contributor to and editor of a variety of literary-cum-artistic reviews of the period (including *The Studio*), and one of the principal figures behind the artistic scenes in the 1890s. The previous year Walter Crane paid glowing tribute to Frederick Sandys in his *Decorative Illustration* ('It is impossible to speak too highly of Mr Sandys' draughtsmanship and power of expression by means of line; he is one of our modern English masters who has never, I think, had justice done to him'[1]) and Joseph Pennell contributed an equally enthusiastic testimonial (illustrated with a

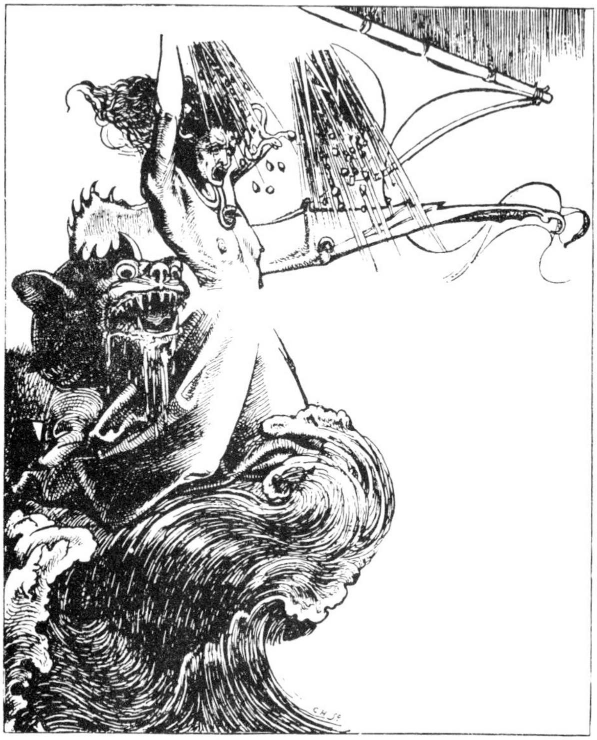

Frederick Sandys:
'The Spirit of the Storm',
unfinished drawing first published
in *The Quarto*, 1896

remarkably ninetyish-looking unfinished block) to *The Quarto*, as well as writing an article on the whole school, 'A Golden Decade in English Art', for *The Savoy*.[2] In 1897, too, Ricketts himself, in his 'Note on Original Wood Engraving',[3] finds kind words for the craftsmen who engraved the illustrations of these artists, 'interpreters whose value is at last being felt'. Other individual artists were also noticed: in 1896 Laurence Housman edited an extensive selection from the works of Arthur Boyd Houghton, and 1900 brought forth G. C. Williamson's vague but well-meaning book on Pinwell.
So, clearly, those actively involved in the Nineties revival in book design were quite well acquainted with the illustrators of the 1860s. What exactly they derived from this acquaintance is not always so easy to see. It is evident from the writings of the time that the most favoured among the illustrators were Sandys, Houghton and Pinwell, in that order. Sandys (1832-1904), I suppose, appealed largely because of his brilliant draughtsmanship (of course), his crowded and intricate compositions (suggestive

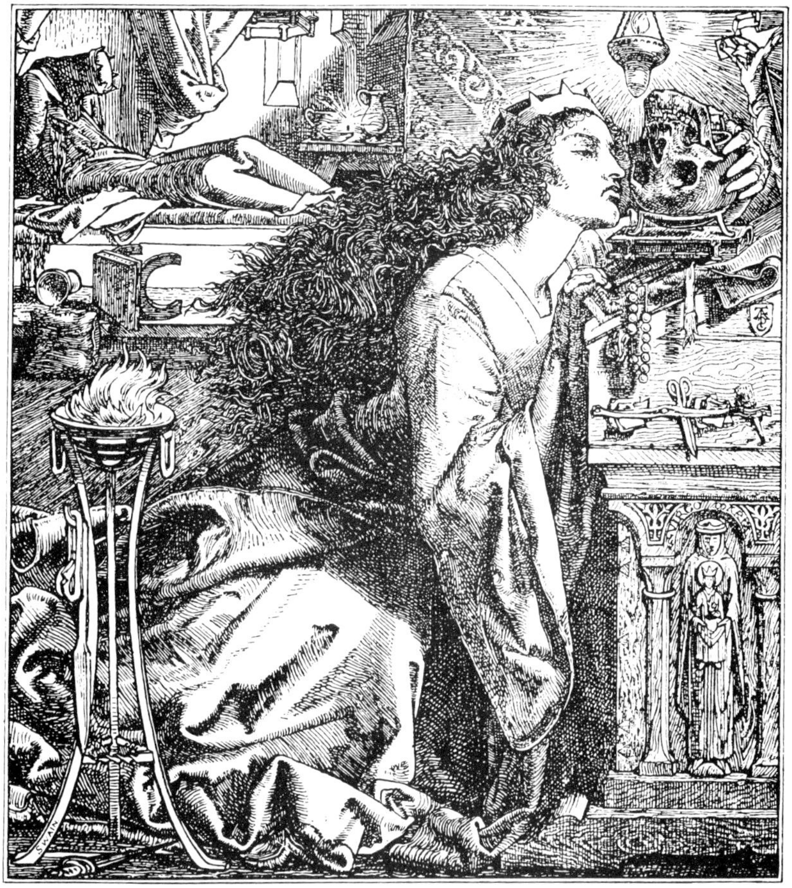

Frederick Sandys: 'Rosamund, Queen of the Lombards' (*Once a Week*, 1861)

of Ricketts's pictorial style during his most ornate and finicky phase in the early 1890s, and of Housman's throughout his career as an illustrator), and his weakness for 'decadent' subject-matter. In fact, meticulous craftsmanship apart, he represents most of the things that the more advanced British art nouveau designers, those who had already thrown off the influence of Rossetti and his circle, were busy reacting against in favour of sophisticated simplicity and spare elegance: in this context it is instructive to compare Sandys's 'Rosamund, Queen of the Lombards' (1861), with Beardsley's treatment of a comparable subject in 'Isolde' (1895). ❧ Houghton (1836-75) is a more interesting case. At first glance there would seem nothing to connect him with art nouveau and the 1890s. And yet there is no doubt that Laurence Housman was a genuine admirer, and in at least one instance practised on him the sincerest form of flattery: the germ from which Housman's series of illustrations to Meredith's *Jump to Glory Jane* (1892) developed is clearly to be found in one of Houghton's *Graphic America* series (1870), of Shakers dancing, which was subsequently included in Housman's 1895 volume of selections. Moreover, in his introduction to that volume Housman makes a shrewd and relevant point when he contrasts Houghton with 'his Pre-Raphaelite predecessors'[4]: 'In their designs for wood engraving it is, as a rule, difficult to find even a square inch of blank space left to represent ground or sky: they worked with jewel-like effect, regarding the wood they drew on as a sort of precious metal whose surface was of too much value to be thrown away. In Houghton's work, on the other hand, we find the value of 'whites' asserted almost by the yard. Broad white upon black, black upon broad white, these were the general lines upon which he worked for his effects.' The value of whites was also a basic tenet of British art nouveau design, in books and elsewhere – though oddly enough not in Housman's own work, for when he wrote these words he was still himself crowding his illustrations in the 'pre-Raphaelite' manner, just as Ricketts in his first period, and while Ricketts learnt the value of whites Housman increasingly gave up design in favour of writing, refusing till the last to accept the implications of his own insight. ❦ Pinwell (1842–75) is rather a mystery. Much of his work was relatively conventional, though often beautiful, but towards the end of the 1860s he developed an extraordinarily mannered and personal style, quite unlike that of any of his contemporaries and immediately recognisable. The most evident characteristic of this style is an odd indeterminateness about perspective: wherever possible the picture is constructed in a series of overlapping parallel planes with all evidence of recession suppressed. And this is so even when by normal convention it should not be: in the illustration to 'The High Tide on the Coast of Lincoln-

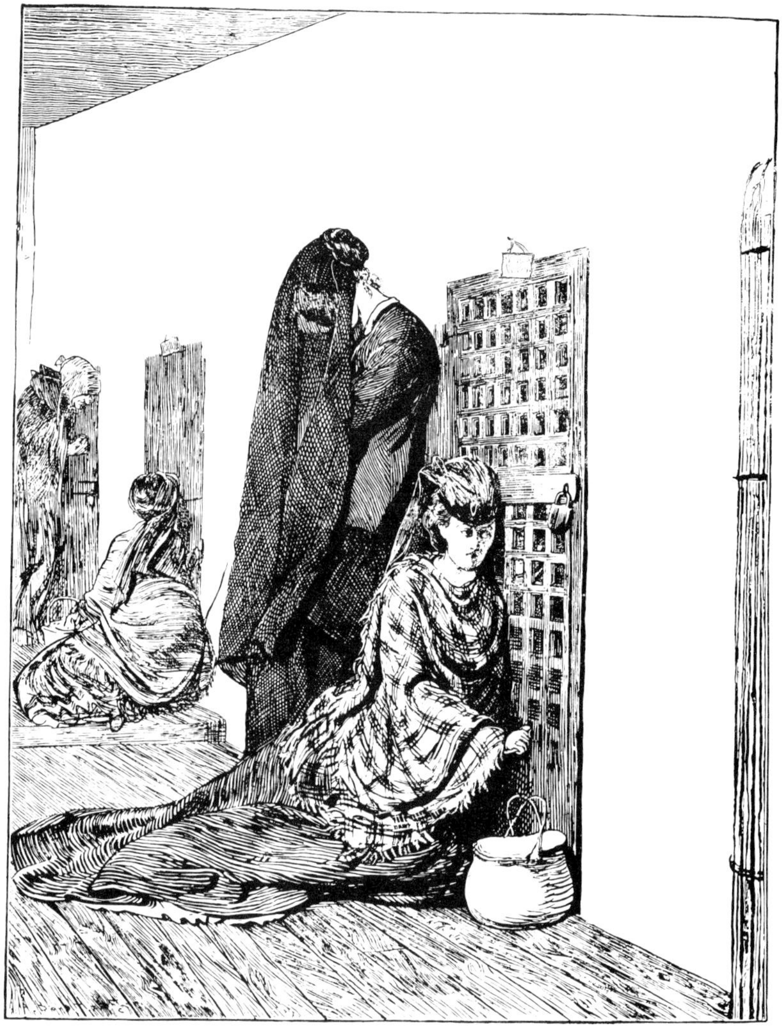

Arthur Boyd Houghton
'The Tombs'
(*Graphic America*, 1870)

shire' (Jean Ingelow's *Poems*, 1867), for example, the smooth recession of the 'level pasture' referred to in the poem is rendered by a series of flat bands imposed one on another up the page, with no feeling of recession at all; the children, particularly the left-hand boy and girl, seem to be hovering mysteriously in mid-air, and the cow in the centre middle-distance might be a cardboard cut-out in the same plane as the children's heads. How Pinwell came to evolve this strange style I cannot explain; his development seems to have been quite solitary, with few parallels in the work of even such close friends

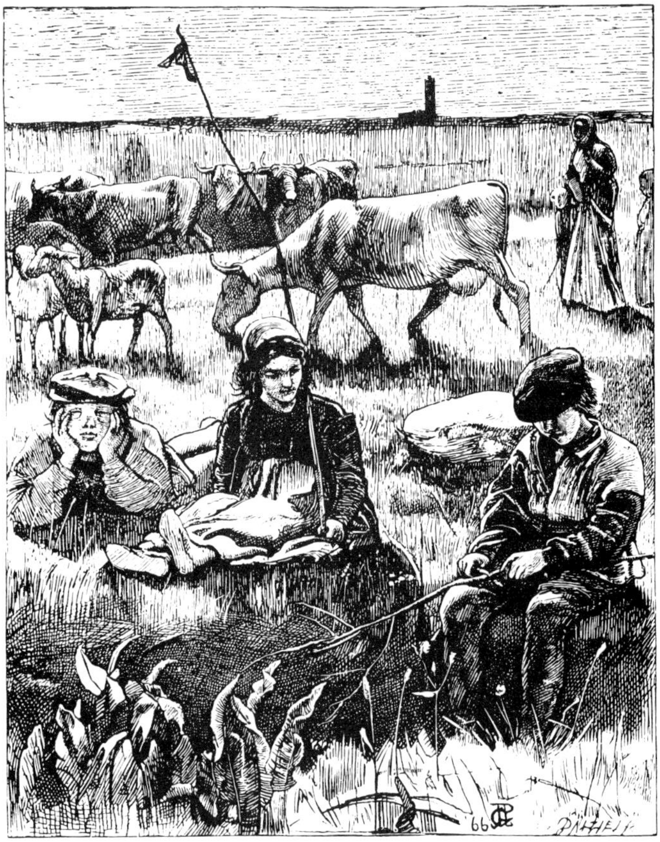

G. J. Pinwell: Illustration for 'The High Tide on the Coast of Lincolnshire' (*Poems by Jean Ingelow*, 1866)

as J. W. North, Frederick Walker or Boyd Houghton, and with little in the way of outside influence. It is unlikely that he can have seen much in the way of Japanese prints, for instance, though there are sometimes elements in his management of pictorial space which make one wonder; again, the fact that he began his artistic career as a designer of carpets and embroideries may have left a permanent mark on his work. Be that as it may, during the later 1860s he arrived at a style which anticipates many of the most marked characteristics of British art nouveau; moreover, no one seems to have thought it at all peculiar. In his short biography of Pinwell[5] the engraver Joseph Swain makes one or two slighting remarks about Pinwell's later work, reproducing an example which he calls 'curious, unconventional, but by no means attractive', but otherwise Pinwell seems to have been generally approved. In his book on the illustrators of the 1860s Gleeson White makes much of Pinwell, though taking some of his later work to task for its 'immobility', which he claims was mainly the fault of the engravers. And yet it is this very immobility, Pinwell's inclination to drain his pictures of drama and movement, rendering them instead as flat decorative patterns, that one would have expected to make him sympathetic above all his contemporaries to the art nouveau sensibility. Still, it is evidently quite possible that the eloquent pictures in Gleeson White's book had more immediate effect than his heavily reference-packed text. ❧ After the 1860s and their rich crop of illustrators there was something of a relapse in standards of book-illustration and production until the revival heralded by the Century Guild's *Hobby Horse* in 1884. The period is notable, indeed, almost solely for the work of two totally dissimilar, entirely individual book-designers. One of them, Andrew Tuer of the Leadenhall Press, is remembered mainly for the chapbooks and broadsides he produced in collaboration with Joseph Crawhall (already, since the 1850s, a designer and publisher of chapbooks in his native Newcastle), which were a deliberate and sophisticated harking-back to the crude popular publications of the eighteenth and early nineteenth centuries. The main immediate significance of their work is that it marked, in the most general way, a breaking-away from the anaemic regularity of 'respectable' book-production at the time: the types used were deliberately rough and irregular, to give the desired crude, penny-plain, tuppence-coloured effect, and Crawhall's bold, splodgy woodcuts exactly matched this, dotted about the text with artful arbitrariness. At first glance it is difficult to think of anything more remote from the refined, expensive products of the great book-designers of the 1890s, and yet those booklets, though cheap and popular in intention (and indeed in achievement) were designed

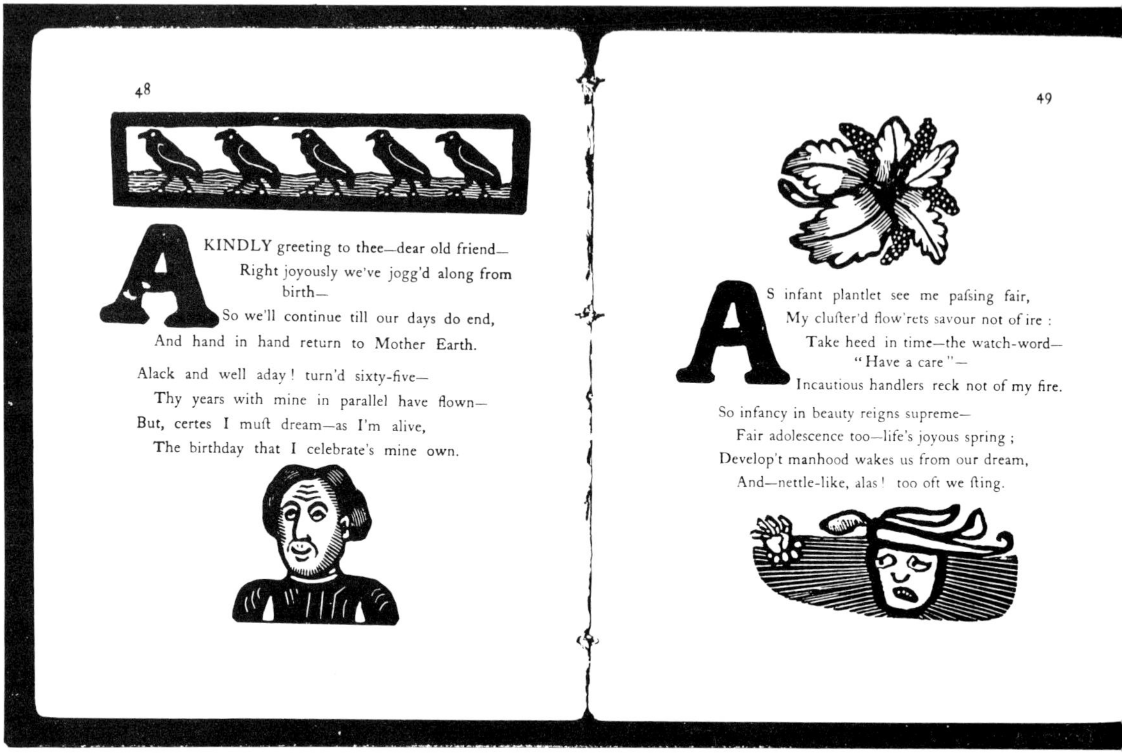

48

A KINDLY greeting to thee—dear old friend—
Right joyously we've jogg'd along from birth—
So we'll continue till our days do end,
And hand in hand return to Mother Earth.

Alack and well aday! turn'd sixty-five—
Thy years with mine in parallel have flown—
But, certes I muſt dream—as I'm alive,
The birthday that I celebrate's mine own.

49

AS infant plantlet see me paſsing fair,
My cluſter'd flow'rets savour not of ire:
Take heed in time—the watch-word—"Have a care"—
Incautious handlers reck not of my fire.

So infancy in beauty reigns supreme—
Fair adolescence too—life's joyous spring;
Develop't manhood wakes us from our dream,
And—nettle-like, alas! too oft we ſting.

Joseph Crawhall: Opening from his own *A Jubilee Thought* (Newcastle-on-Tyne, Mawson, Swan and Morgan, 1887) 7½ x 6 in.

in a way that most more pretentious books in the 1870s and early 1880s were not, with real care and feeling for overall mise-en-page. Moreover later, in the 1900s, they were the model and inspiration of Claud Lovat Fraser in his 'Flying Fame' chapbooks[6] while it is perhaps not entirely insignificant, at one remove further, that Sir Francis Meynell's father Wilfred Meynell was in the 1880s Tuer's literary adviser and friend, so that the creator of the Nonesuch Press spent his childhood in the ambiance of the Leadenhall Press. ❧ The second original to emerge in this period is James McNeill Whistler (1834-1903). Whistler, among his other interests and preoccupations, just qualifies as a black-and-white illustrator of the 1860s, contributing with fair regularity to *Once a Week* and *Good Words*. But it is more as a book-designer than as an illustrator that he is significant in the present context. In the early 1870s he began to devise a highly personal and original typographical arrangement for the catalogues of and invitations to his exhibitions. In 1874 his famous butterfly signature was first seen on an invitation, and in 1878 he published his first booklet, *Whistler v. Ruskin – Art and Art Critics*. This was bound in plain brown paper covers, from then on a regular feature of all his publications and at that time highly original, if not quite without precedent. In it and such later works as *Mr Whistler's 'Ten O'Clock'* (1888), *The Gentle Art of Making Enemies* (1890) and *The Baronet and the Butterfly* (1899), not to mention all his exhibition catalogues from 1881 on and a number of books about him (T. R. Way's book

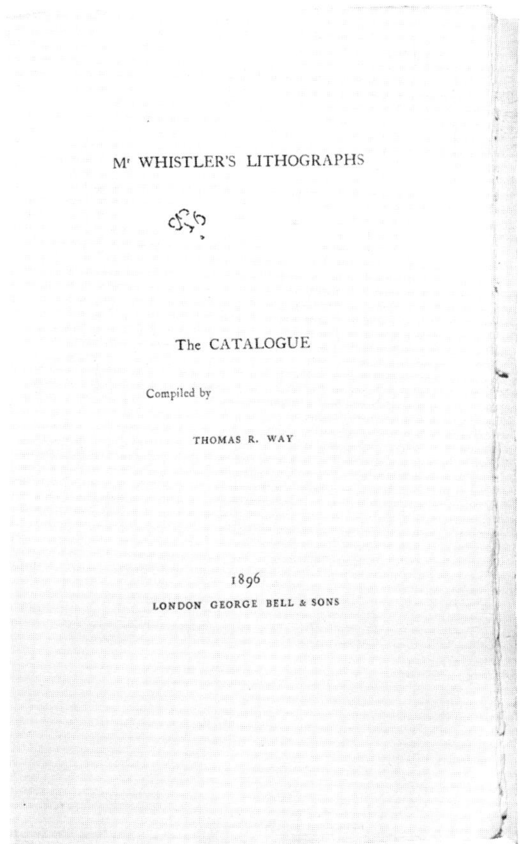

Mr WHISTLER'S LITHOGRAPHS

The CATALOGUE

Compiled by

THOMAS R. WAY

1896

LONDON GEORGE BELL & SONS

James McNeill Whistler: Title-page for *Mr. Whistler's Lithographs* (1896) $8\frac{3}{4} \times 5\frac{1}{8}$ in.

on his lithographs, Joseph Pennell's *Life of Whistler* and *Whistler Diary*) the style of binding and layout which were characteristically his own are established and, once established, remain constant and instantly recognisable. The most obvious feature of

Whistler's book design is his meticulous and wholly idiosyncratic disposition of black and white on the page. None of Whistler's own books is, strictly speaking, illustrated, though they all use his butterfly signature as a sort of graphic punctuation, varied to suit its context: prettily decorative, equipped with a barbed tail or, a famous instance, landing on a farthing – the amount of damages awarded Whistler in his legal tussle with Ruskin – at the end of *Whistler v. Ruskin*. Instead of illustration, Whistler chose to make patterns with the print itself. To begin with, he had a passion for plenty of white on a page, so that the text is generally a neat dark block islanded in tremendously wide margins. Secondly, he had a taste for asymmetrical arrangements, so that the basic block of print is placed not square in the middle of the page (or, strictly speaking, slightly nearer the inner edge) as in a conventional book then and since, but much nearer the inner than the outer edge and noticeably nearer the top than the bottom. To throw conventional balance off still further, he has a habit of annotating in small print not, as is more usual, at the bottom of the page, but above and down the side of the main text. Page numbers and running titles are generally suppressed, the butterfly in its various forms is scattered among the text and in the margins, and the title-pages are as delicately tense, precariously balanced 'arrangements in black and white' as any of his most 'Japanese' paintings. Whistler's books are unlike anyone else's, but he is not the completely anomalous, irrelevant figure one might suppose. His off-centre title-pages started a fashion which is not even now altogether dead, and the luxurious elegance of dropping a small, compact body of text in the middle of a sea of white paper also had its effect, often on the layout of otherwise highly conservative books. Another area in which Whistler led the way was in his insistence on producing his effects by the simplest means at his disposal. He required no special types for his books, no virtuoso

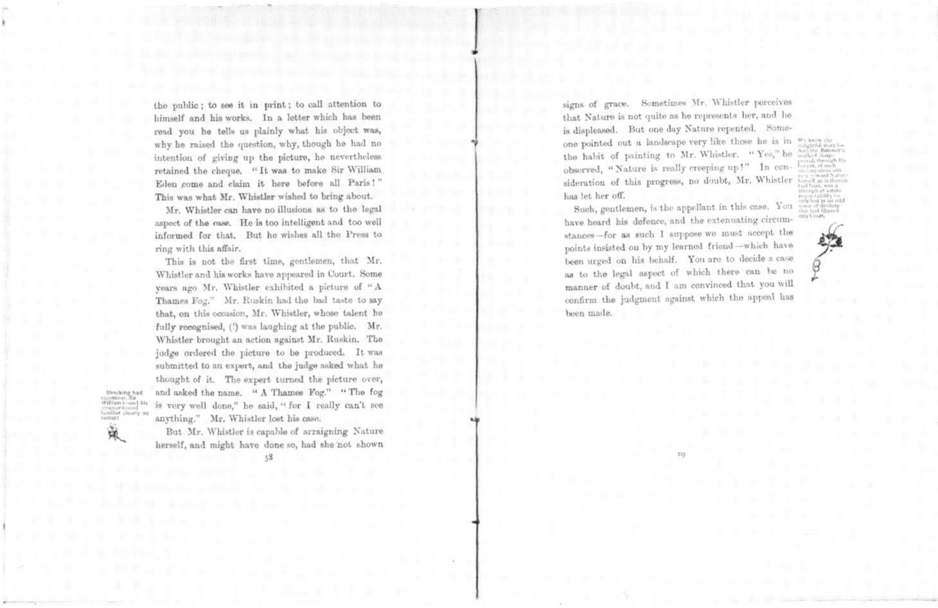

the public; to see it in print; to call attention to himself and his works. In a letter which has been read you he tells us plainly what his object was, why he raised the question, why, though he had no intention of giving up the picture, he nevertheless retained the cheque. "It was to make Sir William Eden come and claim it here before all Paris!" This was what Mr. Whistler wished to bring about.

Mr. Whistler can have no illusions as to the legal aspect of the case. He is too intelligent and too well informed for that. But he wishes all the Press to ring with this affair.

This is not the first time, gentlemen, that Mr. Whistler and his works have appeared in Court. Some years ago Mr. Whistler exhibited a picture of "A Thames Fog." Mr. Ruskin had the bad taste to say that, on this occasion, Mr. Whistler, whose talent he fully recognised, (!) was laughing at the public. Mr. Whistler brought an action against Mr. Ruskin. The judge ordered the picture to be produced. It was submitted to an expert, and the judge asked what he thought of it. The expert turned the picture over, and asked the name. "A Thames Fog." "The fog is very well done," he said, "for I really can't see anything." Mr. Whistler lost his case.

But Mr. Whistler is capable of arraigning Nature herself, and might have done so, had she not shown

58

signs of grace. Sometimes Mr. Whistler perceives that Nature is not quite as he represents her, and he is displeased. But one day Nature repented. Someone pointed out a landscape very like those he is in the habit of painting to Mr. Whistler. "Yes," he observed, "Nature is really creeping up!" In consideration of this progress, no doubt, Mr. Whistler has let her off.

Such, gentlemen, is the appellant in this case. You have heard his defence, and the extenuating circumstances—for as such I suppose we must accept the points insisted on by my learned friend—which have been urged on his behalf. You are to decide a case as to the legal aspect of which there can be no manner of doubt, and I am convinced that you will confirm the judgment against which the appeal has been made.

59

James McNeill Whistler: *The Baronet and the Butterfly* (1899) 8 × 6⅛ in.

effects in printing. He had no difficulty in working within the framework of ordinary commercial publishing, using the types normally available in a normal printer's office in the 1880s and the papers on which everyday books were printed, and moreover devising for himself a form of binding (brown paper boards lettered in black; yellow cloth just covering the spine) which was practical, inexpensive, and, when arranged with his own flair for inspired simplicity, both elegant and distinctive. His influence on the book of the 1890s and 1900s was enormous – not so much in precisely what he did as in the attitude he had to the doing of it. The Pennells describe[7] the infinite care he took to get the arrangement of each and every page exactly right, constantly plaguing his printers and sometimes spending days on a single opening. ❧ This dedication to the book as a whole, as an artefact designed in every detail by one man, could not but have its effect. A. J. A. Symons in his essay 'The Typography of the Nineties'[8] says that it was his 'personal example, more than any other, that influenced later comers', and though this is possibly an over-statement it is true at least to the extent that Whistler's practice in book-production was essentially forward-looking and indicated the way things would inevitably develop, had to develop in fact if the beautiful, well-designed book was going to be read as well as merely looked at (no one in his senses would choose a typical product of Morris's Kelmscott Press for actual reading) and was to be made available to the general public instead of merely the small minority of rich connoisseurs who could afford the luxurious productions of the private presses. More immediate evidence of Whistler's personal influence in this field is also forthcoming, however: Sir John Rothenstein records[9] that it was Whistler who got Wilde interested in book production and Wilde who passed on the message to Ricketts, arousing his enthusiasm for book design, getting him his first commissions (with commercial publishers, incidentally) and setting in motion, indirectly, the whole business of the Vale Press, with all its significance as a model and a standard for later work. With Whistler, in fact, we are already within striking distance of the art nouveau concept of the book at once functional and beautiful; on the threshold, indeed, of the modern book.

Arts and Crafts and Art Nouveau

A friend of mine was recently rung up by someone preparing a television discussion on the newly fashionable subject of art nouveau. The speaker wanted to ask one simple question: was Walter Crane art nouveau? That, as it happens, is very nearly the 64,000 dollar question. Where do we draw the line and what precisely do we mean by art nouveau? *Is* Walter Crane art nouveau? All the great, famous, original pieces of art nouveau come from the Century Guild, or thereabouts, in the heart of the Arts and Crafts Movement: does that mean that Arts and Crafts is the same as art nouveau, and if not, why not? Is Selwyn Image art nouveau; are the Birmingham Art School group art nouveau; is – perish the thought – William Morris himself art nouveau in his later days? There are few easy answers, and the fact that such questions often serve no reasonable purpose but degenerate rapidly into intellectual parlour games does not permit us to avoid asking them. After all, our terminology must mean something, or what use is it? First of all, let us admit, *pace* Walter Crane, who in 1911 called art nouveau 'that strange decorative disease' and was indignant because 'some writers have actually asserted that it was the offspring of what properly considered was really its antithesis – the Morris School of decoration',[1] that there is a lot of common ground between Arts and Crafts and art nouveau.

I personally, as I have already indicated, would extend it further than any Continental or American theorist on the subject that I know of, since it is my contention that much which has been dismissed as irrelevant, merely Arts and Crafts, because it does not fit in with Continental theories based on the sinuous line as the hallmark of true, 'high' art nouveau, is in fact an integral part of British art nouveau right from the outset, and that the true nature of British art nouveau can be understood aright only if we accept this. However, the fact remains that there are artists who are decidedly art nouveau and yet have no touch of Arts and Crafts (Beardsley, for instance). It is possible, also, that there are artists who are Arts and Crafts in their allegiances without any real hint of art nouveau in their work, though in fact almost anyone you like to mention shows some sign of art nouveau influences at work some of the time. ❧ Certain rough lines of demarcation can however be drawn. To begin with, Arts and Crafts is essentially, as the label suggests, direct, unaffected, simple (or at least simpliste); it is fairly stolid and robust; and it is solidly traditional, often with a sort of revivalist fervour. Art nouveau, on the other hand, is essentially sophisticated and eclectic, accepting and assimilating influences from here, there and everywhere – Japanese, Greek, Celtic, Pre-Raphaelite (literally as well as figuratively), Rococo, Dutch, Blake, Victorian industrial design, architectural drawing, etc., etc. Moreover, art nouveau is above all highly mannered. Arts and Crafts is mannered too, of course, but without preciosity and only in certain specific directions: the gothic hankerings of Morris, the striving after black-letter simplicity and directness, the cult of unrefinement and sturdy usefulness. But art nouveau often deliberately plays with affectation, reserving the right to take up and drop a style entirely as the mood takes it, to put motifs from one style to uses quite undreamt of by its creators and to mix and fuse styles entirely on decorative instinct.

First page of the Kelmscott *Chaucer* (1896); illustration by Edward Burne-Jones, border by William Morris $16\frac{3}{4} \times 11\frac{1}{2}$ in.

HERE BEGINNETH THE TALES OF CANTERBURY AND FIRST THE PROLOGUE THEREOF

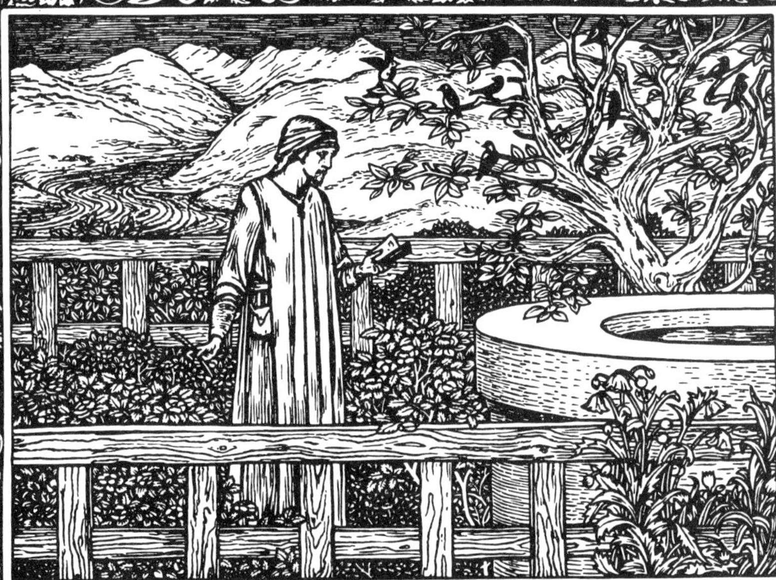

WHAN THAT Aprille with his shoures soote
The droghte of March hath perced to the roote,
And bathed every veyne in swich licour,
Of which vertu engendred is the flour;
Whan Zephirus eek with his swete breeth
Inspired hath in every holt and heeth
The tendre croppes, and the yonge sonne
Hath in the Ram his halfe cours yronne,
And smale foweles maken melodye,
That slepen al the nyght with open eye,
So priketh hem nature in hir corages;
Thanne longen folk to goon on pilgrimages,
And palmeres for to seken straunge strondes,
To ferne halwes, kowthe in sondry londes;
And specially, from every shires ende
Of Engelond, to Caunterbury they wende,
The hooly blisful martir for to seke,
That hem hath holpen whan that they were seeke.

BIFIL that in that seson on a day,
In Southwerk at the Tabard as I lay,
Redy to wenden on my pilgrymage
To Caunterbury with ful devout corage,
At nyght were come into that hostelrye
Wel nyne and twenty in a compaignye,
Of sondry folk, by aventure yfalle
In felaweshipe, and pilgrimes were they alle,
That toward Caunterbury wolden ryde.

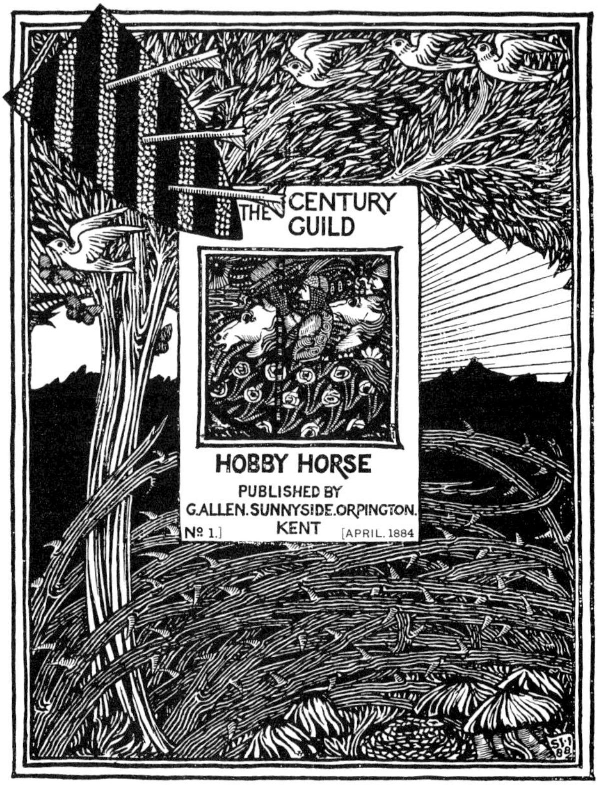

Selwyn Image: Title page to *The Century Guild Hobby Horse* (1884) $10\frac{3}{4} \times 8\frac{1}{2}$ in.

It is capable, even, of adopting all the trappings of Arts and Crafts, but purely for their decorative effect, their value as a piquant ingredient in a stylistic mélange, without a hint of Arts and Crafts crusading fervour. And yet, such is the paradoxical nature of art nouveau, the final product is nearly always much simpler and less cluttered than Arts and Crafts. Though direct, uncomplicated communication is a prime aim of Arts and Crafts designers, they are, just because of their high ideals and almost religious principles, to a considerable extent prisoners of their own style and their own time. Much Arts and Crafts design is infected by a mid-Victorian fussiness and ornateness. Selwyn Image's title-page to *The Hobby Horse*, for example, is quite claustrophobic in its insistent detail, its determination to pack every corner with significance. Even Morris's most famous works at the Kelmscott Press, like the sumptuous and overpowering *Chaucer*, suffer from the same defect – they are over-decorated (as Morris himself remarked, his books are those of 'a decorator by profession'), over-elaborate, airless.

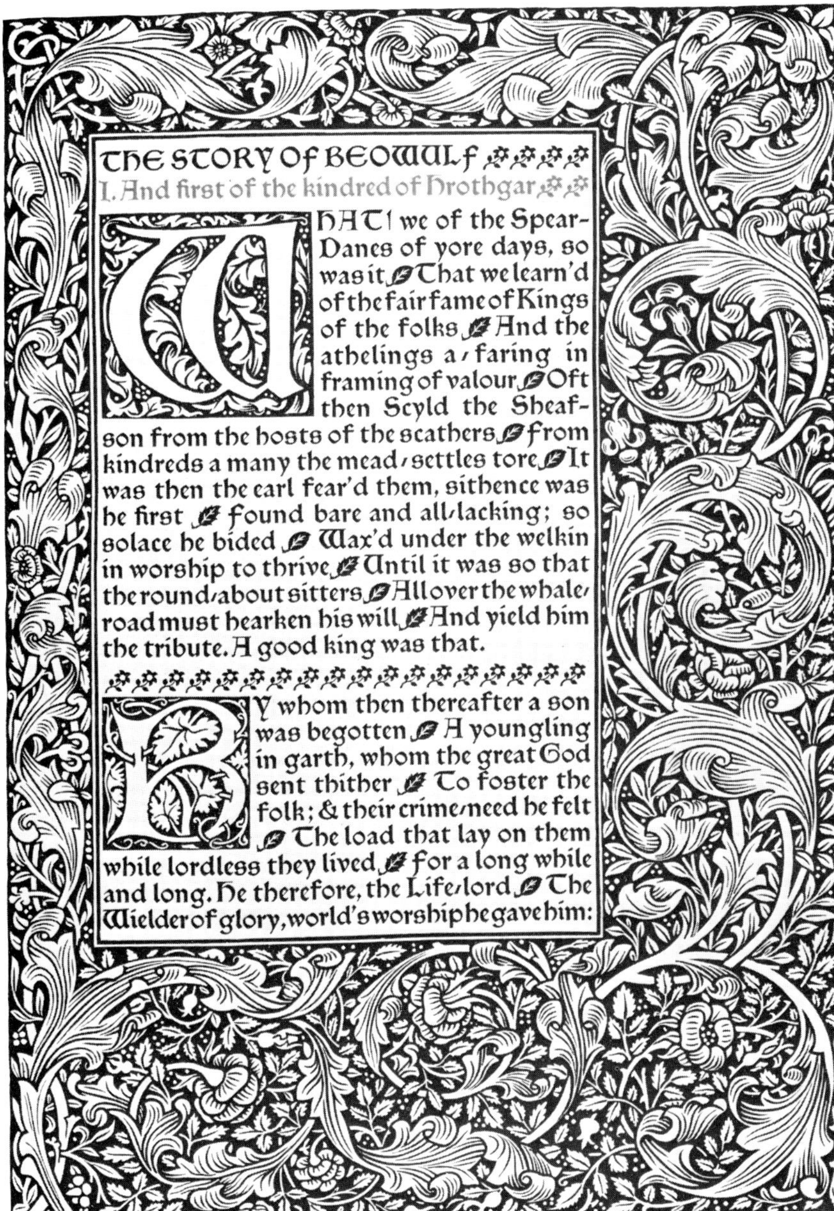
THE STORY OF BEOWULF

I. And first of the kindred of Hrothgar

WHAT! we of the Spear-Danes of yore days, so was it That we learn'd of the fair fame of Kings of the folks And the athelings a-faring in framing of valour. Oft then Scyld the Sheaf-son from the hosts of the scathers from kindreds a many the mead-settles tore. It was then the earl fear'd them, sithence was he first found bare and all-lacking; so solace he bided Wax'd under the welkin in worship to thrive Until it was so that the round-about sitters All over the whale-road must hearken his will And yield him the tribute. A good king was that.

BY whom then thereafter a son was begotten A youngling in garth, whom the great God sent thither To foster the folk; & their crime-need he felt The load that lay on them while lordless they lived for a long while and long. He therefore, the Life-lord The Wielder of glory, world's worship he gave him:

William Morris: First page of *Beowulf* (Kelmscott, 1895) $11\frac{3}{8} \times 8\frac{1}{4}$ in.

White is mistrusted, and so, as often as not, are the resources of purely typographical arrangement; art in book production tends to become the somewhat indiscriminate elaboration of ornament rather than its careful positioning, its scrupulous selection in relation to the book as a whole and the text which it accompanies. Any opening of a Morris book, or one by those who subscribed to his ideas of the book beautiful, is probably splendid: it is only when one comes to leaf through an entire volume, or worse still tries to read one, that aesthetic indigestion sets in. ❦ But this is just where the art nouveau book scores. British art nouveau represents above all a sense of proportion. Being, in effect, the stage after Arts and Crafts, art nouveau can throw out the elements of established convention which most hampered Arts and Crafts designers. In their woodcut illustrations Arts and Crafts designers, while seeking to emulate the ease and directness of the decorations in early printed books, were constrained still to observe nineteenth-century rather than sixteenth-century conventions about the rendering of pictorial space, so that the effect is often, despite the intentions, fussy and cluttered, and quite unlike that of the ostensible models. Part of the art nouveau reaction is the rejection of the three-dimensional effect still considered necessary by Arts and Crafts: the page is accepted as what it is, a flat, white surface ready for decoration by patterns in two dimensions, the patterns to be made by arrangement of print, or illustrative designs, or both. Compare, for instance, the exactly contemporary designs for the English and American editions of R. D. Blackmore's book of poems *Fringilla* (1895). The English edition (Elkin Mathews), illustrated largely by Louis Fairfax Muckley, is a fair if undistinguished example of Arts and Crafts taste – though even this was apparently a little much for the author (admittedly seventy at the time and crotchety with it), who remarks in his introductory note that the illustrations, at which

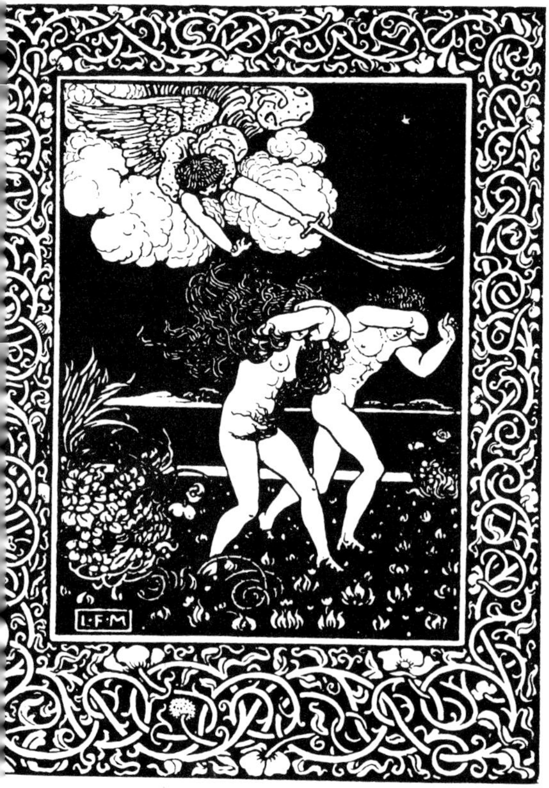

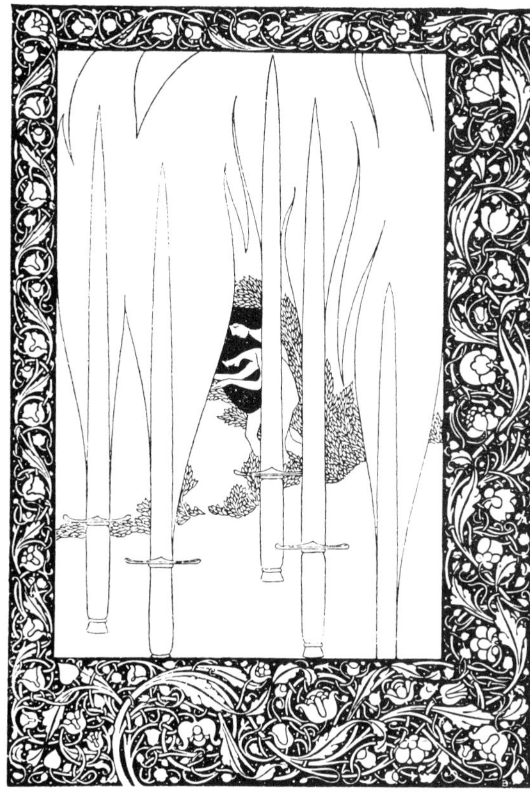

Louis F. Muckley: Adam and Eve Driven out of Eden, from R. D. Blackmore's *Fringilla* (English edition, 1895) 8 x 6 in.

Will H. Bradley: Adam and Eve Driven out of Eden, from R. D. Blackmore's *Fringilla* (American edition, 1895) $8\frac{7}{8}$ x 6 in.

he 'gazes with doubt', 'have conquered the taste of the day, perhaps, and high art announces them as her latest transfiguration'. What, if anything, he made of Will Bradley's illustrations to the American edition (Cleveland: Burrows Brothers) is not recorded: here we find at once the bold use of masses of black and free, open areas of white, the abandonment of all attempt at a 'realistic', three-dimensional rendering of space and recession, and the highly mannered, anti-traditional approach to pictorial composition characteristic of art nouveau proper. Also, Fairfax Muckley's designs are unmistakably illustrations of the text; Bradley's are equally unmistakably decorations. In that distinction, perhaps, is to be found the key to the difference between the Arts and Crafts and the art nouveau approaches to the book.

Having suggested some sorts of distinction between the two schools of thought, we had better see how they turn out in practice. To begin with, it must be said that the writings of various artists and theorists involved are frequently little or no help. Nobody seems to like what by rights he should like, approve in theory of what by his practice he seems to be advocating. Walter Crane, in his admirably comprehensive *Of the Decorative Illustration of Books Old and New* (1896), shows a remarkable faculty of appreciating almost everything on its own terms, though stating that in his choice of illustration he has 'endeavoured to draw the line between the purely graphic aim, on the one hand, and the ornamental aim on the other – between what I should term the art of *pictorial statement* and the art of *decorative treatment*; though there are many cases in which they are combined, as indeed, in all the most complete book-pictures, they should be' – a view, one might say, distinctively more Arts and Crafts than art nouveau in its final proviso, but broadly enough phrased to stand for both. Equally, in his two handbooks of decorative art, *The Bases of Design* (1898) and *Line and Form* (1900), Crane puts forward and expounds such a variety of styles and motifs, of alternative approaches to composition and the rendering of pictorial space, that one could reach any conclusion, or none at all, about his real sympathies. ❧ Other writers are not so obliging. Not only did Ricketts admire Morris, with reservations, but Morris, we are told, was reduced to tears of admiration when, on his deathbed, shown the books of the Vale Press.[2] Though Whistler's example had an important place in the formation of Vale Press ideals, Joseph Pennell, Whistler's devoted admirer and biographer, dismisses the Ricketts–Shannon *Daphnis and Chloe* contemptuously in his *Modern Illustration* as bound to 'serve to perpetuate the imperfections of the Middle-Age woodcutter'.[3] And consider this, by Gleeson White, in an essay entitled 'The Rococo, and After' in an 1896 number of *The Quarto*[4]: deploring the rise of 'sprawling, lawless ornament of the most vulgar decoration that ever grew to be recognized as style' he writes:

Flamboyant and voluptuous curves of this gorgeous and ornate decoration have already conquered the simpler lines of the Queen Anne period and the spiky stiffness of modern Gothic. The lily and the sunflower are dethroned to allow the extraordinary and unnatural possibilities of the rococo flora to reign in their stead. The thing like an old-fashioned jam-tart, the foliage like a limp head of celery or an acanthus run to seed, the tortured capital C's writhing in agonies, the wicker-work baskets of ultra-naturalistic flowers, the sprawling rotund cupids, and all the motley motives belonging to this carnival of artistic licence are, for the moment, rampant in our homes.

Whatever is he talking about? Not, surely, Beardsley's and Conder's deliberate revival of rococo motifs, for that came too late (Beardsley's earliest, the *Rape of the Lock* designs, towards the end of 1896). And in fact he is talking specifically of mass-produced interior decoration and furnishing; he is speaking of a sort of 'new rococo' which we should call high or Continental art nouveau, and he is contrasting its decadence and eclecticism with the strength and purity of Arts and Crafts (note the lilies and sunflowers, the reference to the Queen Anne style). And yet this same Gleeson White had been editor of *The Studio* when its first number (1893) gave publicity to Beardsley in an article by Pennell and sported a Beardsley cover; in 1896 he was editing, with Shannon, a literary and artistic magazine, *The Pageant* (1896-97), decorated with these same old-fashioned jam-tarts and limp heads of celery (as, indeed, are the end-papers of *The Quarto* itself); he was a friend of Ricketts and had Ricketts design him a book-plate in his most ornate Continental manner, and seems to have noticed no inconsistency whatever in his attitude. All very puzzling. ❦ Matters become a little clearer, though, when we come back to what the artists of the period did, rather than what they thought they were doing.

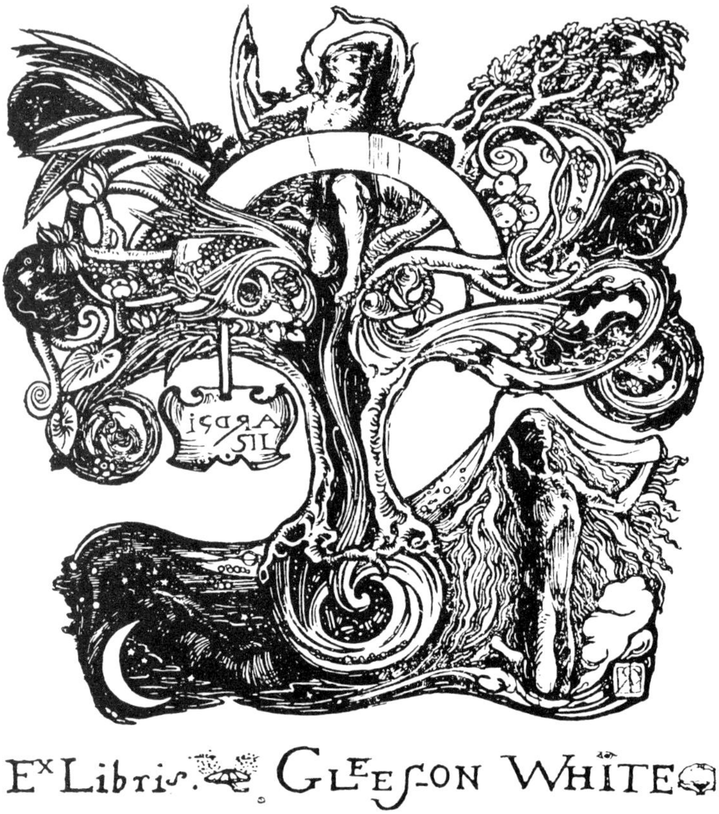

Charles Ricketts: Bookplate for Gleeson White

'The tree of Creation (Igdrasil) springs from a swirl of water and flame which breaks into little gems; the flame, continuing, flows through the trunk of the tree, which branches on each side into composite boughs suggesting the different plant kingdoms. This central flame envelopes the figure of a man, placed in the midst of the tree in the action of awakening. The fruit on the eastern end of each bough represent in embryo the fish and water fowl; the reptile and creeping insects; the larger animals; and finally the creatures with wings. The rainbow shooting through the centre composition signifies the atmosphere; the two figures under one cloak in the lower part of the design represent night and day, i.e., the planets.' – Charles Ricketts, in Egerton Castle: *English Book-Plates*

The best place to start this study is with the first group religiously devoted to Arts and Crafts, the Century Guild, and, more specifically, with their spiritual father Walter Crane. Crane (1846-1915) is really too big and unmanageable a figure to be fitted neatly into any single pigeonhole, but it is clearly with Arts and Crafts that he properly belongs. He was, in fact, a craftsman in a sense that few others in the movement were: by necessity and practical training from youth rather than by intellectual conviction and on adult moral principle. He was apprenticed at the age of thirteen to the wood-engraver W. J. Lintot. He contributed during the 1860s to the great magazine-outlets for the designer's work, *Once a Week* and *Good Words*, but unlike most the other notable illustrators of the 1860s he did not merely draw for a skilled engraver to translate into wood-blocks: he understood the processes of wood-engraving from practical experience, and he was sometimes designer, sometimes engraver, and sometimes both together. In 1865 he branched out with the first of his famous 'toy-books', which continued to appear regularly until 1876, and meanwhile and later wrote or compiled, designed and illustrated any number of other books for children. From the first he has a recognisable, individual style,

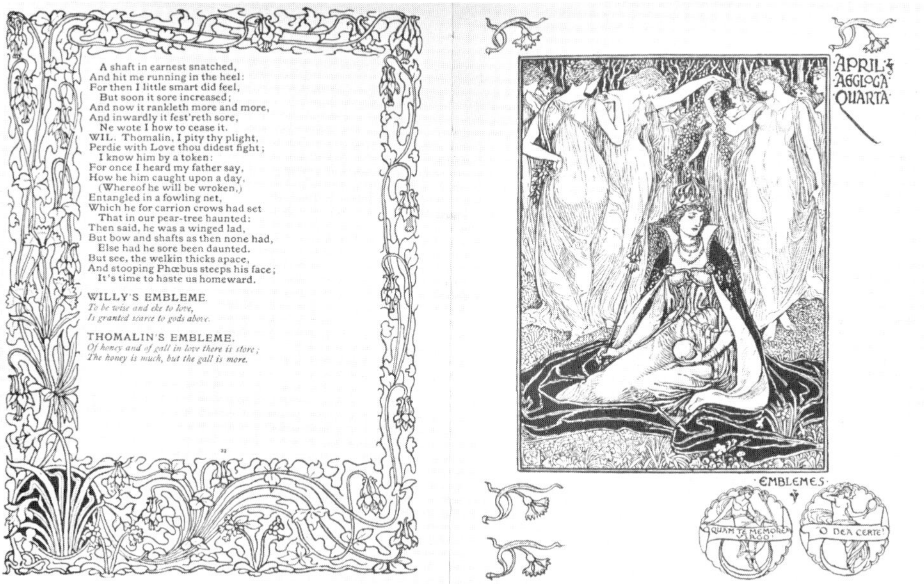

Walter Crane: *The Shepheard's Calender* (1898) 8 x $6\frac{1}{4}$ in.

marked above all by the strength and solidity of his line, which at times suggests more the woodcut than the wood-engraving. These qualities already stood him apart from other illustrators of the 1860s, and so did his intense interest in what was going on around him in other areas of art. He was one of the first artists in Britain to take serious notice of Japanese art, especially colour-prints, and their influence on his compositions and to a certain extent on his decorative motifs is apparent in the later toy-books. He was also one of the first English illustrators to take an active interest in the possibilities of commercial colour-printing as a medium in its own right, with special qualities, instead of as a more or less effective way of reproducing the effects of other media: in *Decorative Illustration*[5] he attributes this also to Japanese influences – 'It was the influence

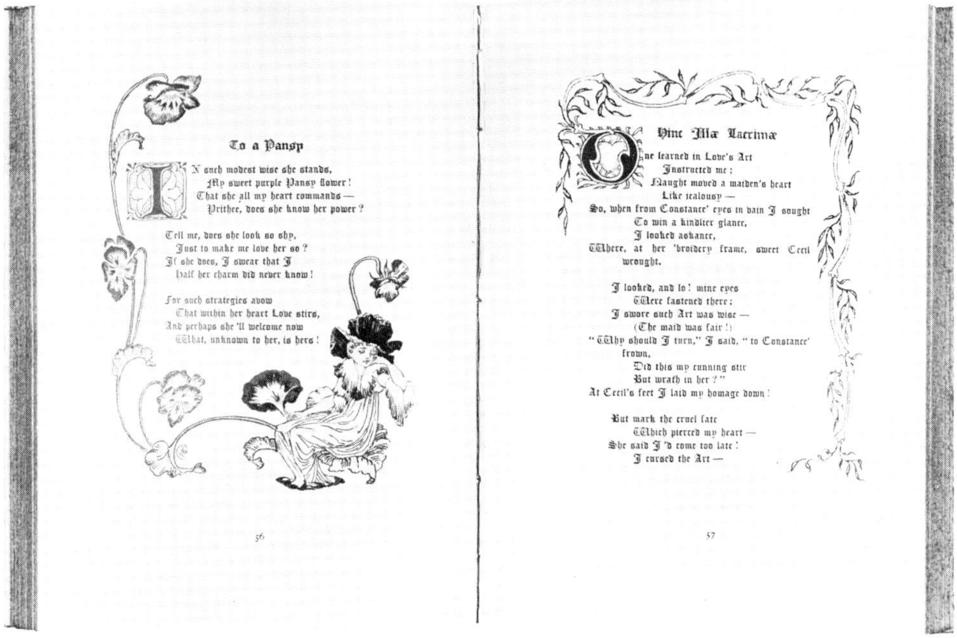

Walter Crane: *The Old Garden* (1893) $7\frac{3}{4} \times 5\frac{3}{8}$ in.

of some Japanese printed pictures given to me by a lieutenant in the navy . . . which I believe, though I drew inspiration from many sources, gave the real impulse to that treatment in strong outlines, and solid tints and flat blocks, which I adopted with variations in books of this kind [colour-printed children's books] from that time (about 1870) onwards'. But he had reservations about too whole-hearted an acceptance of Japanese modes, remarking[6] that the Japanese possess merely 'a decorative sense – the *finesse* which goes to the placing of flowers in a pot, of hanging a garland on a wall, or of placing a mat or a fan – taste, in short, that is a different thing from real constructive power of design, and satisfactory filling of spaces'. ❧ In fact, though not unsympathetic to the elements which were to contribute so importantly to the make-up of art nouveau, when it came to the point Crane held fast to more traditional, academic views of construction, design, and the 'satisfactory filling of spaces'. He has taste, certainly, particularly in his use of colour, and a clear if limited notion of overall design in a book. He has, too, a decided style, though not finally, to me at any rate, a very attractive one, remaining as it does from first to last just a trifle heavy, stodgy, puddingy. He was an early and passionate admirer of Blake, and the famous sinuous line of Blake may be found in a few of his designs – those, as it happens, which had the strongest influence abroad, particularly *Flora's Feast* (Cassell, 1889) and *The Old Garden* (Osgood, McIlvaine, 1893), where the subject-matter of personified flowers inevitably suggested Blakean pictorial equations of tendrils, waves and flames. But though these works have been much commented on by Continental writers on art nouveau,[7] they are not really at all characteristic of the ensemble of Crane's work. This is more fairly represented by the stable, respectable combination of Greek architectural motifs and draperies à la Edwin Godwin and Albert Moore[8] and Morrisian medievalism to be seen in, say, his designs for Grimm's *Household Tales* (Macmillan, 1882) or the Kelmscott edition of Morris's *The Glittering Plain* (1894), in which he actually collaborated harmoniously with Morris, or Spenser's *Shepheard's Calender* (Harper, 1898). Really, from first to last Crane was an Arts and Crafts man, and though his books have their sober charms they are nearly all fatally lacking in the grace, elegance or imaginative lift of real art nouveau. ❧ Almost exactly the same set of provisos and qualifications would go equally well for much of the work of the Century Guild and its followers, the Birmingham Guild of Handicraft, some associates of which, such as A. J. Gaskin and C. M. Gere, also figure among the lesser workers for the Kelmscott Press, and other minor figures on the fringes of the Arts and Crafts movement. However, in the case of the principal figures of the Century Guild there are significant enough deviations from the norm to make a closer examination of their decorative work worthwhile. In particular they, Mackmurdo and Heywood Sumner (1853-1940) especially, stand as we have already remarked for the

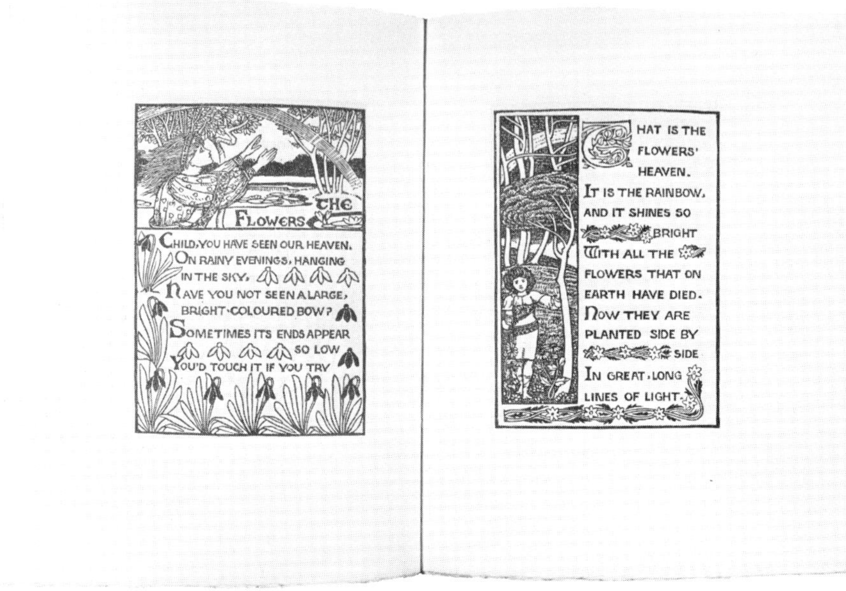

Bernard Sleigh: Designs for *The Sea King's Daughter* (Amy Mark), printed at the Birmingham Guild of Handicraft (1895) $8\frac{3}{4} \times 6\frac{3}{4}$ in.

initiation of sinuous, 'high' art nouveau in England; its initiation and virtually its conclusion. The sinuous element comes almost entirely from Blake: Blake was one of their idols, and Blake is appreciably behind Mackmurdo's flower-flame decorations in the first number of *The Hobby Horse*, the title-page of his *Wren's City Churches* and the back of his 1881 chair, as well as in Heywood Sumner's designs for *Cinderella* (Novello, Enser, 1882), *Sintram* (Seeley, Jackson and Halliday, 1883) and *Undine* (Chapman and Hall, 1888), though these latter also contain many designs which might almost be by Crane, and the lucid, flowing forms of the *Undine* cover are the exception rather than the rule. ❧ But from the very start these Blakean elements go hand in hand with others which seem at first glance not art nouveau at all – not, anyway, as we normally understand the term. There are, for example, Mackmurdo's interest

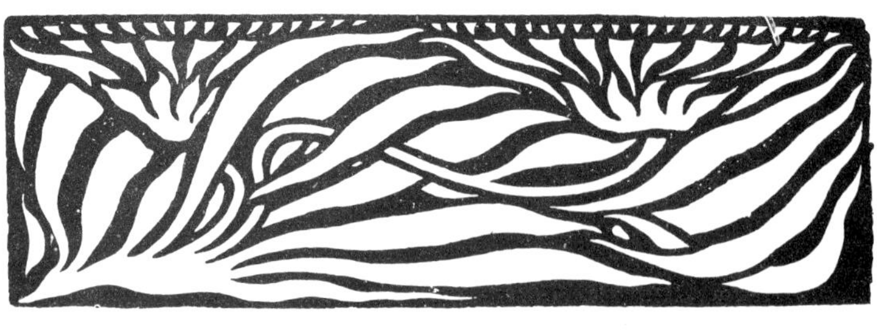

Arthur Heygate Mackmurdo: Decoration in *The Hobby Horse* (1884)

in Wren and in seventeenth-century Dutch art, and Herbert Horne's in Inigo Jones, which produced an enthusiastic essay in *The Hobby Horse* (1886); there are the Dutch motifs of tulips, Gleeson White's sunflower and small round-topped orange-bushes in pots, and the weakness of many Century Guild designers for the upright, elongated rectangles of Dutch brick architecture. The title-page by Selwyn Image (1849 - 1930) to Ernest Radford's *Old and New* (Fisher Unwin, 1895) is a latish but fully representative example, and the book designs of Herbert Horne (1864 - 1916), who was a professional typographer as well as an architect, writer and general

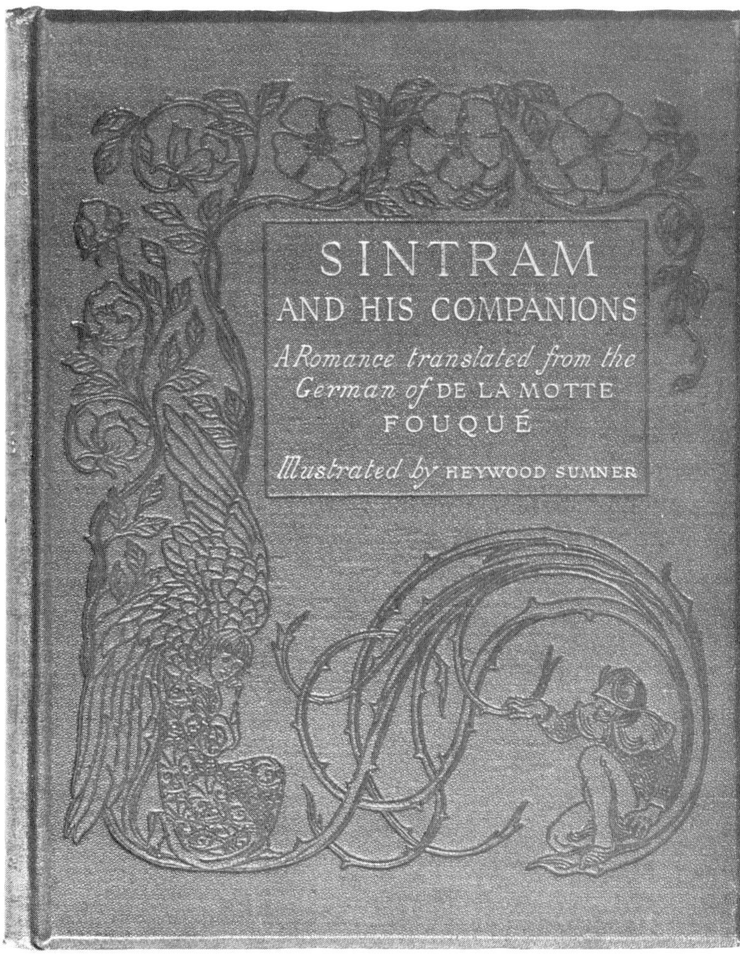

eywood Sumner: Binding for *Sintram and his Companions* (1883) $8\frac{3}{8} \times 6\frac{3}{8}$ in.

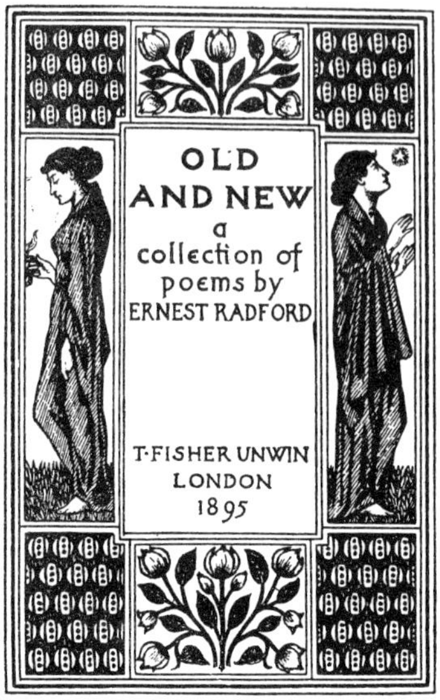

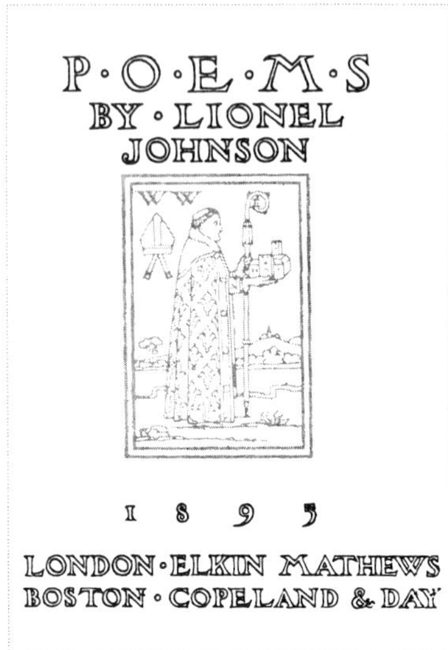

Selwyn Image:
Title-page for
Old and New (1895) $7\frac{3}{8} \times 5$ in.

Herbert Horne: Title-page for
Poems by Lionel Johnson (1895)
red and black $8\frac{1}{4} \times 5\frac{1}{2}$ in.

craft-designer, might also be instanced; they show a quite classical severity and restraint – his *Poems by Lionel Johnson* (Elkin Mathews, 1895) is the perfect demonstration – and make their effects almost entirely by the exercise of an immaculate sense of massing and proportion. But these other characteristics, when we consider them more closely, prove to have had a more important and lasting influence on British art nouveau than the Blakean free sinuous curves. ❧ The most important distinction between the Century Guild artists and the practitioners of the fully developed British art nouveau of the 1890s and 1900s, in fact, is not so much in the elements that go to make up their style (though the later artists add many other heterogeneous elements) but in the way these elements are combined. In Mackmurdo, Heywood Sumner and Selwyn Image the elements co-exist, and often quite happily, without ever quite fusing into one easy, reasonably consistent, reasonably coherent new style. In Ricketts, in Beardsley, in Laurence Housman, in Mackintosh, Talwin Morris and Jessie M. King, in Alastair, and even in Rackham and Dulac, the elements have fused – in different ways and in different combinations, of course, but the ultimate unity of effect is not in doubt.

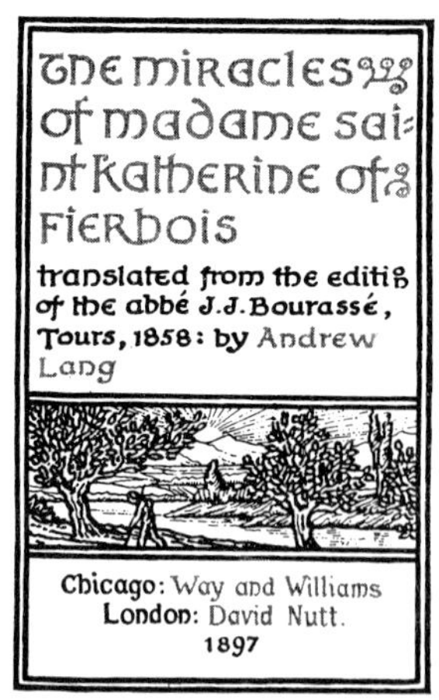

Selwyn Image: Title-page for
The Miracles of Madame Saint Katherine of Fierbois (1897)
red and black $7\frac{1}{2} \times 4\frac{3}{4}$ in.

Art Nouveau in the Nineties

(i) Charles Ricketts

Whichever way one looks at it, Ricketts seems somehow to come out as the hero of any study of the art nouveau book – even, in certain respects, of art nouveau in general. Ricketts was born in 1866, and Charles Haslewood Shannon, his life-long personal and professional partner, in 1863; Ricketts died in 1930 and Shannon, after some years as a complete invalid following a brain injury, in 1937. Most of their important work in book design and production was done between 1889, when the first number of their artistic periodical *The Dial* appeared, and 1914, though even in the 1920s Ricketts continued occasionally to design bindings for books. The period of most intense activity was between 1893, when the first published book completely designed by Ricketts (with the collaboration of Shannon in some of the illustrations[1]), *Daphnis and Chloe*, appeared, and 1903, when *Danaë*, the last book published by Ricketts's Vale Press (founded 1896), was issued. During this period Ricketts was entirely responsible – with some assistance from Shannon and T. Sturge Moore, and latterly from C. Keats in the cutting of borders – for the design of eighty-eight volumes, eighty-five of them from the Vale Press (thirty-nine a complete Shakespeare), preceded by *Daphnis and Chloe*, *The Sphinx* and *Hero and Leander* (1894) published in Vale Press style before the press itself

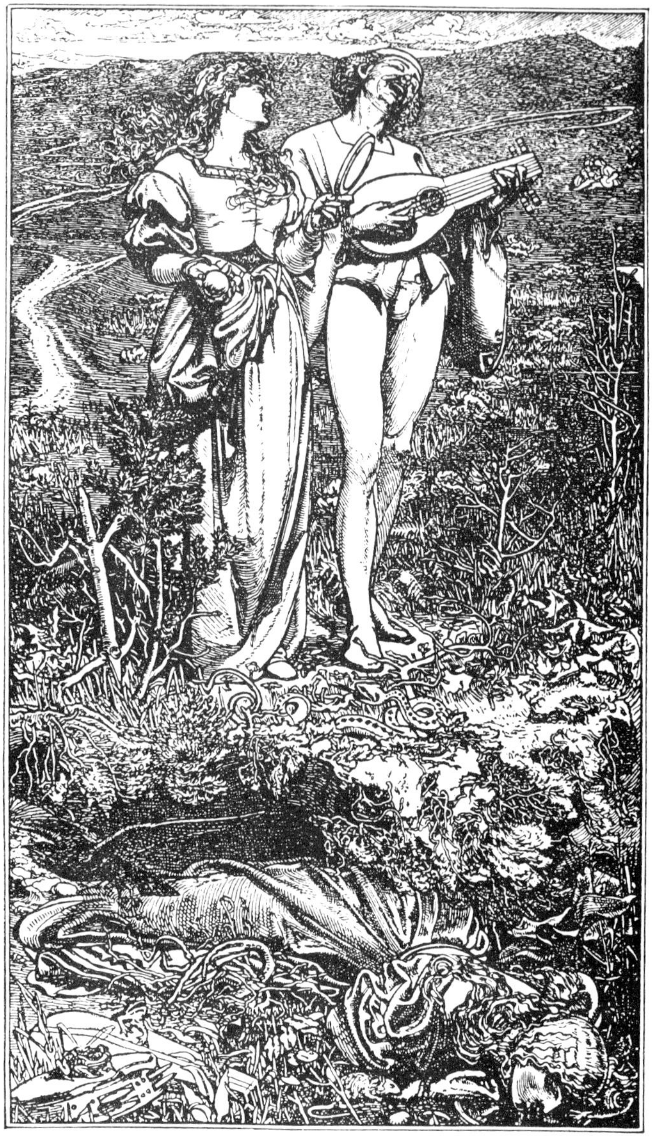

Frederick Sandys: 'Amor Mundi' (*Shilling Magazine*, 1865)

had been set up. And this, apart from his writings on art, his designs for commercially produced books and for the elaborate leather bindings executed by Sybil Pye in the 1900s, his painting (taken up seriously in the early 1900s), his collecting and innumerable other activities. Moreover, whatever one may think of his other works (and his oil paintings in particular tend to be rather disappointing), his graphic work remains not only of unique influence and importance, but frequently extremely beautiful in its own right – the Vale Press books in particular remain for me the most pleasurable to look

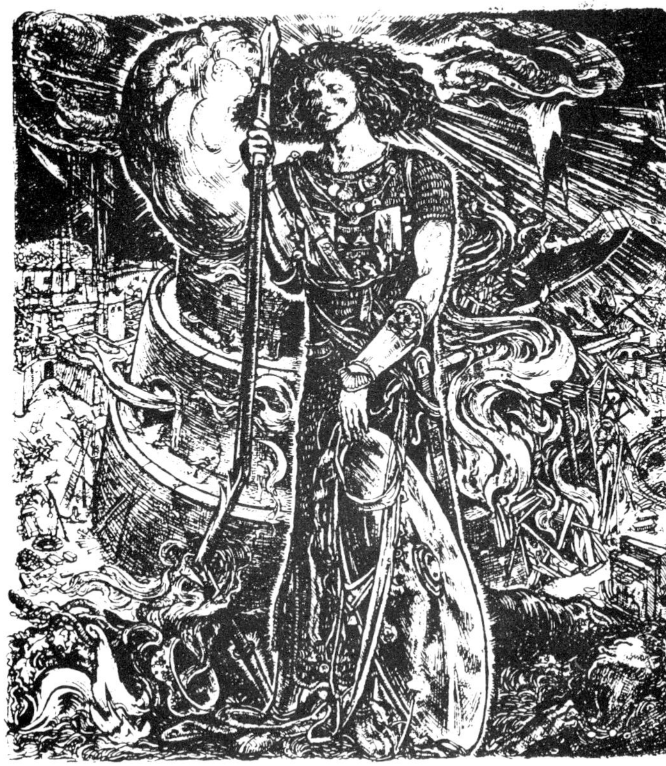

Charles Ricketts:
Poems, Lyrical and Dramatic,
by Lord de Tablay (1893)

at, to handle and, yes, even to read of all that emerged from private presses in that turn-of-the-century heyday of the private press. ❧ Perhaps the first reason why Ricketts is not only such an important but such a symptomatic figure in art nouveau is that he was a born eclectic. With complete (and in general justified) confidence in his own powers of assimilation he accepted influences and ideas from all sorts of conceivable and inconceivable sources, using them only in so far as, and only in the way that, they had any relevance to the object in hand, and discarding or drastically modifying them when their immediate usefulness ceased; his books are, in A. J. A. Symons's phrase, 'the products of an historically learned mind applied unhistorically', presenting 'a fantastic mixture of archaic pedanticism and revolutionary defiance of precedent.'[2] Thus, though his development can be divided very roughly into phases, we often find alarmingly divergent styles appearing side by side in contemporary work. ❧ Some of his earliest book-bindings, for instance, among them those for Wilde's *A House of Pomegranates* (Osgood, McIlvaine, 1891), John Addington Symonds's *In the Key of Blue* (Elkin Mathews and John Lane, 1893) and the *Poems, Lyrical and Dramatic* of Lord de Tablay (Mathews and Lane, 1893), are very much in the 'old-fashioned jam-tart' style of Continental high art nouveau. Yet oddly enough the illustrations to the latter volume are just as unmistakably in the manner of Rossetti, slightly exaggerated and tinged with self-conscious decadence (though not much more so than, say, Sandys's 'Amor Mundi' of 1865). And for the cover of the *Poetical Works* of James Thomson (Dobell) two years later, where considering the subject-matter of the contents a morbid, decadent style would be thoroughly justified, Ricketts reverts unpredictably to a simple, artless, almost 1850-ish brand of Pre-Raphaelitism.

Charles Ricketts bindings.

Top row: *Poems, Lyrical and Dramati* of Lord de Tablay (1893) $7\frac{3}{4} \times 5$ in.; *Collected Poems* of Lord de Tablay (1903) $7\frac{3}{4} \times 5$ in.; *Poems of Adoration* b Michael Field (1912) $7\frac{3}{4} \times 5$ in.; Bottom row: *Mystic Trees* by Michael Field (1913) $7\frac{3}{4} \times 5$ in.; *The Poetical Works* of James Thomson (1895) $7\frac{5}{8} \times 4\frac{5}{8}$ in.; *Wild Honey* by Michael Field (1908) $7\frac{5}{8} \times 4\frac{5}{8}$ in.

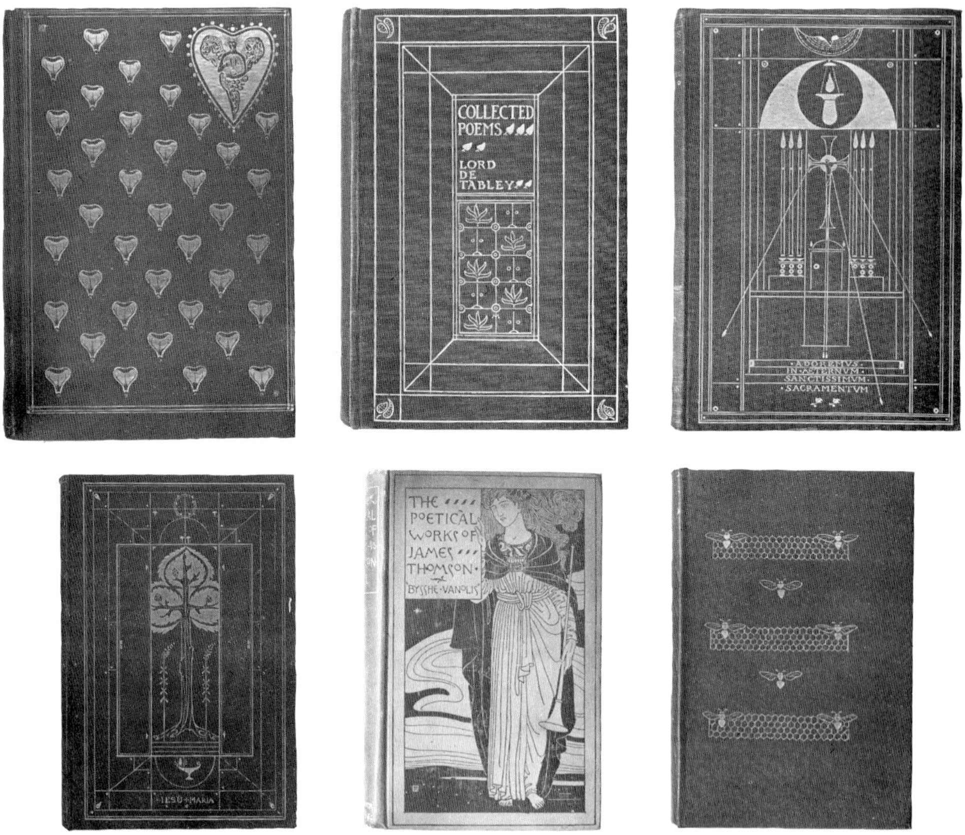

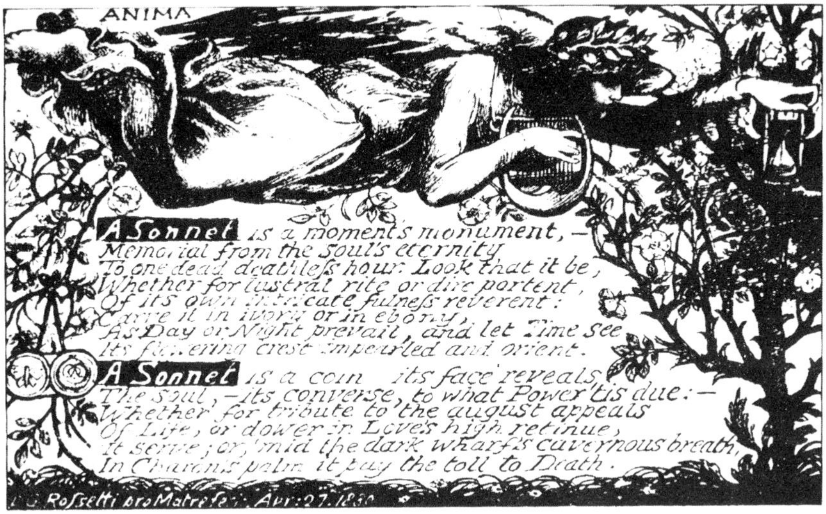

Dante Gabriel Rossetti: 'A Sonnet', written 1880

In 1903, on the cover for Lord de Tablay's *Collected Poems* (Chapman and Hall), we encounter the severe, 'architectural' later manner in which abstract patterns of straight lines and small circles are broken up by only the smallest tokens of representationalism; but then again five years later still the cover of Michael Field's *Wild Honey* (Fisher Unwin) is patterned with a honeycomb design obviously suggested by the title but equally obviously deriving directly from Rossetti's binding for his *Poems* of 1881. But the curious thing is that for all this diversity, every one of the covers (except probably that for Thomson's poems) is instantly recognizable as the work of Ricketts and no one else. And the same is true, despite an even greater diversity of inspiration, about his illustrations. Ricketts the illustrator was early influenced by the Pre-Raphaelites, certainly, by the illustrators of the 1860s,

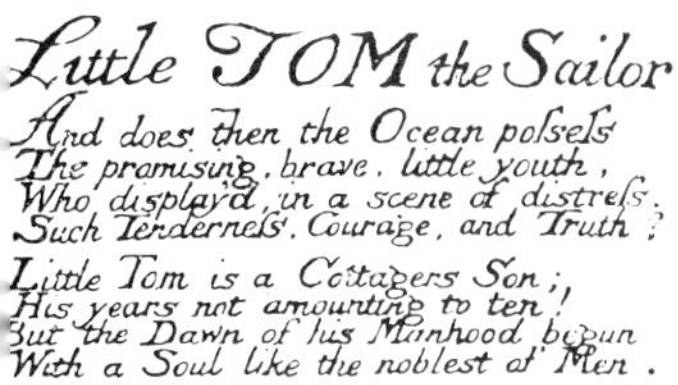

Villiam Blake: Broadside ballad,
Little Tom the Sailor' (1800),
s reproduced in *The Hobby Horse* (1886)

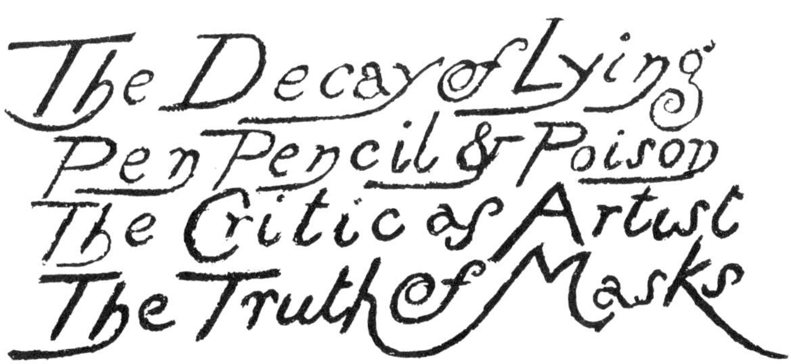

Charles Ricketts: Lettering from the cover of Oscar Wilde's *Intentions* (Osgood, McIlvaine, 1891)

particularly Sandys, and by the later, post-Pre-Raphaelite work of Rossetti. In particular he is said[3] to have modelled the free script seen on many of his early covers and illustrations (notably the cover of Wilde's *Intentions*, 1891) on Rossetti's handwriting, though Rossetti in his turn must surely have modelled his on Blake's engraved script, so lavishly praised by Herbert H. Gilchrist in *The Hobby Horse*,[4] and since Ricketts admired Blake as well, Blake's script could just as easily have been the model. In addition he had a deep admiration for Morris, though admitting that his first impression of the first Kelmscott book *The Glittering Plain* (1891) was 'one of disappointment' ('in this I thought the type very noble indeed, but the decoration less so'), and his mature taste was more for the severity and simplicity of the books Morris had printed by the Chiswick Press under his close supervision, *The House of the Wolfings* (1889) and *The Roots of the Mountains* (1890), which, Ricketts said, had he known them when he began as a book designer, 'might have initiated me at the time to a better and more severe style'.[5] But though the debt that some of the Vale Press books owe to some aspects of Kelmscott Press books is obvious (and the divergences are often even more revealing), Morris's models were basically gothic and even the types he designed, Golden, Troye and Chaucer, were strongly influenced by gothic types, the latter two being fully gothic and the first a roman modified in such a way as to look gothic. Ricketts's models, on the other hand, were from the beginning Renaissance; *Daphnis and Chloe*, according to its prospectus, was intended 'to emulate the build and style of the finest Italian books'. And so, despite his interest in fifteenth-century woodcuts,[6] handed on to Sturge Moore, who carried out some of the researches on the subject indicated by Ricketts,[7] his own books were about as un-gothic as possible, reflecting instead the lightness and sparkle of the best sixteenth-century Italian books. Needless to say,

Poliphili Hypnerotomachia (149
– Methuen facsimile of 190

Charles Ricketts
Daphnis and Chloe (189

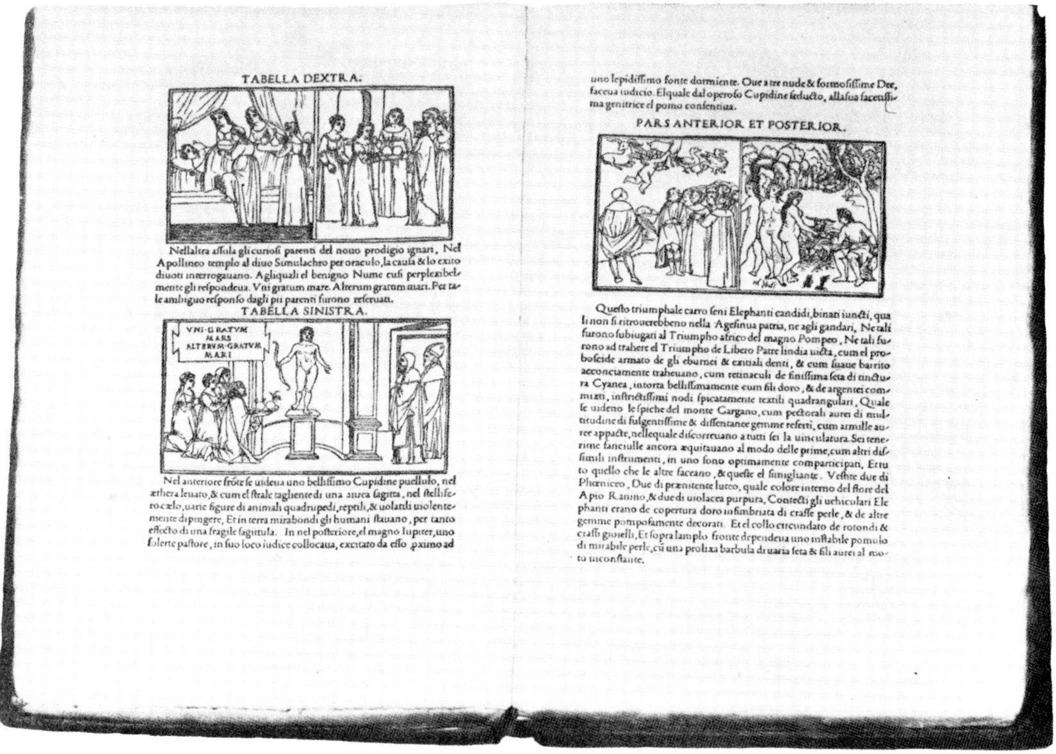

TABELLA DEXTRA.

Nellaltra assola gli curiosi parenti del nouo prodigio ignari, Nel Apollineo templo al diuo Simulachro per oraculo, la causa & lo exito diuoti interrogauano. Agliquali el benigno Nume cusi perplexibelmente gli respondeua. Vni gratum mare. Alterum gratum mari. Per tale ambiguo responso dagli pii parenti furono reseruati.

TABELLA SINISTRA.

Nel anteriore frōte se uideua uno bellissimo Cupidine puellulo, nel æthera leuato, & cum el strale tagliente di una aurea sagitta, nel stellifero cælo, uarie figure di animali quadrupedi, reptili, & uolatili uiolentemente dipingere, Et in terra mirabondi gli humani stauano, per tanto effecto di una fragile sagittula. In nel posteriore, el magno Iupiter, uno solerte pastore, in suo loco iudice collocaua, excitato da esso ꝓximo ad uno lepidissimo fonte dormiente. Oue a tre nude & formosissime Dee, faceua iudicio. Elquale dal operoso Cupidine seducto, allasua facetissima genitrice el pomo consentiua.

PARS ANTERIOR ET POSTERIOR.

Questo triumphale carro seni Elephanti candidi, binati iuncti, quali non si ritrouerebbeno nella Agesinua patria, ne agli gandari, Ne tali furono subiugati al Triumpho africo del magno Pompeo, Ne tali furono ad trahere el Triumpho de Libero Patre lindia uicta, cum el proboscide armato de gli eburnei & exitiali denti, & cum suaue barrito acconciamente traheuano, cum retinaculi de finissima seta di tinctura Cyanea, intorta bellissimamente cum fili doro, & de argentei commixti, instrictissimi nodi spicatamente textili quadrangulari, Quale se uideno le spiche del monte Gargano, cum pectorali aurei di multitudine di fulgentissime & dissentanee gemme referti, cum armille auree appacte, nellequale discorreuano a tutti sei la uinculatura. Sei tenerime fanciulle ancora æquitauano al modo delle prime, cum altri dissimili instrumenti, in uno sono optimamente comparticipati, Et tuto quello che le altre faceano, & queste el simigliante. Vestite due di Phœniceo, Due di prænitente luteo, quale colore interno del fiore del Apio Ranino, & due di uiolacea purpura, Contecti gli uehiculari Elephanti erano de copertura doro infimbriata di crasse perle, & de altre gemme pomposamente decorati. Et el collo circundato de rotondi & crassi gioielli, Et sopra lamplo fronte dependeua uno instabile pomulo di mirabile perle, cū una prolixa barbula di uaria seta & fili aurei al moto inconstante.

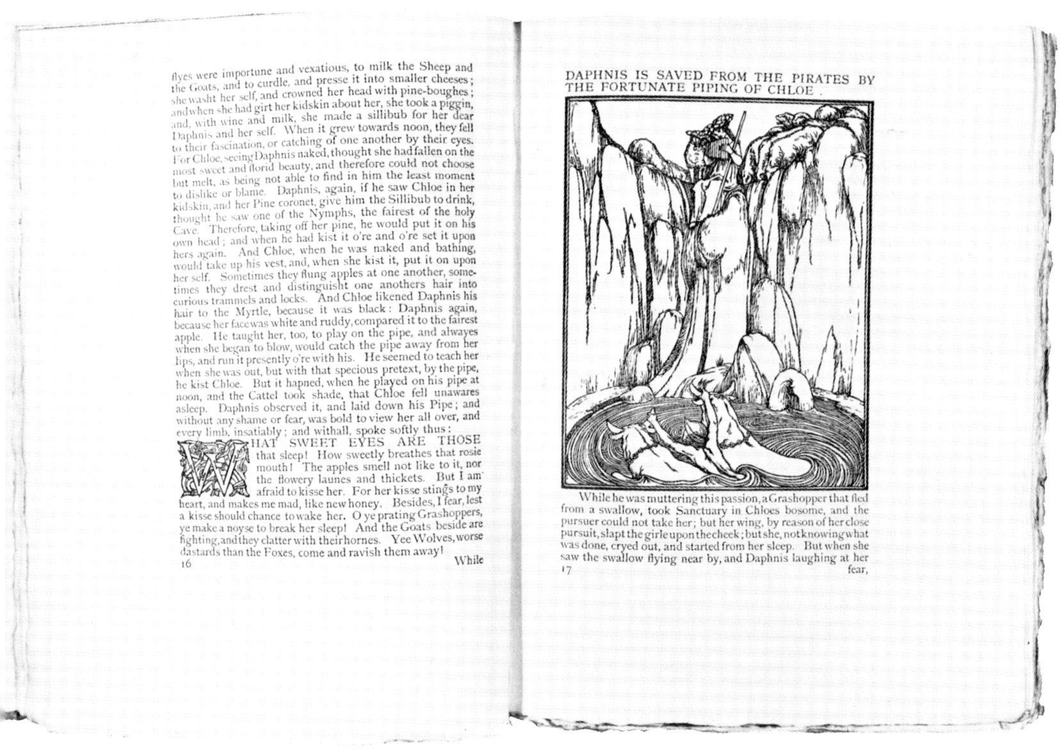

flyes were importune and vexatious, to milk the Sheep and the Goats, and to curdle, and presse it into smaller cheeses; she washt her self, and crowned her head with pine-boughes; and when she had girt her kidskin about her, she took a piggin, and, with wine and milk, she made a sillibub for her dear Daphnis and her self. When it grew towards noon, they fell to their fascination, or catching of one another by their eyes. For Chloe, seeing Daphnis naked, thought she had fallen on the most sweet and florid beauty, and therefore could not choose but melt, as being not able to find in him the least moment to dislike or blame. Daphnis, again, if he saw Chloe in her kidskin, and her Pine coronet, give him the Sillibub to drink, thought he saw one of the Nymphs, the fairest of the holy Cave. Therefore, taking off her pine, he would put it on his own head; and when he had kist it o're and o're set it upon hers again. And Chloe, when he was naked and bathing, would take up his vest, and, when she kist it, put it on upon her self. Sometimes they flung apples at one another, sometimes they drest and distinguisht one anothers hair into curious trammels and locks. And Chloe likened Daphnis his hair to the Myrtle, because it was black: Daphnis again, because her face was white and ruddy, compared it to the fairest apple. He taught her, too, to play on the pipe, and alwayes when she began to blow, would catch the pipe away from her lips, and run it presently o're with his. He seemed to teach her when she was out, but with that specious pretext, by the pipe, he kist Chloe. But it hapned, when he played on his pipe at noon, and the Cattel took shade, that Chloe fell unawares asleep. Daphnis observed it, and laid down his Pipe; and without any shame or fear, was bold to view her all over, and every limb, insatiably; and withall, spoke softly thus:

WHAT SWEET EYES ARE THOSE that sleep! How sweetly breathes that rosie mouth! The apples smell not like to it, nor the flowery launes and thickets. But I am afraid to kisse her. For her kisse stings to my heart, and makes me mad, like new honey. Besides, I fear, lest a kisse should chance to wake her. O ye prating Grashoppers, ye make a noyse to break her sleep! And the Goats beside are fighting, and they clatter with their hornes. Yee Wolves, worse dastards than the Foxes, come and ravish them away!

16 While

DAPHNIS IS SAVED FROM THE PIRATES BY THE FORTUNATE PIPING OF CHLOE.

While he was muttering this passion, a Grashopper that fled from a swallow, took Sanctuary in Chloes bosome, and the pursuer could not take her; but her wing, by reason of her close pursuit, slapt the girle upon the cheek; but she, not knowing what was done, cryed out, and started from her sleep. But when she saw the swallow flying near by, and Daphnis laughing at her

17 fear,

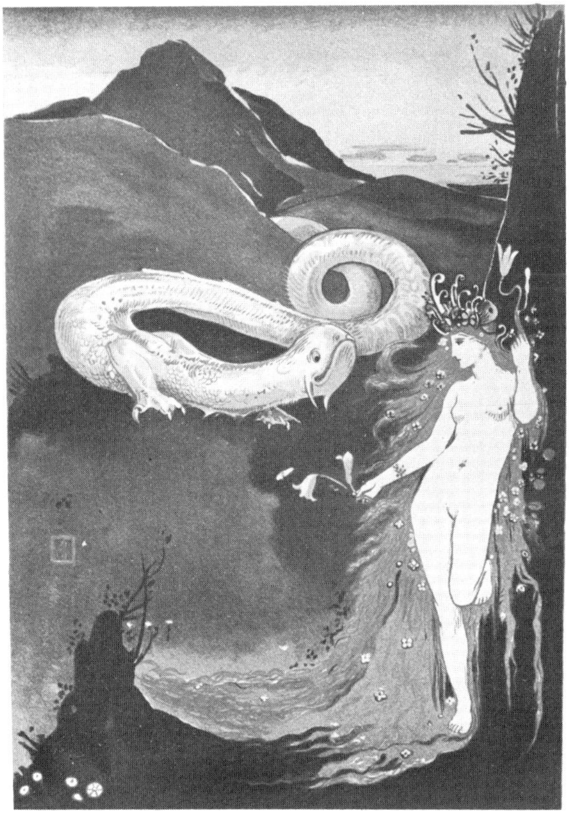

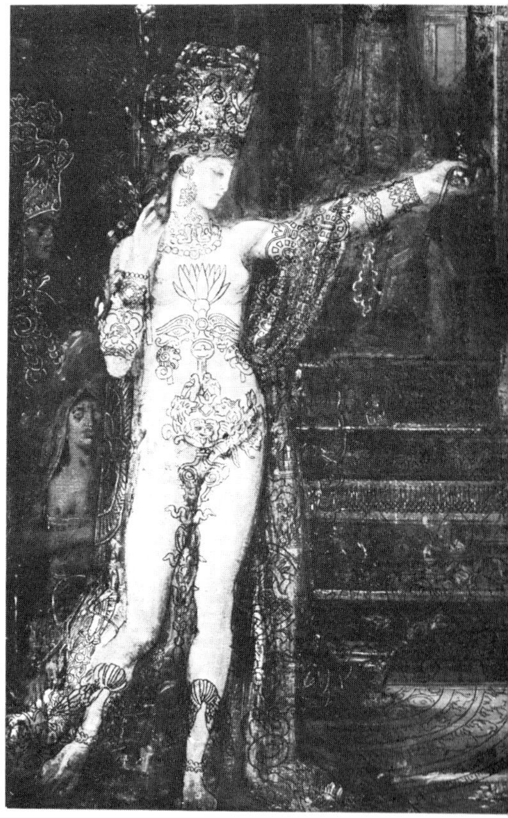

Charles Ricketts: *The Great Worm*. Coloured lithograph from *The Dial* No. 1 (1889)

Gustave Moreau: *La Salomé Tatouée* (Musée Moreau, Paris)

Botticelli was also an object of Ricketts's worship, as he was earlier (and less knowledgeably) of Rossetti's.[8] ❧ But along with these traditional, 'respectable' influences drawn from the main-stream of European art and design, there are in Ricketts's work all sorts of more idiosyncratic, exotic influences. First of all there is the Japanese: Ricketts shared with Whistler and with all the major figures of art nouveau a profound admiration for Japanese styles and conventions – an admiration which makes itself felt as a piquant element in the composition of designs otherwise apparently quite traditional, almost Pre-Raphaelite (by either interpretation of that ambiguous term) in their stylistic allegiances. The influences of the Frenchmen Puvis de Chavannes and Gustave Moreau are also marked, especially in his early works; the figure in his coloured lithograph in the first number of *The Dial*, for instance, is clearly a virtual pastiche of Moreau. The list of influences could be extended almost indefinitely: Ricketts was passionately interested in Greek vase decorations, and the conventions there used in the flat, frieze-like renderings of rounded forms recur more or less modified in his designs; Celtic intricacies of intertwining shapes occur in the decorative borders of a number of Vale Press books; much of Ricketts's admiration – unlikely in the general context of art nouveau taste – for Titian and Delacroix comes out in his oil paintings, and less evidently, but nevertheless appreciably when one knows what to look for, in his woodcuts (which in some cases are rehandlings of the same subjects as the oil paintings). And so on and so on. Rarely can so many heterogeneous influences and so much eccentric learning have gone into the formation of one man's style.

However, all the same one can talk of *a* style, the Ricketts look in design. To begin with, this comes from Ricketts's complete technical control of his media. He began his working life apprenticed to a wood-engraver, Roberts of the City and Guilds Technical Art School, as did Shannon, and he had a thorough mastery of the woodcutter's and engraver's craft, which enabled him not only to design with complete knowledge of the intended technique's possibilities, but actually to cut the blocks himself, whereas even Morris called in professional engravers to translate his and Burne-Jones's designs into blocks for the Kelmscott Press. Moreover, Ricketts started work as a book designer with a succession of commercial companies, selecting from the types and materials they or their printers had available, and even when he set up his own firm and had types cast to his own designs – Vale, Avon (smaller, for the Shakespeare) and his own favourite, the curious King's, a revised roman returning to half-uncial form – he never owned a printing press himself, but continued to have his books set and printed by commercial printers, the Ballantyne Press, though under his own most detailed and demanding supervision. He never hesitated, any more than Whistler had, to use common materials – plain white buckram, flowered and gaily patterned papers for front and back of books – and though the Vale Press books are designed and made with every possible care and attention, they never have the rarified *noli-me-tangere* air of most Kelmscott Press books or the later products of the Doves Press, founded in 1900 by Morris's disciple T. J. Cobden-Sanderson and Morris's one-time associate Emery Walker – the same Emery Walker whose lecture on printing, delivered first in 1888 and later included in *Arts and Crafts Essays* (1893) as the joint work of Walker and Morris, is really the first definitive statement of the printing revival. ❧ Rather, they seem to be an extension of Ricketts's ordinary commercial practice, the putting together of books at once beautiful and practical, to be used as well as admired. Morris, despite his important pioneering work of design for printers on *The House of the Wolfings* and *The Roots of the Mountains*, both printed for him by the Chiswick Press in pre-Kelmscott days, seems to have regarded such activity as a largely irrelevant second-best, though in fact these volumes were in the last analysis more influential on subsequent practice than the more pretentious products of Kelmscott. Ricketts, on the other hand, not only started in commercial publishing, but graduated to what was in effect his own rather special form of it, applying there the lessons he had learnt, and went quite happily back to designing for commercial publishers after winding up the Vale Press with a small but undoubted profit. ❧ The Vale Press was actually set up after the Kelmscott Press, and of course Ricketts was Morris's junior by some thirty-two years, but much of Ricketts's thinking about book-design is independent of Morris's, and a tendency in writers earlier this century to list the Vale Press as one of the many which followed more or less closely in Kelmscott's wake is unfair. Ricketts's first attempts at page-layout and book-design date back to 1889, only a year after Emery Walker's influential lecture and the same year as Morris's first venture, *The House of the Wolfings* (which, however, as noted above, Ricketts did not know until some years later); they are to be found in the first number of *The Dial.* This, it must be said, is in many respects a disappointment if one comes to it with some knowledge of Ricketts's later work. The cover is an undistinguished jumble designed by Ricketts but engraved by Shannon (the cover of the other four numbers was designed and engraved by Ricketts); the full-page designs – a coloured lithograph by Ricketts, an etching by Shannon and other oddments – are bundled together at the front, and hardly seem to belong to the rest of the magazine; and the text itself is printed, not very appetizingly, on a smooth, creamish paper. And yet there are already all sorts of signs of the way Ricketts would develop. The way that the pages are scattered with small decorative vignettes, ornamental capitals and tailpieces (all of them, the editors note, 'printed *from the wood* to ensure the greater sweetness of the printing') demonstrates an ease and freedom already far in advance of the somewhat staid *Hobby Horse*, *The Dial's* main precurser in this field. ❧ During the next year Ricketts was introduced, through the influence of Wilde, into the world of commercial book-design, his first commission being for Wilde's *The Picture of Dorian Gray* (Ward Lock, 1891), followed immediately by *A House of Pomegranates* (1891),[9] published by Osgood, McIlvaine and Co., for whom he subsequently designed a number of other books, 'not always strictly shaped according to my wishes',[10] including Wilde's *Intentions* (1891), *The Bard of the Dimbovitza* by Hélène Vacaresco (1891) and *Tess of the d'Urbervilles* (1891). In these, even more evidently than in *The Dial*, he is feeling his way towards a personal style of book-design, quite different from and infinitely more forward-looking than Morris's. By the time the second issue of *The*

Dial came out in 1892 he had nearly found it: the sometimes fussy over-ornateness of *A House of Pomegranates* has largely given way to the elegant sparseness and discretion of his cover for *Intentions* and the overall design of John Gray's *Silverpoints* (John Lane and Elkin Mathews, 1893), in which the decoration was confined to a few of the capitals, the rest being left in plain roman, with the body of the text in italics. In *Silverpoints* too he made his one notable contribution in format, evolving for it a curious upright shape based on 'one of those rare Aldus italic volumes with its margins uncut' which in their turn, he notes, probably came from the Persian saddle-book, designed to be slipped easily into the pocket of a saddle.[11] It would not be true to say that Ricketts's books after 1892 were never

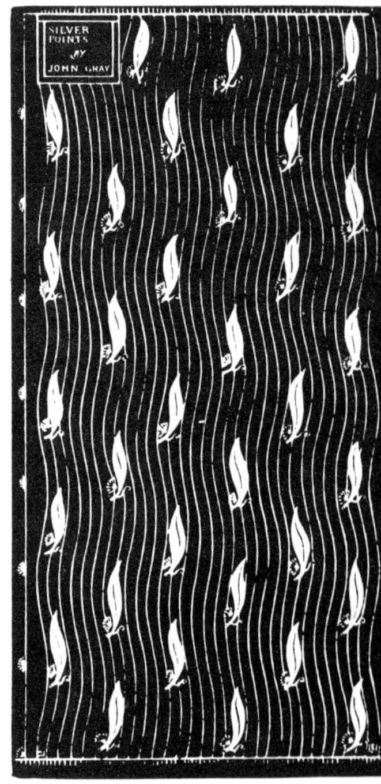

Charles Ricketts:
Silverpoints binding (1893)
$8\frac{1}{2} \times 4\frac{1}{4}$ in.

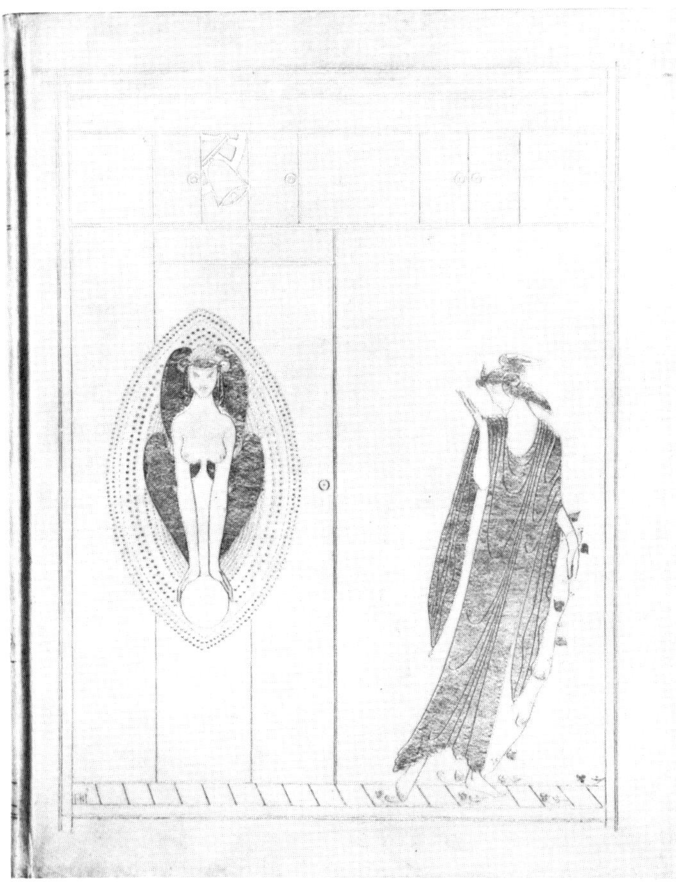

Charles Ricketts:
Binding for Oscar Wilde's
The Sphinx (1894) $8\frac{3}{4} \times 6\frac{5}{8}$ in.

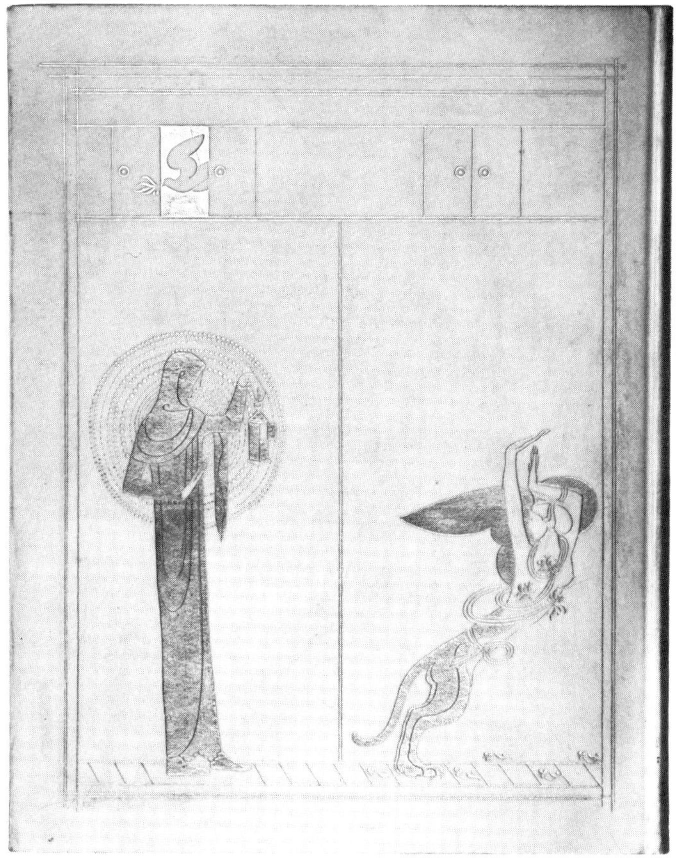

Charles Ricketts:
Binding for Oscar Wilde's
The Sphinx (1894)

ornate, though the general tendency of the Vale Press books is towards greater and greater simplicity. At least two of the books after that date for which Ricketts had complete overall responsibility, *Daphnis and Chloe*, which he published himself (1893) and *The Sphinx*, which he designed at Wilde's behest in 1893 and which was published by John Lane in 1894, are ornate in the extreme. But the secret of Ricketts lies in his ability to vary the expressions of his style to match with almost uncanny precision the form and nature of the text upon which he is working. Morris and his associates at the Kelmscott Press tended to apply much the same treatment to every text they handled, with greater or lesser degrees of elaboration depending on the size and importance of the book; the Doves Press, even more severely,

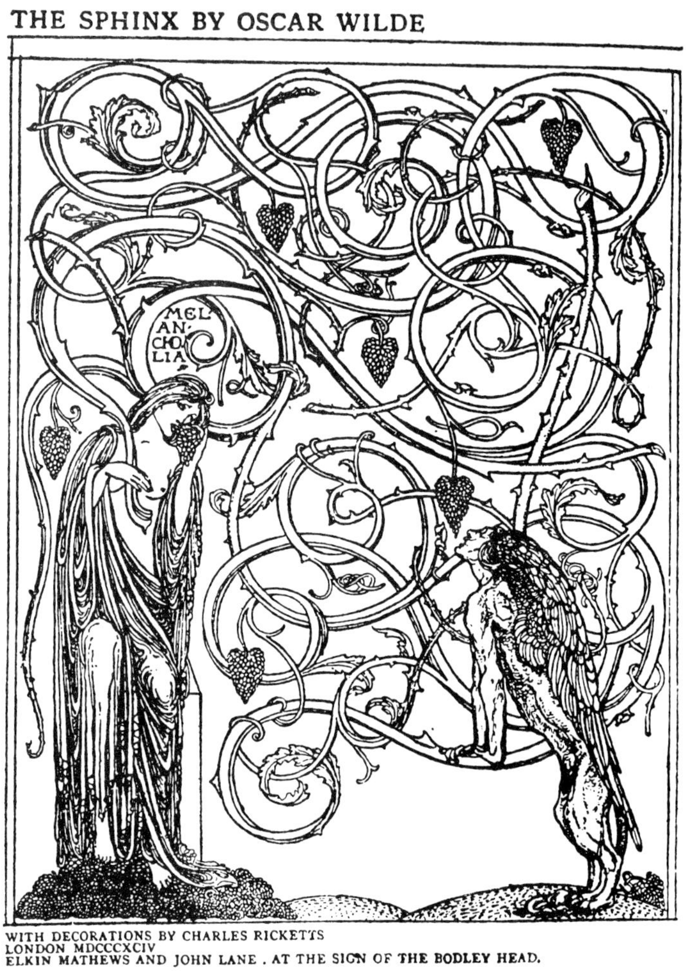

Charles Ricketts:
Title-page for Oscar Wilde's
The Sphinx (1894)
black, brown and green $8\frac{3}{8} \times 6\frac{1}{4}$ in.

fixed right from the start on a formula using no non-typographical decoration beyond an occasional hand-drawn initial, and applied it to everything – as Sir Francis Meynell remarks of Cobden-Sanderson's books, 'They are lovely, impeccable, taut and silky like young muscles in play; but they are in series a little automatic, a little boring: typographical Tiller girls.'[12] Not so Ricketts's books: each is conceived freshly in terms of its literary materials, the design sometimes chiming with, sometimes counterpointing the qualities of the subject, and the illustrations (if any) following Ricketts's own precept that 'illustration ought to give to the book an accompaniment of gesture and decoration, perhaps also an added element of visual poetry.' In *Daphnis and Chloe* 'the

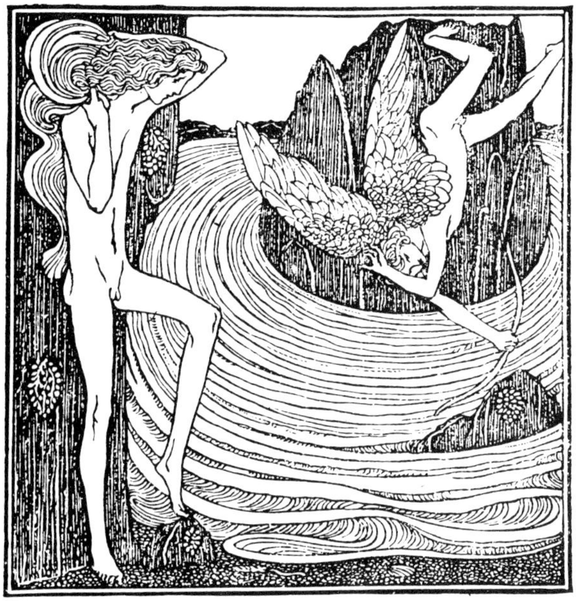

Charles Ricketts: *Hero and Leander* (1894)

lightness of the subject carries triumphantly the luxuriance of the decorations'[13]; in *The Sphinx* the extreme elaboration of the book's form – it is printed, the text entirely in capitals ('more classical than Renaissance'[14]), in rust, green and black, profusely decorated, and bound in ivory vellum with designs in gold – mirrors exactly the luxuriant and self-consciously perverse exoticism of Wilde's text; perversity, indeed, is even indulged graphically to the extent of having a left-hand title page. In contrast to these two volumes, Ricketts's edition of Marlowe's *Hero and Leander* with Chapman's conclusion (1894; published for Ricketts by Mathews and Lane) offsets the lush eroticism of the poem, especially Marlowe's cantos, with a design of great sobriety, confining the decoration mainly to formally framed pictorial headpieces for each book. ❧ In the books published by the Vale Press proper from 1896 onwards there is considerable variation within the basic limits of Ricketts's style. One of them, Michael Field's *The World at Auction* (1898), has what Ricketts described as his only pure Renaissance border; most of the others, from the first, *The Early Poems of John Milton* (1896), onward, contain instead borders of freely-ranging intertwined foliage in the

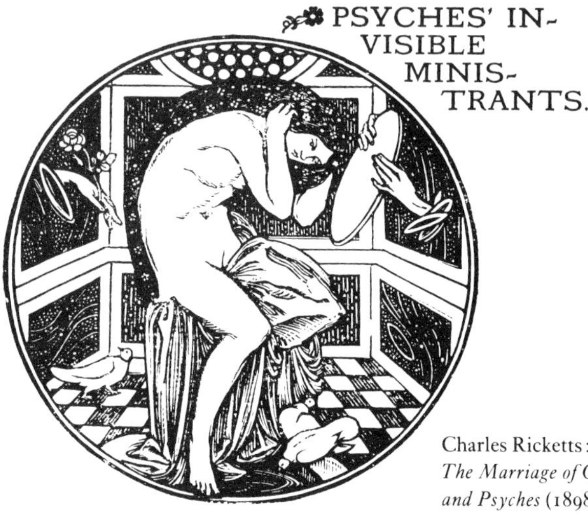

Charles Ricketts:
The Marriage of Cupide and Psyches (1898)

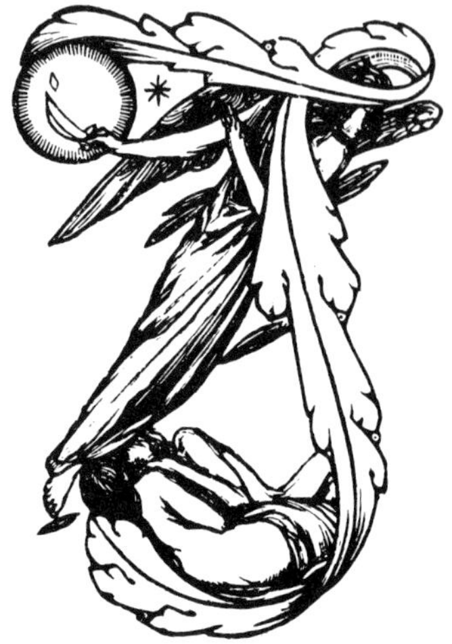

Charles Ricketts:
Initial to Blake's *Poetical Sketches* (1899)

style Ricketts maintained he had arrived at quite instinctively, probably because 'the usually solid ground of the Ratdolt and Morris borders forced me towards open decoration, if I may give it this name'.[15] Certainly the often-suggested influence of Morris on this particular aspect of Ricketts's books would seem to be entirely negative: as H. C. Marillier remarks, 'There is nothing in all the flowering tracery of William Morris which remotely resembles the intricate knot-work and geometrical orderliness of the Milton borders'.[16] Some of the books – Blake's *Poetical Sketches* of 1899 is a beautiful example – are decorated in addition with pictorial illustrations and initials; others have the main decorative accent placed on an elaborate title-page design. ❦ None of the Vale books is so elaborately decorated as the *Daphnis and Chloe*, and some of the most successful, such as the *Lyrical Poems* and *In Memoriam* of Tennyson (both 1900) contain no illustrations at all, but only a few foliate borders distributed with apparent (but only apparent) arbitrariness through the text. Holbrook Jackson takes mild exception to this practice (he is writing particularly of the Vale Press Shakespeare): 'In the use of leaf figures as a kind of super-punctuation, an intellectual process seems to have taken the place of the subtle and indefinable taste which dominates matters of art. The leaves seem to have been *thought* into their

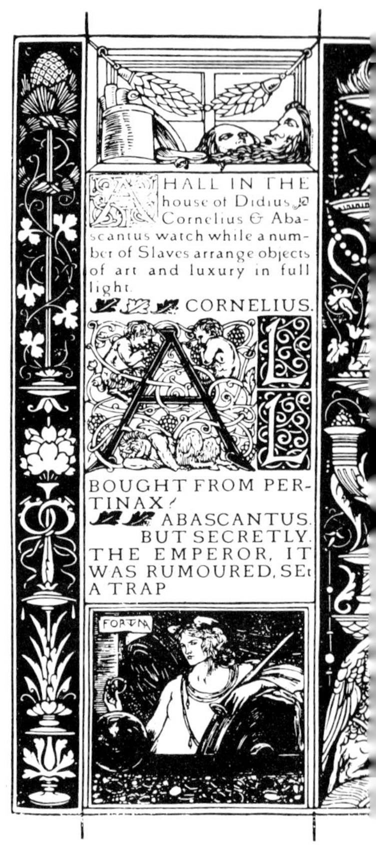

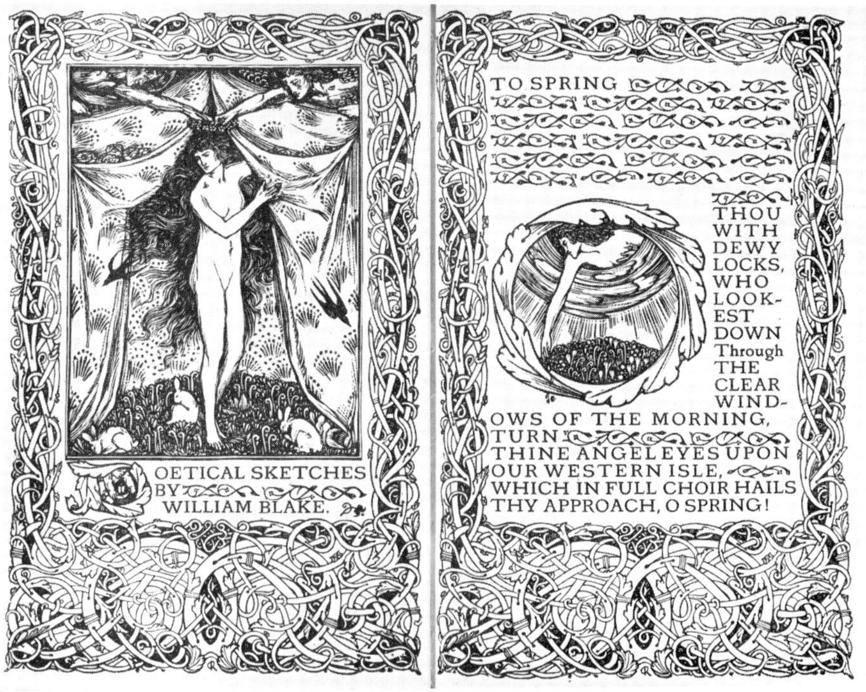

Charles Ricketts: Title-opening of Blake's *Poetical Sketches* (1899) $7\frac{1}{2} \times 4\frac{3}{4}$ in.

places, and the result is not always happy.'[17] This seems to me a perhaps hyper-sophisticated view of the question – especially since it appears as part of a contrast between the 'refinement' of Vale Press books and the 'naturalness' of Kelmscott, a rather surprising view of matters Jackson apparently accepted in 1913 but later had second thoughts about.[18] Surely if the average observant user of the books raised the question at all – and in all probability he would not – it would be rather to wonder whether there was any system in the placing of the decorated leaves than to be disturbed by the intellectual calculation with which they were distributed. ❦ However, the general point that Jackson is making seems fair enough: he characterizes the Vale Press books as having 'all the supersensitiveness of things which have been deliberately made according to a fastidious though eclectic taste and a strict formula . . . Yet at the same time, although Ricketts does not suggest organic growth in his decorated books, he suggests growth by segregation – by a rearrange-

Charles Ricketts: *The World at Auction* (1898) $9 \times 5\frac{1}{2}$ in.

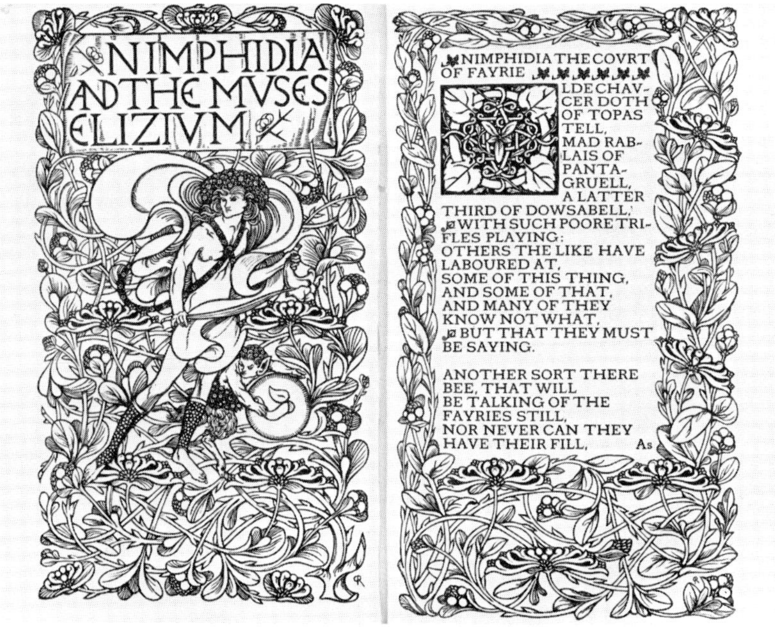

Charles Ricketts: Title-opening of Drayton's *Nimphidia and the Muses Elizium*, Vale Press (1896) 9 × 5½ in.

ment of parts which seem to have come together mathematically, or which are built up in a counterpoint like a theme in music.' The only dubious point in that is the implication that this is necessarily a disadvantage, that the Romantic air of organic growth (supposing one grants that Morris's books have it) is in some way absolutely preferable. To many tastes one of the great advantages of Ricketts as a book-designer is just this 'classical' quality in even his most ornate work, this feeling of mathematical precision which informs and disciplines even his most informal and extravagant early work and early in the 1900s, in the cover-designs for the Vale Press Shakespeare and the *Collected Poems* of Lord de Tablay, becomes overtly his inspiration. It is, in fact, the severe, geometrical character underlying all British art nouveau, right from Mackmurdo on, and it is hardly surprising if some of Ricketts's designs, such as that for *Daphnis and Chloe*,[19] not only look back in their spare elegance to seventeenth-century Dutch interiors and the White House Godwin designed for Whistler, but forward to Van de Velde, de Stijl, Mondrian, Corbusier and New Brutalism. After the winding-up of the Vale Press in 1904[20] Ricketts devoted himself increasingly to painting and to stage design, in which field he was also a powerful innovator, even finally being let loose in 1926 on *The Mikado*, in the very heart of English traditionalism represented by Gilbert and Sullivan. Earlier he seems to have felt some slight bitterness about the way his innovations in book-production and stage design had both been forgotten or discounted; writing to Gordon Bottomley in 1915, in answer to a query, [21] he says:

> *No, my dear chap, the Russians [Diaghilev's designers, that is] owe me nothing. (My book-illustration work has been swamped for ever by the success of Beardsley – whom they know.) My stage-work, which anticipated much of theirs – the all-red Attila scene, the all-blue Salome and Lear tent-scene, the all-green* Miracle *scenc, and countless details, too long to describe, such as huge patterns and fantastic head-dresses, are unknown to them; they are known here and remembered only by the theatrical profession. Any chance likeness you may detect lies in a common indebtedness to Moreau, or I should say, to things initiated and discovered by Moreau; remains a certain local and semi-Oriental element which is spontaneous, and which, with me, is replaced by many complex currents of experience.*

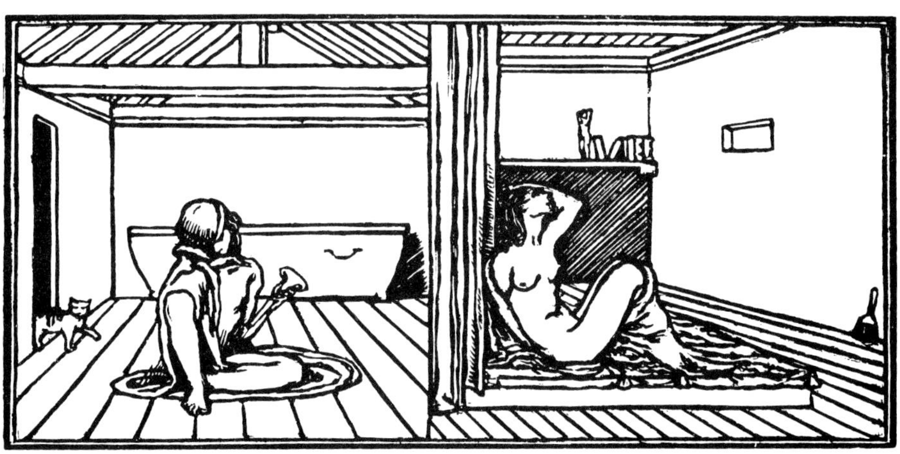

Charles Ricketts: *Daphnis and Chloe* (1894)

Nevertheless, Ricketts continued occasionally to design covers, sometimes illustrate and to some extent plan the layout of his own books – *Beyond the Threshold*, (privately printed, 1928); *Recollections of Oscar Wilde*, (Nonesuch, posthumously published in 1932); *Unrecorded Histories*, (Martin Secker, 1933) – those of his friends – Michael Field's *Poems of Adoration*, (Sands, 1912), and *Mystic Trees*, (Everleigh Nash, 1913); Laurence Binyon's *For Dauntless France*, (1918); Gordon Bottomley's *King Lear's Wife* (Constable, 1920), *Gruach and Britain's Daughter* (Constable, 1921), *A Vision of Giorgione* (Constable, 1922) and other books by the same author – and one or two others, such as Humbert Wolfe's *Troy* (Faber, 1928) and *Twenty-five Years of the National Art Collections Fund* (de luxe edition only, Maclehose, 1928). He also produced at least two elaborate series of designs in later years for works of Wilde, a second set of illustrations for *The Sphinx* and one for *Poems in Prose* (both c. 1914) which were sold to an American collector and remain largely unpublished. ❧ There is something very strange and mysterious about these later designs, and something I think very private. The more abstract designs for book-covers in particular have the air of meaning more than meets the eye, so that one suspects some esoteric system of symbolism at the back of them. What exactly – if anything specific – did these squares and triangles, these intersected circles, these minute circles, sometimes with dots at the centre, 'punctuating' the grander architectural designs mean to Ricketts? (In the cover-design for *The Sphinx*, when they first appear, the dots-in-circles are appreciably Japanese-style sliding-door fittings, but later all immediate representational significance vanishes.) They seem very much in the spirit of the various mystical associations of the 1900s, such as the Golden Dawn to which Yeats belonged, or again of the various offshoots of Freemasonry, Rosicrucianism and Theosophy (though one cannot imagine that the Michael Field ladies, both devout Roman Catholics, would have been very happy if their devotional poems had been, to their knowledge, clothed in Masonic symbolism). I have found no direct evidence that Ricketts was actively interested in any of these movements, and in 1904 he remarked in his journals[22] of the Michael Fields that they were 'unable to understand that an interest in religion and a sense of the effectiveness of its mythology or circumstances do not imply a religious spirit'. ❧ Even so, he was very much a child of his time, and the decoration from the first number of *The Dial*, with the visible odours diffusing from the resting place of the dead pauper girl, clearly hint at the synaesthesia which Yeats refers to in his introduction to W. T. Horton's *Book of Images*,[23] suggesting that

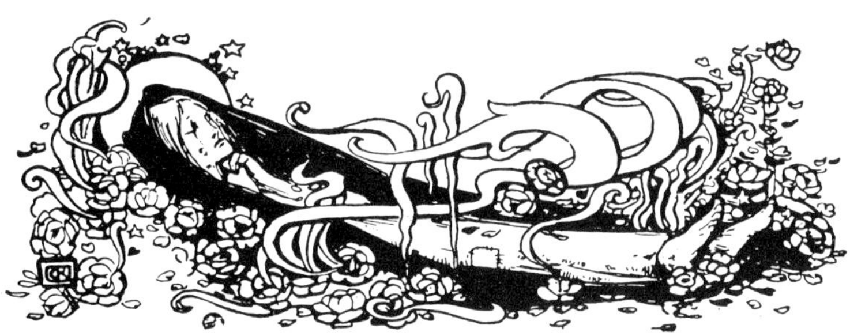

Charles Ricketts: *The Dial* (1889)

Horton's drawing and symbolist designs in general evoke 'a world where nothing is still for a moment, and where colours have odours and odours musical notes . . .', and which remained for some years, under Theosophist influence, the aim of many art nouveau artists (Scriabin, for instance, with his colour organ in *Prometheus* (1910) and his plan for a Mystery in the performance of which music would blend with architecture, dancing, colours and perfumes). Some support for the notion that Ricketts's later designs do in fact embody some sort of esoteric symbolism may perhaps be found in Sturge Moore's note to his own designs – very closely modelled on Ricketts's style of the period – for an edition of Villiers de l'Isle-Adam's symbolist drama *Axel*, published with an introduction by Yeats in 1925 (Jarrolds). Here Moore explains the significance of the designs in the sort of terms which might equally apply to Ricketts – 'The minor decorations are symbols: for the "uncreated light", an unfigured circle; for the great renunciation, a crucifix; for heaven-reflecting life, a rose . . .', etc. Or again, they might not. Whether they do or no, however, these later Ricketts designs have an oddly haunting quality which makes one regret intensely that he did not continue to work regularly in the field of book-design after the 1900s, feeling that he was regarded as, and perhaps was, 'a back number'. Nevertheless, the best of his work in this medium marks one of the high points, possibly *the* high point, of British book-design, and it is hard to over-estimate its influence, direct and indirect, on later-comers – on Sir Francis Meynell and the Nonesuch Press, which actually published Ricketts's last book, the *Recollections of Oscar Wilde* (which he intended to call *Roses of Shadow*); on Eric Gill, both in figure design and composition (compare a characteristic Gill design with Ricketts's book-plate for John Morgan) and in the ideals of page layout he practised in his own books; and through them on the whole range of modern book design. 'The essential point to remember', Emery Walker had said in his lecture of 1888,[24] 'is that the ornament, whatever it is, picture or pattern-work, should form *part of the page*, should be part of the whole scheme of the book'. Morris subscribed to this, and in his Kelmscott books it is in a sense true, though often only at the expense of making the ornament dictate the form of the book rather than vice versa. Ricketts in his books was the first really to apply the principle in all its implications; and for this he was and remains the one indispensable figure in the evolution of all that is worthwhile in the book today.

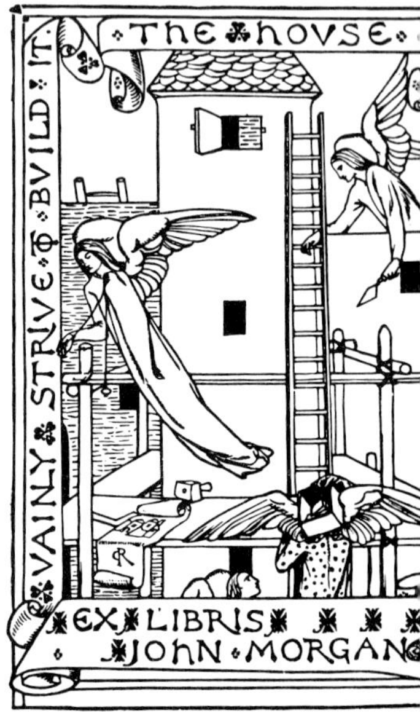

Charles Ricketts:
Book plate for John Morgan

(ii) Aubrey Beardsley

Aubrey Beardsley (1872-98) is the other key figure of the art nouveau book in the 1890s, though the nature and extent of his influence is very different from that of Ricketts. Ricketts, though frequently a superlative illustrator, was first and foremost a designer of books in which pictorial illustration played only a part, and sometimes not even that. Beardsley, on the other hand, was an illustrator before all else. For several books he designed elaborate series of illustrations, title-page, endpapers, covers, and obviously in these, especially when published by his friend Leonard Smithers – *Lysistrata*, 1896; *The Rape of the Lock*, 1896; *The Pierrot of the Minute*, 1897; *Mademoiselle de Maupin*, 1898 – he must certainly have had some say in the general layout and design, though it is difficult to say from the evidence left to us exactly how far his responsibility extended.[1] In any case, neither they nor *The Yellow Book*, of which he was art-editor from 1894 to 1895, for the first four numbers, and *The Savoy*, of which he was art editor for all eight numbers, January–December 1896, suggest that he had any specially adventurous approach to the overall design of books, particularly since *The Savoy*, for which he was more completely responsible, is much less distinguished typographically than *The Yellow Book*; at best one can say that the illustrations are placed in the books and magazines with unexceptionable taste and that the covers are often supremely elegant.[2] No, it is as a designer of illustrations, and above all as an artist in black-and-white, that Beardsley achieved and has retained his special eminence. Like Ricketts – but in general how unlike him in final effect – Beardsley was an eclectic, welding his highly personal style, or succession of styles, from a wide and varied range of materials. Moreover he, unlike Ricketts, provided for the perpetuation and dissemination of his products by all the latest methods; he accepted wholeheartedly from the beginning the photo-engraved line-block; some of his later illustrations, such as those for *Mademoiselle de Maupin* (1898) were actually designed for half-tone reproduction from wash drawings. ❦ He was extremely precocious, and drawings made by him when as young as eight survive.[3] His earliest enthusiasm in art was for the Italian primitives, and this devotion to Mantegna and Botticelli remained to the end of his life. The first major influence he underwent was, hardly surprisingly, that of Burne-Jones. When he was sixteen he entered an architect's office in London, and in 1892 he met Burne-Jones himself, who advised and encouraged him, and Watts, who was suspicious, as well as becoming more widely known in the London art world generally. In 1892 also he was commissioned by J. M. Dent to design and illustrate an ambitious edition of Malory's *Le Morte d'Arthur* (published 1893) which was intended to rival the Kelmscott Press books on their own ground, using the methods of mass-production. Presumably the motive behind this commission was largely the resemblance of Beardsley's work at this time to Burne-Jones's, not to mention the young artist's great facility and relative cheapness. The result probably did not turn out quite as intended, though, since other elements beside the pale remnants of Pre-Raphaelitism were at work fertilizing his developing talent, and what was seen by its devisers as an emulation of Morris and Burne-Jones turned out in the execution more like a parody of them – a parody which annoyed Morris to the point at which he contemplated legal action. ❦ It may well not have been a deliberate parody: it is simply that already, willy-nilly, the 'strong medieval decorative feeling' of Morris was mixed, as Walter Crane noted,[4] 'with a curious, weird Japanese-like spirit of *diablerie* and grotesque, as of an opium dream'. The design reproduced gives a clear indication of the way this heady and unstable mixture worked.

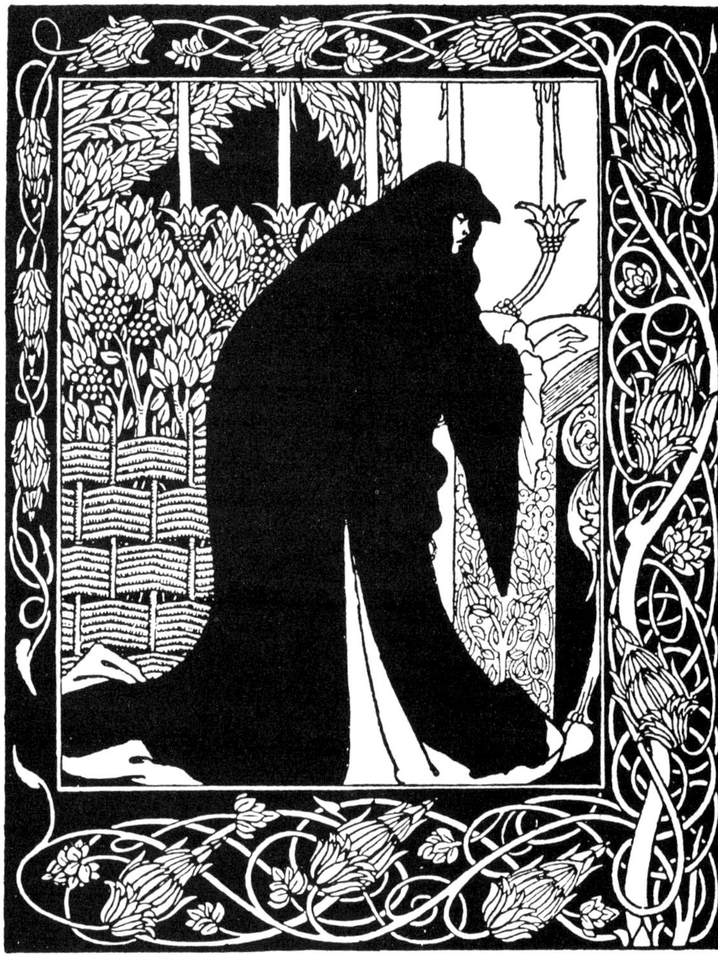

Aubrey Beardsley:
Le Morte d'Arthur (1893)

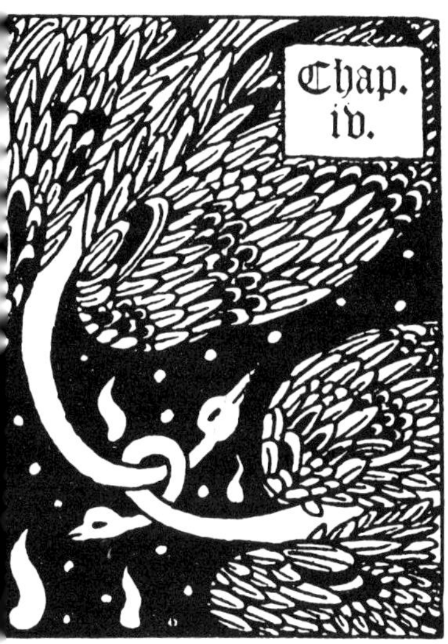

Aubrey Beardsley:
Le Morte d'Arthur (1893)

The general inspiration of a Kelmscott page layout, with a pictorial design enclosed in a formal floral border, is obvious enough, but note too the significant deviations and eccentricities: the illustration proper is not placed squarely on its frame, but moved towards the upper left-hand corner; the floral border becomes a casually informal and irregular business of wandering intertwined tendrils, arranged so as to intensify the asymmetry of the page; and the illustration itself is composed not in the regular, classical fashion of a Burne-Jones design, but in the much more tense, elusive manner of a Japanese print, with its bold massing of flat black in the figure's cloak set off by patches of clear white and two areas of flat, conventionalized patterning, all conspiring to falsify or suppress any possible feeling of perspective or recession – the whole composition remains resolutely a pattern in two dimensions. ❧ Obviously the days of medievalizing were over for Beardsley, and indeed before *Le Morte d'Arthur* finally appeared he had already been spectacularly introduced to the public by Joseph Pennell with an article devoted to him in the first issue of a new magazine, *The Studio* (April 1893), for which he also designed the cover. The eleven illustrations which accompanied this article, 'A New Illustrator', ranged from a drawing of 'Siegfried, Act II', much admired by and presented to Burne-Jones, through four designs for *Le Morte d'Arthur*, to two drawings, 'The Birthday of Madame Cigale' and 'Salome with the Head of St John the Baptist', in which Beardsley's capitulation to Japanese modes seems complete. In the Salome design particularly we find, save for a certain tendency to uncontrolled elaboration of detail which rapidly disappears (a comparison of this with the later version of the same design in the *Salome* set of 1894 is instructive), a complete example of what we would think of as characteristic Beardsley. Not only is the subject-matter suffused with a morbid and perverse eroticism, but the bold two-dimensional pattern-making, the uncompromising and unerring placing of an area of elaboration in an unwrought, entirely abstract setting, all point to Beardsley's first phase of maturity. ❧ But this, of course, though in general estimation 'typical' Beardsley, is not by any means all of Beardsley. The Beardsley who was influenced by Japanese prints (it is recorded that he kept a couple of the more subtly obscene ones on his walls to startle observant visitors), and perhaps even more by the art of Japan as refracted through the opulent imagination of Whistler's Peacock Room, was at the same time the devotee of Mantegna and the early Italians,[5] and an impassioned student of the collection of Greek vases at the British Museum, which acted as a valuable corrective to the Burne-Jones influence and

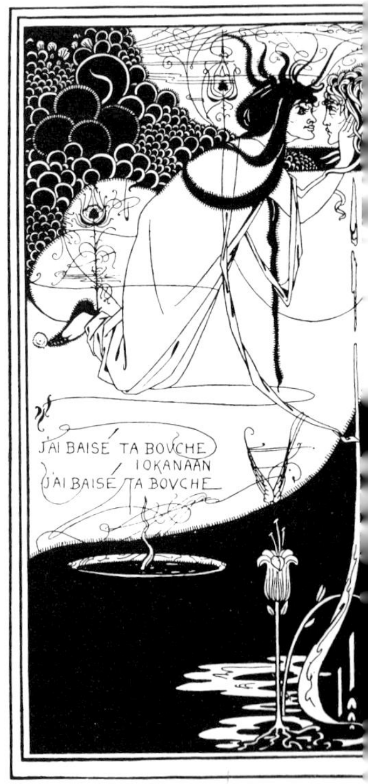

Aubrey Beardsley: 'Salome with the Head of St John the Baptist' *The Studio*, 1893

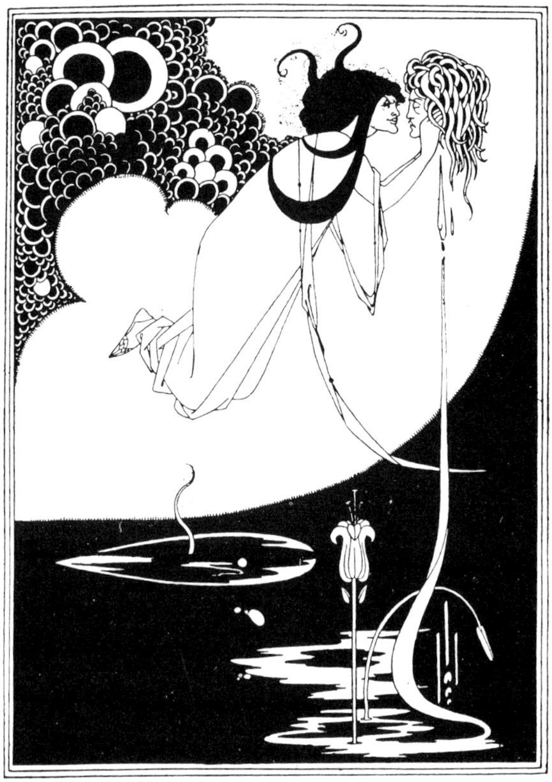

Aubrey Beardsley: *Salome* (1894)

supplement to the Japanese by teaching him how to indicate draperies with a minimum of lines and no shading at all.[6] In the designs for Wilde's *Salome* (John Lane, 1894), all these influences come together (along, possibly, with that of Ricketts's *Sphinx* designs, which he had seen before starting work on *Salome*[7]) in the creation of a new style, at once opulent in detail and severe in general effect. The opulence anyone could imitate, after a fashion, and many did – it was a trick that parodists of Beardsley in particular rapidly picked up – but the severity and self-discipline which lay beneath it remained Beardsley's own. ❦ In terms of popular fame and international influence the illustrations for *Salome* probably represent the peak of Beardsley's career: the type of female figure he here favours is the 'Beardsley woman' (who became for a year or two a fashionable type in life as well as in art); the sumptuous, vaguely oriental trappings seized the imagination of Europe and beyond (as Ricketts remarked in the letter quoted on p. 89, Bakst and other of Diaghilev's Russian designers were early familiar with Beardsley's illustrations); and the sparse, formalised shapes of such designs as 'The Woman in the Moon' (who is given the face of Wilde) and 'The Toilet of Salome' can be found haunting the imagination of the illustrators who came after. But 'The Toilet of Salome' already has suggestions – in the masked figure of the dresser, in the dress half seen beneath the cloak – of another influence which was about to overtake the mercurial, ever-receptive artist: that of the rococo. ❧ Beardsley was throughout his life a voracious but selective reader, and he early developed a taste for the eighteenth-century French novel, the plays of Congreve and the poetry of Pope. Around 1896, partly as a result of his literary preoccupations at the time – with *Les Liaisons Dangereuses* particularly – he began a detailed study of Watteau and other eighteenth-century French masters, bombarding Smithers with orders for the rare French illustrated books from his catalogue. Even before this he had begun his most extensive literary experiment, the rococo fantasy version of the Venus and Tannhäuser legend best known as *Under the Hill*, and in 1894-95 had sketched a frontispiece in an appropriate style (possibly under the influence, as Aymer Vallance suggests, of Ricketts or Laurence Housman[8]), but the eighteenth-century phase of Beardsley's work really begins with the two great illustrated books of 1896, *The Lysistrata of Aristophanes* and *The Rape of the Lock*. *The Rape of the Lock* series are better known, for obvious reasons: Pope's fantasy demands no illustrations which may not be put into the hands of the most sheltered young lady, while Aristophanes's unblinkingly sexual farce not only suggests but positively requires illustrations of comparable broadness and directness – a requirement Beardsley happily meets by decorating his drawings with a variety of lovingly delineated penises in various

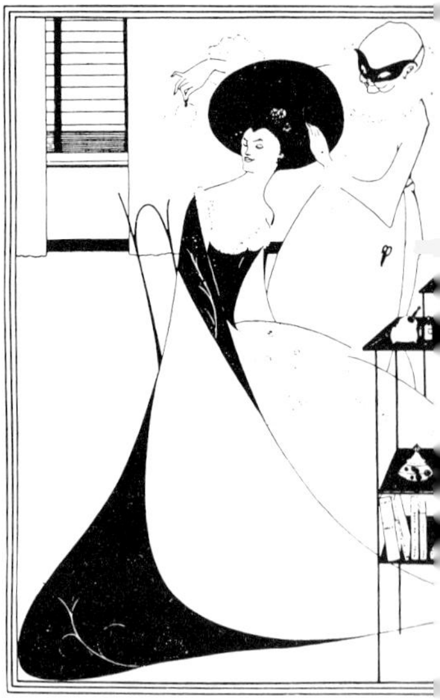

Aubrey Beardsley: *'The Toilet of Salome'* (1894)

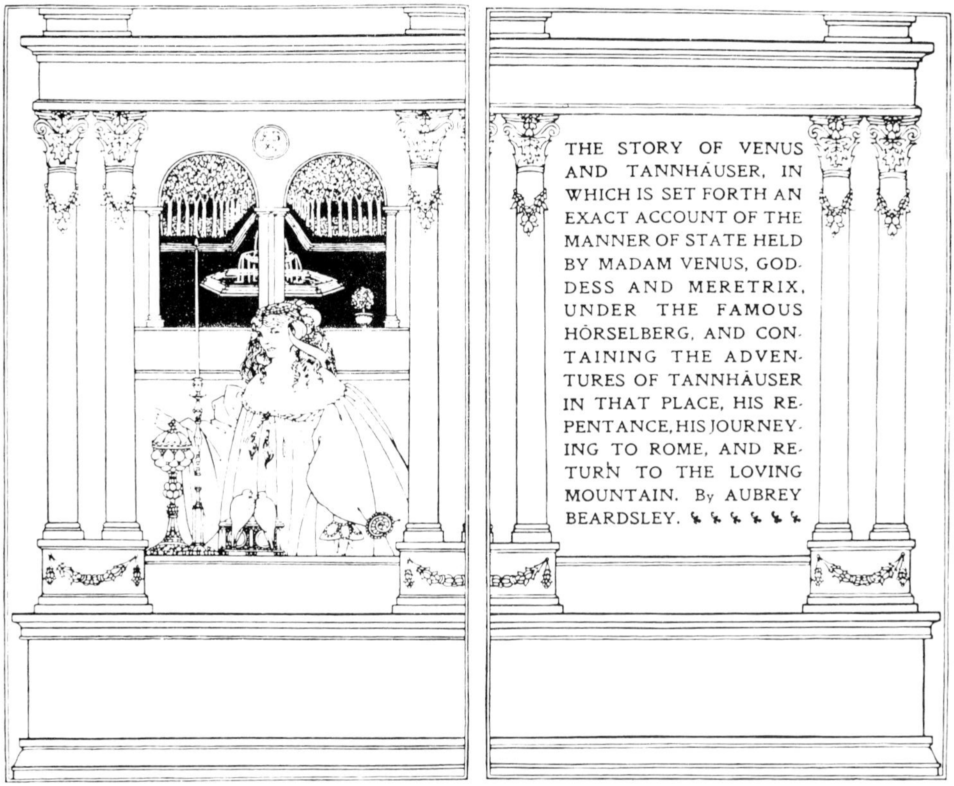

Aubrey Beardsley: Design for the title-opening of a projected edition of his own unfinished novel *Under the Hill* (Venus and Tannhäuser) 1896. First published in *The Early Work of Aubrey Beardsley* (Lane, 1899)

states of monstrous erection.[9] And the designs for the *Rape of the Lock* are certainly a unique tour de force, both imaginatively and technically. Instead of the bold, clear juxtapositions of black and white, the glitter and sparkle of the *Salome* drawings, everything here is light and fragile, fine and graceful as gossamer. Beardsley has not abandoned altogether his earlier decorative conventions: the compositions are still devised with extreme skill to suppress all evidence of recession, to preserve the spacial ambiguity which has always been such a telling feature of his work – the *Rape of the Lock* drawings are very much, like their predecessors, patterns in two dimensions. But here the form of the patterns has changed radically: the hard, clean lines of the earlier work have been dissolved in many places into shimmering threads of tiny dots, suggesting with extraordinary vividness and economy flounces of fine lace and delicate embroidery. Occasionally, as in 'The Battle of Beaux and Belles' and 'The

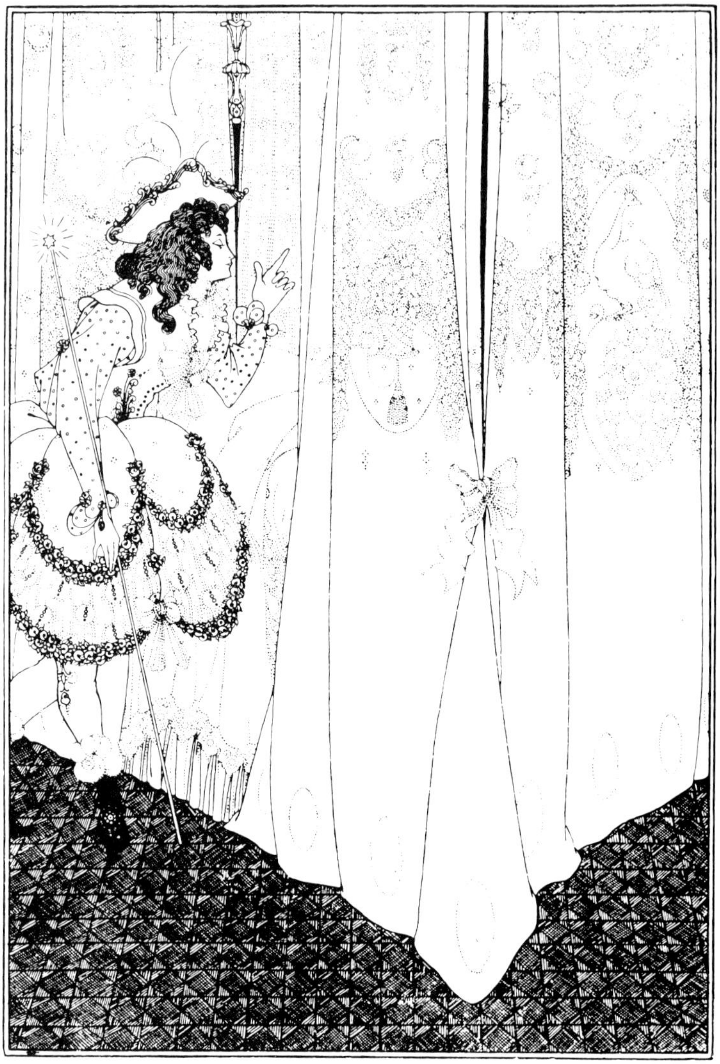

Aubrey Beardsley: 'The Dream' from *The Rape of the Lock* (Smithers, 1896)

Cave of Spleen', the effect is even a trifle over-rich and confused, but in general the series may be regarded as one of Beardsley's most complete achievements – as well as one of his most immediately influential: the ghosts of Belinda and her attendants walk through many of Conder's dreamy evocations of an eighteenth-century never-never land, and inspire the preoccupation of popular designers of the 1900s and 1920s with Pierrots, Pierrettes and such – Charles Robinson, John Austen, Harry Clarke in his illustrations to *Perrault's Fairy Tales* – only to end up ignominiously on the lids of 1930s chocolate boxes. But excellent though the *Rape of the Lock* designs are, the *Lysistrata* are in many ways even more impressive. Most writers who have been familiar with them – Robert Ross,[10] Holbrook Jackson,[11] Sir John Rothenstein[12] – have regarded them as among the finest of all his works, and with such a verdict it is hard to disagree. Baroque rather than rococo in inspiration, they are composed with a grand simplicity and directness, dispensing absolutely with all background and reducing each composition to its bare essentials. They are, as one can hardly say of any other Beardsley, completely unmannered in the impression they create; whereas the compositions of his earlier work have an artful, worked-on rightness (Beardsley drew in pencil and rubbed out and drew again indefinitely before he was satisfied enough to ink in the final result), the *Lysistrata* designs seem to have just fallen uncoaxed yet with unerring instinct straight on to the page.

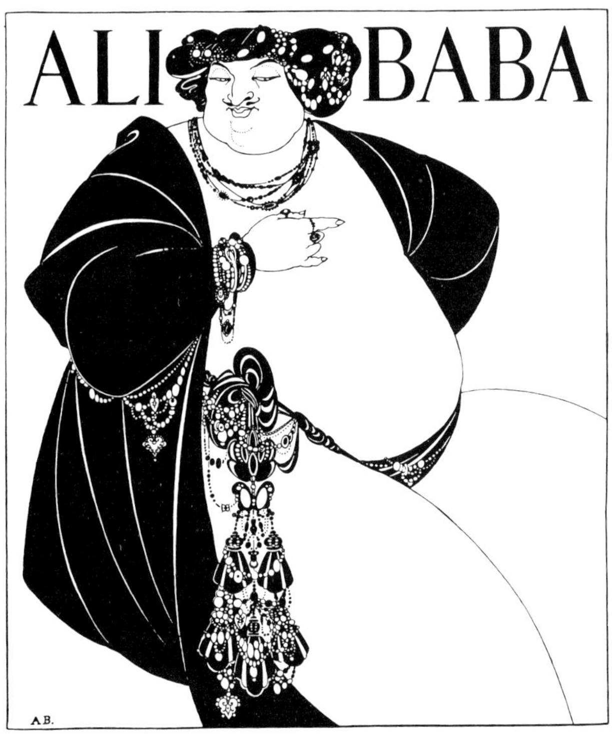

Aubrey Beardsley:
Cover for *Ali Baba* (1897)

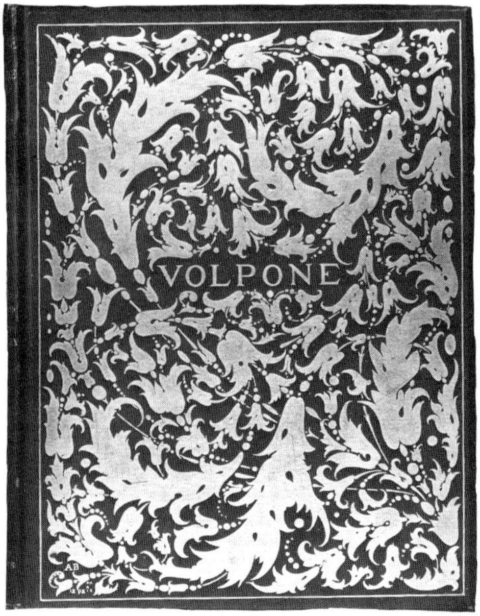

Aubrey Beardsley:
Binding for Ben Jonson's
Volpone (1898) $11\frac{1}{2} \times 8\frac{1}{2}$ in.

They are, too, altogether larger, broader in treatment than any of Beardsley's other work, and seem to be pointing towards yet another development in his style, only partially realized in some of the later *Savoy* drawings ('Mrs Margery Pinchwife' in Number 8, for instance), in the resplendent cover design for *Ali Baba* (1897) and in the six vignettes he completed for Smithers's edition of *Volpone*

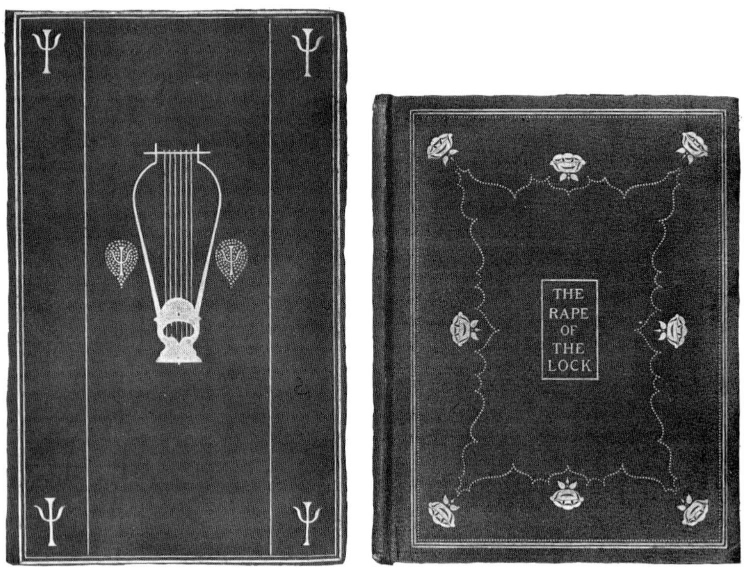

Aubrey Beardsley:
Bindings for H. T. Wharton's
Sappho (1896) $6\frac{7}{8} \times 4\frac{3}{8}$ in.
and the bijou edition of
The Rape of the Lock
(1897) $5\frac{5}{8} \times 4\frac{1}{4}$ in.

(1898), which have an almost Jacobean solidity. Apart from his illustrations, Beardsley was an absolute master of cover-design. Many of his covers are as simple as one could imagine, though with that simplicity which only extreme sophistication and complete technical mastery can achieve. The covers to H. T. Wharton's version of *Sappho* (John Lane, 1896), to Dowson's *Verses* (Leonard Smithers, 1896) and to the original and bijou editions of *The Rape of the Lock* (Leonard Smithers, 1896 and 1897) are among the most telling ever designed, and it would be pleasant to say that they had a large influence. Unfortunately it is not so; that particular secret is one that belonged to Beardsley alone and died with him.

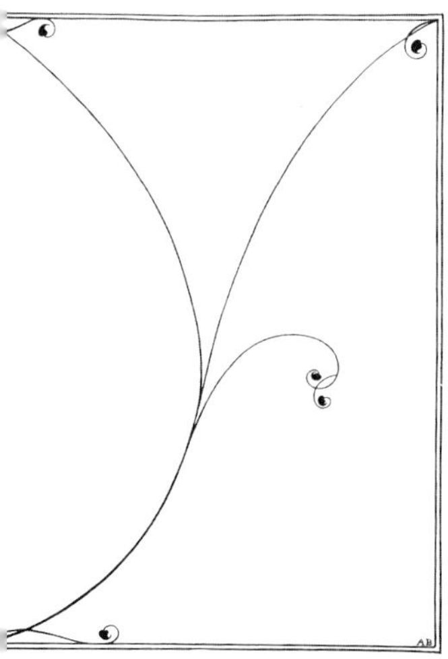

Aubrey Beardsley: Binding for Dowson's *Verses* (1896) $8 \times 5\frac{7}{8}$ in.

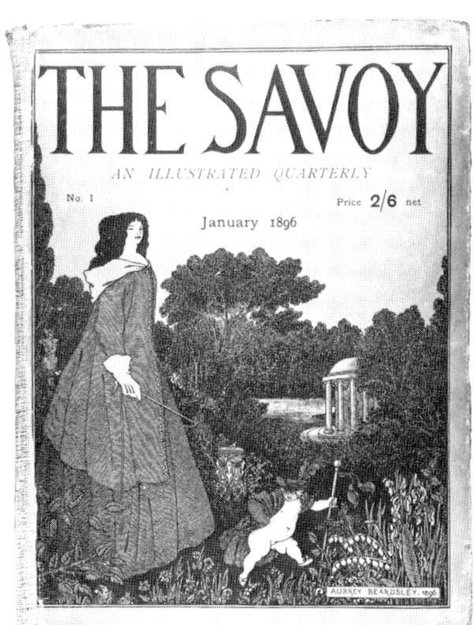

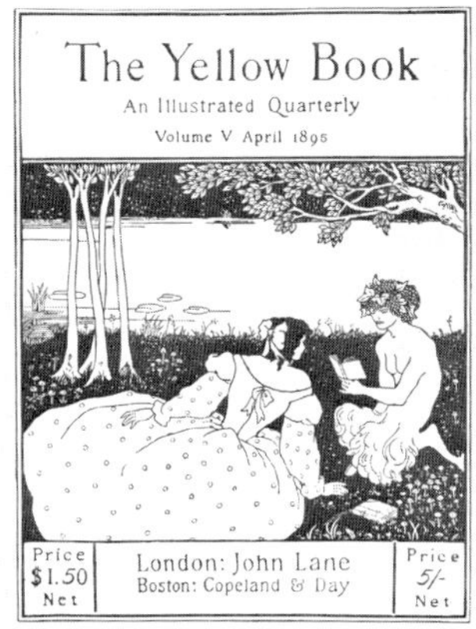

Beardsley as art editor: *The Yellow Book* (John Lane, 1894) $8\frac{1}{8} \times 6\frac{1}{4}$ in. and *The Savoy* (Smithers, 1896) $10\frac{3}{8} \times 7\frac{5}{8}$ in.

(iii) Laurence Housman and some others

The other illustrators of the 1890s relevant to our purpose may be fairly briefly disposed of; to discover how much else was going on at the same time one need do no more than check quickly through the pages of James Thorpe's *English Illustration: The Nineties* (1935), noting what a relatively small proportion of his space is given up to designers who can be classified as either art nouveau or Arts and Crafts. For the Nineties were also the heyday of Phil May, one of the greatest of all English draughtsmen and quite uninfluenced by both movements; Charles Keene, an even greater, lived just into the period; Sir John Tenniel was *Punch's* leading cartoonist all through it; Harry Furniss, Cecil Aldin, C. E. Brock, Hugh Thomson, Jack B. Yeats, Maurice Greiffenhagen, E. A. Abbey – all managed to do much their best work during this decade while blandly disregarding art nouveau, Arts and Crafts, the printing revival and the book beautiful altogether. Even someone as closely involved with this particular world as Charles Conder (1868-1909) could continue happily designing in a pretty, fanciful, pseudo-eighteenth-century style tinged to only the faintest degree with art nouveau, as in his illustrations to Balzac's *La Fille aux Yeux d'Or* (Leonard Smithers, 1896) and *Beauty and the Beast* (John Lane, 1908), and dabble only very briefly in art nouveau in a few line-drawings made for *The Yellow Book*, 1895-97. Yet there are, among all these, quite a number working along our particular line. The most important of them, from every point of view, is Laurence Housman (1865-1959). Better remembered today as a dramatist, essayist and fiction-writer, Housman was nevertheless in the 1890s one of the leading figures in book illustration, in which field, as he explains in his autobiography *The Unexpected Years*,[1] he found at that time much readier employment than in what he felt was his true vocation, literature. He came of a gifted family.

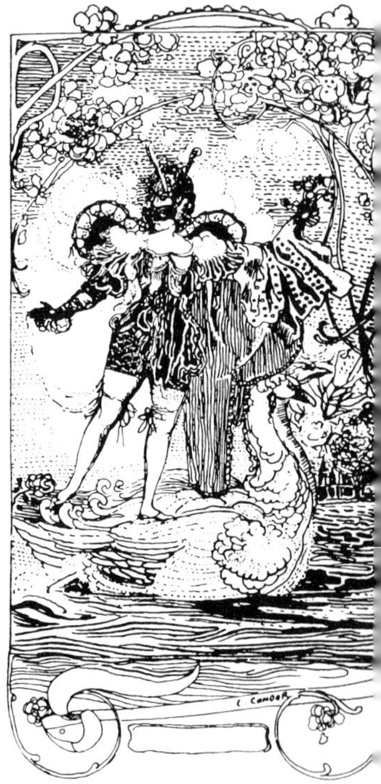

Charles Conder: 'A Fairy Prince' (*The Yellow Book*, 1897)

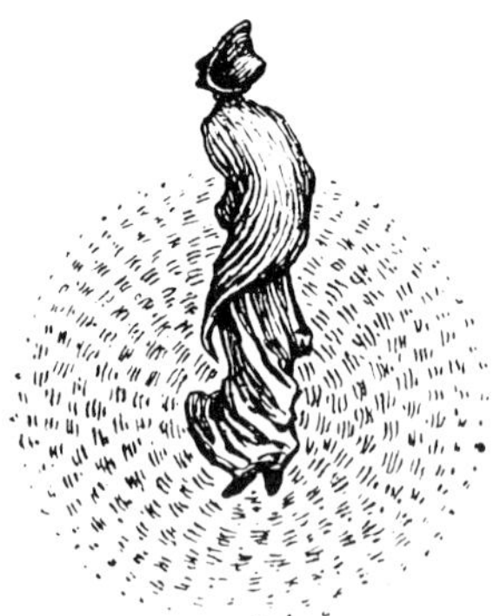

Laurence Housman: *Jump to Glory Jane* (Swan, Sonnenschein, 1892)

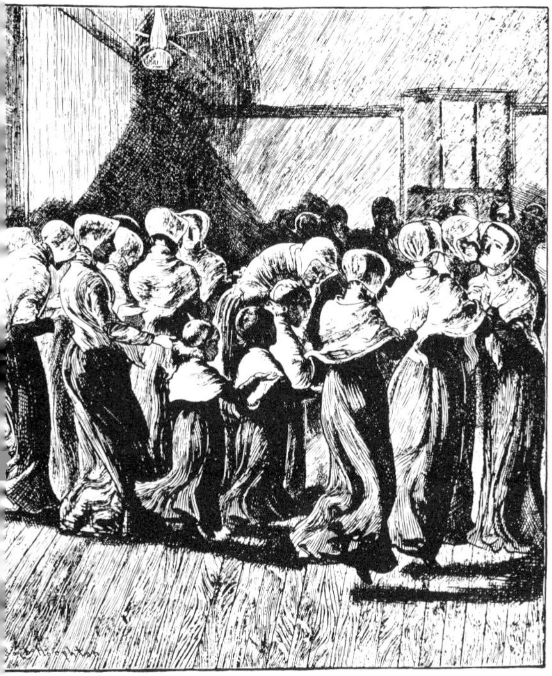

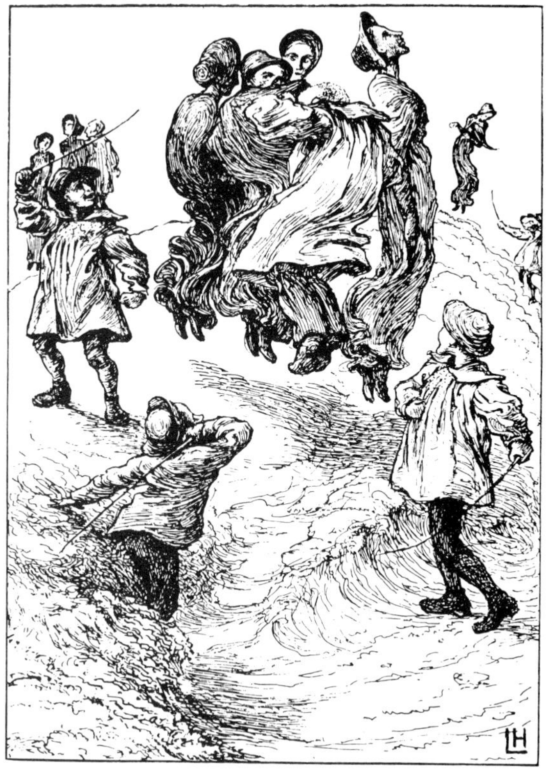

Arthur Boyd Houghton: 'Shakers Dancing' (*Graphic America*, 1870)

Laurence Housman: *Jump to Glory Jane* (Swan, Sonnenschein, 1892) 7⅜ × 5 in.

His brother was A. E. Housman, author of *A Shropshire Lad* and ultimately Professor of Latin at London and Cambridge. His sister Clemence (1861 - 1955) also wrote – some of Laurence Housman's best illustrative work was done for her story, *The Were-Wolf* (John Lane, 1896) – and more importantly was a skilled engraver, one of the last brought up in the classic English wood-engraving tradition; she translated a number of his later designs into wood, though in his earlier he had readily exploited the new process of photo-engraving line-blocks direct from pen drawings. His first training was artistic, and more or less by accident he gained a reputation with his first major commission, to write out in his own script and to illustrate George Meredith's ballad *Jump to Glory Jane* (Swan, Sonnenschein, 1892). This series, of forty-four designs, was commissioned by the poem's editor, Harry Quilter, after he had been impressed by the illustrations which accompanied Housman's story 'The Green Gaffer' in *The Universal Review*

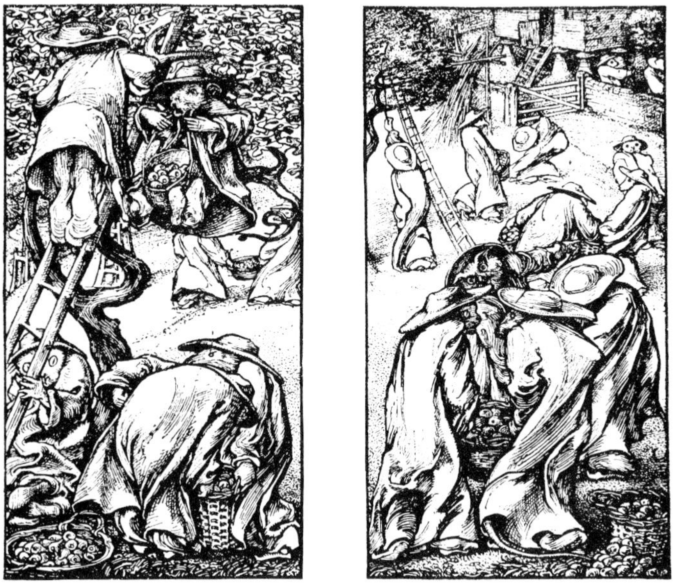

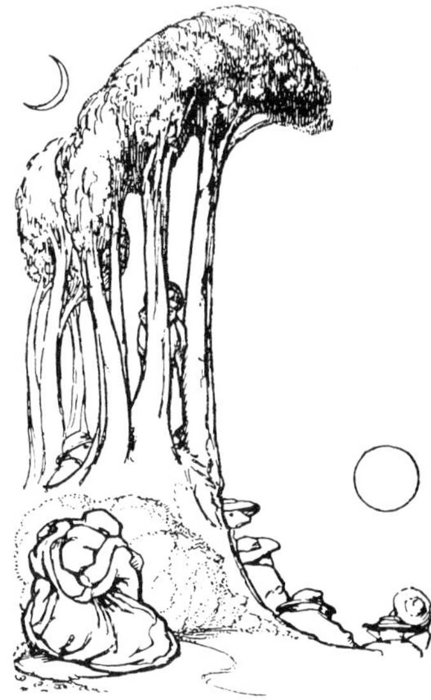

Laurence Housman: Opening from *Goblin Market* (1893)

Laurence Housman: *Goblin Market*, (1893) $7\frac{1}{8} \times 3\frac{7}{8}$ in.

(1890), and embodied the progress of Meredith's ecstatically bobbing evangelist in strange, angular little pictures with a touch of Rossetti and some hints (v. p. 45) from Boyd Houghton, but at the same time with an arching intensity and mannerist exaggeration which were unmistakably Ninetyish. The novelty of the style, and the expressiveness of the way pictures were related to the hand-written text, at once attracted attention, and during the next decade Housman the illustrator and book-designer was rarely idle. During the early 1890s he was an intimate of Ricketts and Shannon (though he later quarrelled with Ricketts) and belongs, in so far as he belongs anywhere, to their 'group'.[2] It was Ricketts who first urged him to take up pen-and-ink as his favoured medium and his illustrations draw on the same sources of inspiration as Ricketts's earliest works. There is a lot of Rossetti, especially visible in the female figures and in some of the grotesque and sinister animals peopling his splendid illustrations to Christina Rossetti's *Goblin Market* (Macmillan, 1893), which are reminiscent of those in Rossetti's designs for *Goblin Market and Other Poems* (1862). His next important piece of book decoration, Jane Barlow's *The End of Elfin-Town*

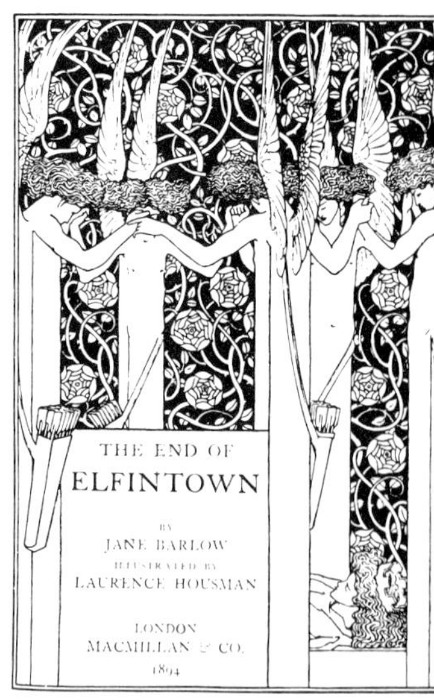

Laurence Housman: Title-page to *The End of Elfintown* (1894) $7 \times 4\frac{5}{8}$ in.

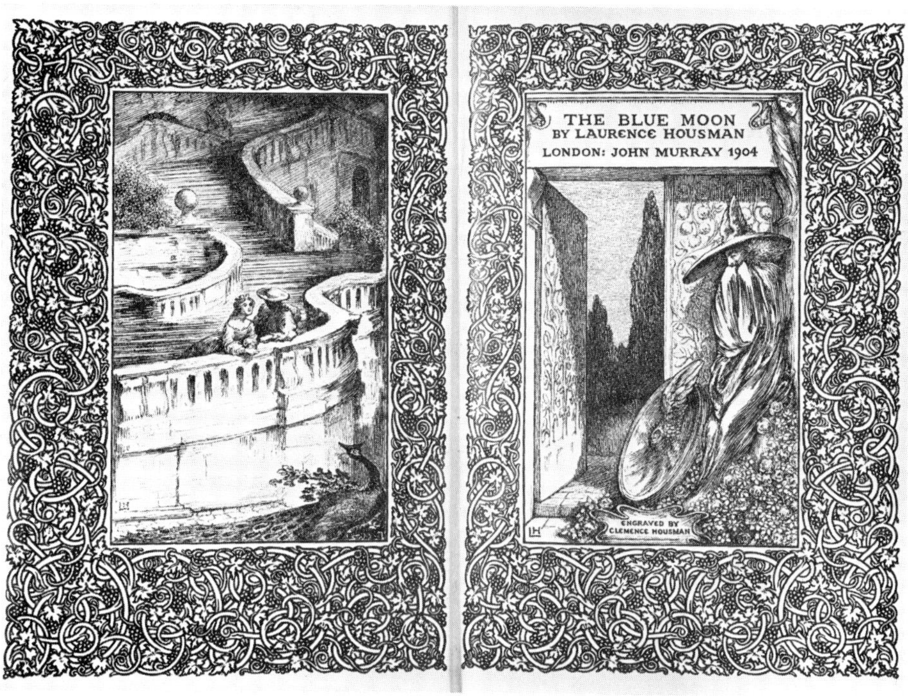

Laurence Housman: *The Blue Moon* (1904) $7\frac{1}{2} \times 5$ in.

(Macmillan, 1894) shows perhaps in its strange attenuated forms some direct influence from Ricketts, and the same year, in his designs for his own *A Farm in Fairyland* (Kegan Paul) the elaborately patterned surrounds of the title-opening, with their vaguely floral design, suggest that he has been studying Morris's Kelmscott borders, and, even more, some of Ricketts's earliest comparable inventions (though the possibility here of reciprocal influences between Ricketts and Housman cannot be entirely overlooked). But in general he established from the first a highly individual, completely recognizable style, and remained true to it throughout his fairly brief career as a book-designer, which ended effectively when he gained an increasing reputation as a writer in the early 1900s, and at the same time discovered that his 'eyesight no longer served me for the very detailed style of drawing which was what most interested me'.[3] Like Ricketts, Housman began as a journeyman designer for commercial publishers; unlike Ricketts, he remained one throughout his career. As we have seen, the text pages of his first book, *Jump to Glory Jane*, were by a fluke designed throughout by him, more completely even than if he had simply been given general control over layout and type. His second book, *Goblin Market*, was set up more normally in type, but was again all his own work: the strange upright format – to become a favourite with art nouveau designers, and standard for the envelope-books of the 1900s on which the illustrators of the Glasgow School regularly worked – seems to have been virtually his invention, the book being almost exactly contemporary with Ricketts's similar *Silverpoints*; the elegantly patterned cover (gold on green cloth in the ordinary edition) was designed by him; and the title-page, the disposition of vignettes in the text and the very unusual arrangement of the full-page illustrations in complete openings altogether uncluttered by text were all arrived at under his supervision. From then on his seems to have been the controlling hand in virtually all the books with which he was associated. In general he favoured a concentration of illustration, the artful distribution of elaborately decorated pages among soberly undecorated (but always meticulously designed) pages of text. His books differ from, say, Beardsley's, which are superficially arranged on the same principle (if one may dignify it in its normal application with the name) in the exquisite care and discretion with which the text pages answer the illustrated or decorated pages in balance and proportion, so that though text and decoration are segregated there is no doubt that they are part of the same ordered design. ❧ Housman's influence on book design is felt during the 1890s and 1900s far beyond the books he actually illustrated. A number of books which are without illustration and most obvious decoration of any sort (e.g. Edmond Holmes's *The Silence of Love*, John Lane, 1899) bear his initials as designer on the colophon, and lessons learnt from his practice may

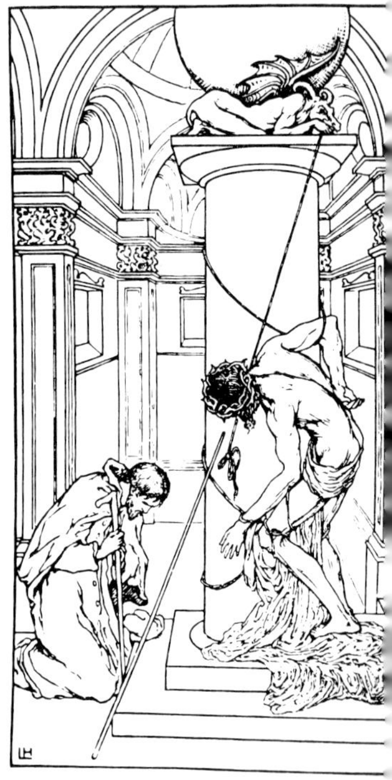

Laurence Housman: *The Imitation of Christ* by Thomas À. Kempis (Kegan Paul, 1898)

be seen applied by his most regular employers, John Lane and Kegan Paul, in publications with which he was, as far as we know, entirely unconnected. In particular, the art nouveau book owes to his fertile invention many of its happiest experiments with format, an area of innovation oddly disregarded by Ricketts, apart from the aforementioned upright format he devised for *Silverpoints* (1893), and hardly touched at all by Beardsley: the dumpy, squarish octavo of *The Yellow Book*, along with its mannerisms of layout, may have been chosen by him, but is anyway only a slight deviation from normal and owes its striking effect more to the bold yellow-and-black colour scheme than to the format itself. But Housman stipulated from the outset that he should have a say in the format of the books he designed, feeling that it was 'as unreasonable to expect a designer always to design within a set format as it would be to expect a painter always to paint within a frame of a fixed size and shape'.[4] And if he may be credited with inventing, or at least publicizing and popularizing, the tall, narrow octavo of *Goblin Market*, he can also be credited with the evolution of the squat, almost square octavo of Francis Thompson's *Poems* (Mathews and Lane) and *Sister Songs* (Lane, both 1895), another shape much used thereafter, and with the very slightly higher, narrower octavo of *The Were Wolf* – both formats used before, if at all, only for children's picture-books rather than for ordinary literature. In each of Housman's books, in fact, some care and deliberation has gone into the exact choice of format; never, seemingly, does he accept a conventional format just because it is the usual thing. ❧ Matching his unusual formats are his varied and unconventional handlings of the title-page. Despite the eccentric and individual practice of Whistler (v. p. 52) the centred, symmetrical arrangement of title-pages had remained the rule. Ricketts in his early title-pages varied the formula, and in the Vale Press books tended to eliminate the title-page as generally understood altogether, noting title and author summarily on the half-title and then starting straight into the text with a decorative opening, frontispiece to the left, headpiece (if any) and beginning of the text on the right, and the rest of the information one would normally expect from a title-page – publisher, date of publication – relegated to the colophon at the back. This, of course, was easy enough to do when he was his own publisher, but commercial publishers, such as Housman always worked for, have an understandable weakness for seeing their names fairly prominently displayed. He therefore had to do what he could with the traditional constituents of the title-page. What he did was to produce a series of ingenious and elaborate off-centre designs, usually with some sort of abstracted, vaguely plant-like pattern on the left, sometimes containing in it, sometimes surmounted

Laurence Housman: Bindings.

Top row: Jane Barlow's *The End of Elfintown* (1894) $7\frac{1}{8} \times 4\frac{3}{4}$ in.; his own *Green Arras* (1896) $7\frac{7}{8} \times 5$ in.; Christina Rossetti's *Goblin Market* (1893) $7\frac{3}{8} \times 4$ i[illegible]
Bottom row: George Meredith's *Jump to Glory Jane* (1892) $7\frac{7}{8} \times 5$ in.; Charles Newton-Robinson's *The Viol o[illegible] Love and Other Poems* (1895) $7\frac{7}{8} \times 5$ in.

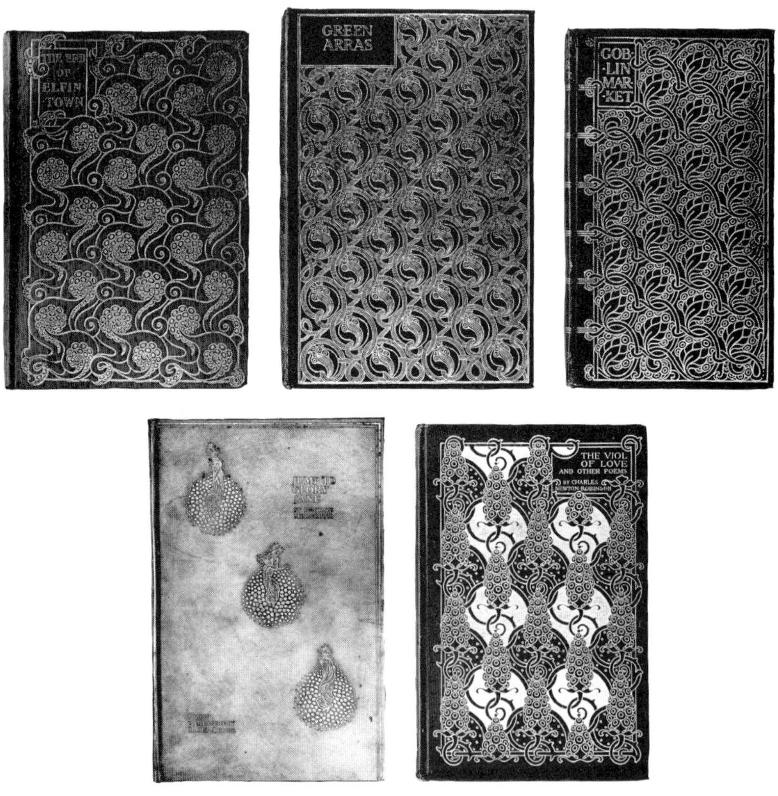

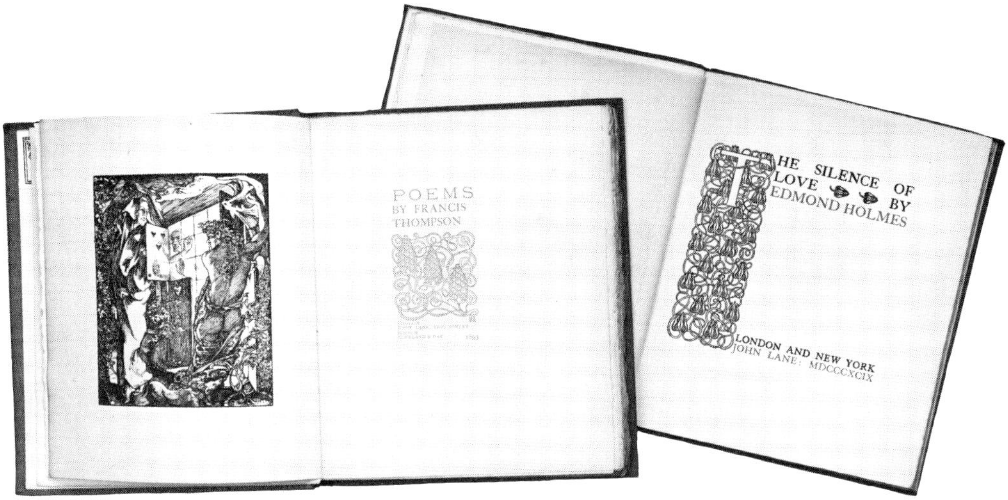

Laurence Housman: Title-pages to *Poems by Francis Thompson* (Lane, 1895) $7\frac{5}{8} \times 6$ in. and *The Silence of Love* (Lane, 1899) $7\frac{5}{8} \times 6\frac{1}{8}$ in.

by, a large, perhaps a decorated, capital letter. One of the best of such title-pages is that for *The Were Wolf*, a highly individual composition of yellow-ochre print and pattern (this colour, a favourite of Housman's, recurs in a number of his book-designs) which manages to accommodate elegantly all the necessary information and at the same time form with the facing frontispiece a completely satisfactory balanced opening. Both Francis Thompson's *Poems* and *Sister Songs* feature equally effective variations of the same basic formula in a kindred format.

Along with Laurence Housman must be mentioned, very briefly, another illustrator, Paul Woodroffe (1875-1955). His first illustrations, closely imitative of Walter Crane, were for *Ye Booke of Nursery Rhymes* (George Allen, 1895) and the *Second Book of Nursery Rhymes* (Allen, 1896), both with music by Joseph Moorat, a friend of Housman's. He would seem to have been adopted early by the Housmans, Clemence engraving his illustrations to *The Confessions of St Augustine* (Kegan Paul, 1900), which Laurence supplied with a title-page, and his illustrations to Laurence's translation of *Aucassin and Nicolette* (John Murray, 1902). In the circumstances it is hardly surprising that when left on his own, as in *The Little Flowers of St Francis* (Kegan

Paul, 1899) and *The Little Flowers of St Benet* (Kegan Paul, 1901) he should prove to be close to Laurence Housman's work in style and, in a rather second-hand sort of way, quite accomplished. Once removed from the direct Housman influence he drifted into other artistic activities; his designs for *The Princess and Other Poems* (Dent, 1904) are very ordinary, and his few later book-illustrations[5] are quite uninteresting. The other important art nouveau book-designer and illustrator to emerge in the 1890s was also a member of the Ricketts circle, and a far more faithful, long-suffering one than Laurence Housman: T. Sturge Moore (1870-1944). Sturge Moore met Shannon and Ricketts when they were students, and contributed his first published woodcuts to *The Dial*, number three (1893). He was another of those many-sided figures the period was so rich in, being also a dramatist, a noted poet and a distinguished critic of art and literature. In 1899 Ricketts persuaded him to illustrate his own translation of Maurice de Guérin's *The Centaur* and *The Bacchante*, published by the Vale Press, and thereafter few of his own works appeared without at least a title page of his own design – probably the most attractive of his books is *The Little School* (Eragny Press, 1905), with four woodcuts. In addition he illustrated his selection of *Poems from Wordsworth* (Vale Press, 1902) and Perrault's *Histoire de Peau d'Ane* (Eragny Press, 1902),

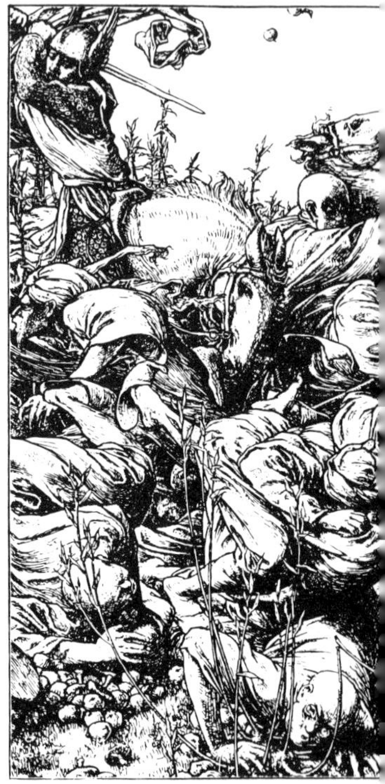

Paul Woodroffe: *Of Aucassin and Nicolet* (1902) showing heavy influence from Housman and, indirectly, from Sandys

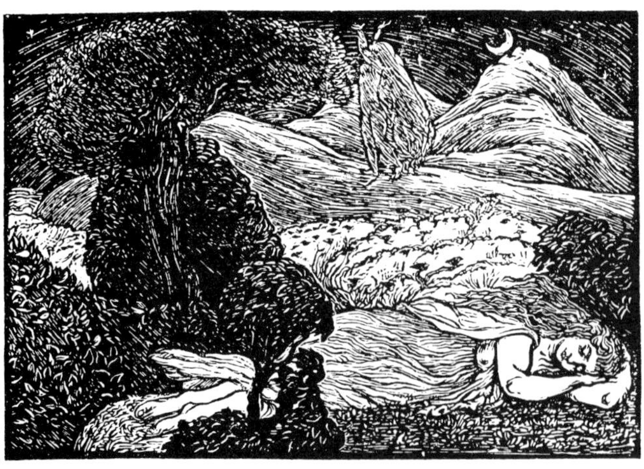

T. Sturge Moore: *The Centaur and The Bacchante* (1899)

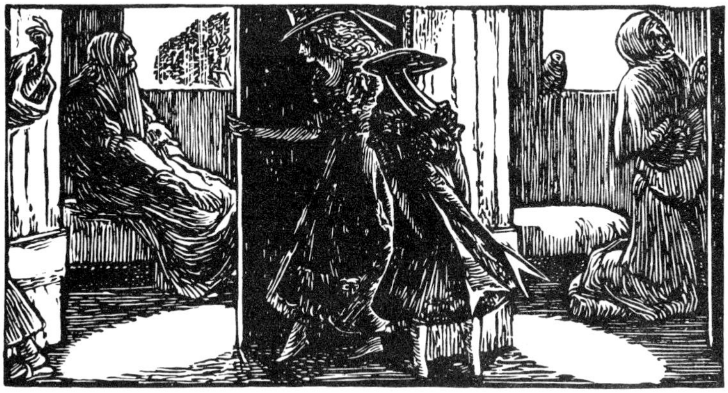

T. Sturge Moore: 'Nuns Fret Not at their Convent's ·ow Room', *Poems from Wordsworth* (1902)

designed title-pages and covers for several books by Yeats, of whom he was a close friend,[6] and was responsible for the overall design – none too happy, it must be admitted – of H. P. R. Finberg's ambitious English edition of Villiers de l'Isle Adam's *Axel* (Jarrolds) in 1925. Ultimately wood-engraving came to play a relatively minor part in his life, but his early works especially have a dark, brooding concentration quite different from those of Ricketts

Paul Woodroffe: *Of Aucassin and Nicolette* (1902) $7\frac{1}{4} \times 4\frac{1}{2}$ in.

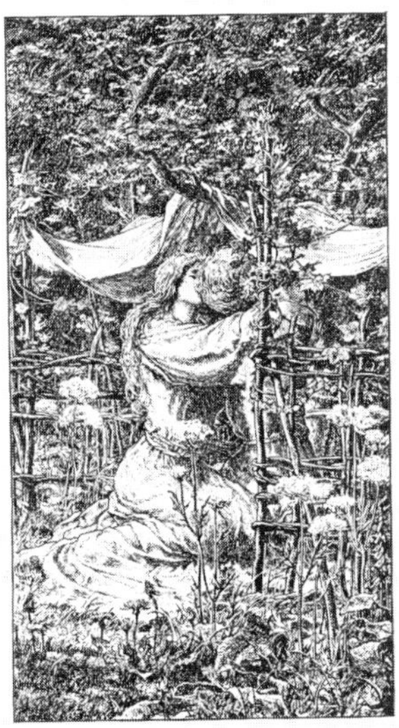

THE LOVERS.

[*Frontispiece.*

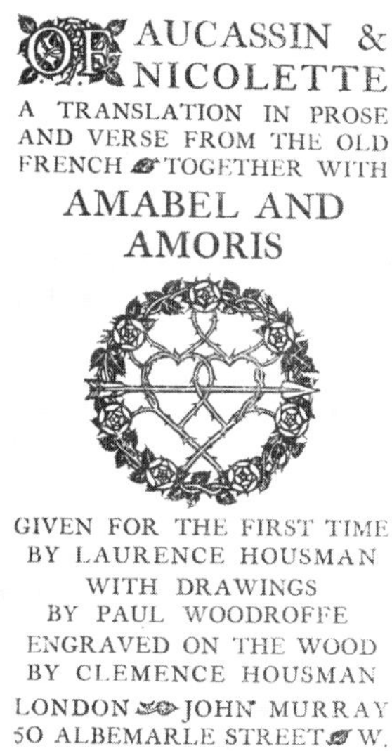

OF AUCASSIN & NICOLETTE

A TRANSLATION IN PROSE AND VERSE FROM THE OLD FRENCH TOGETHER WITH

AMABEL AND AMORIS

GIVEN FOR THE FIRST TIME BY LAURENCE HOUSMAN WITH DRAWINGS BY PAUL WOODROFFE ENGRAVED ON THE WOOD BY CLEMENCE HOUSMAN

LONDON JOHN MURRAY 50 ALBEMARLE STREET W.

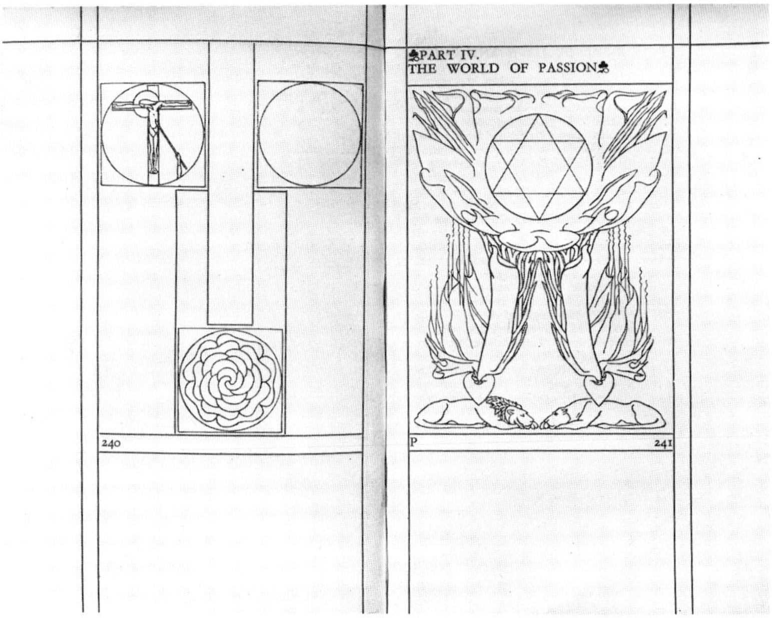

T. Sturge Moore: Title-opening to Part IV of Villiers de l'Isle Adam's *Axel* (1925) 9 × 5½ in.

and reflecting perhaps his enthusiastic study of Blake's woodcuts[7] and Calvert, on whom he announced his intention, never carried out, of producing a monograph.[8] His later designs show him happiest when exploiting the varied textures possible in a woodcut proper, which he thoroughly understood, and weakest in those closest to pure line-engraving, which show up his severe deficiencies (especially in the comparison, which he seems to court, with Ricketts) as a linear draughtsman. It may be significant that by far his most effective work in pure line, the device for the Unicorn Press (1900), not only retains a woodcut solidity of outline, but is modelled very closely on a print, 'The Captive Stag', by Giulio Campagnola reproduced in an enthusiastic article about the artist in *The Pageant* of 1897, to which Moore was also a contributor.[9] Though Moore's woodcuts are in general little remembered now, he was a skilful and individual practitioner of the art and an obvious link between the 1890s vogue for the artist's wood-engraving and the 1920s revival of the woodcut proper. As an artist in books, however, he remains decidedly in the second rank. Among the lesser figures of the Nineties there are all sorts of more or less interesting illustrators, such as J. D. Batten and Patten Wilson,

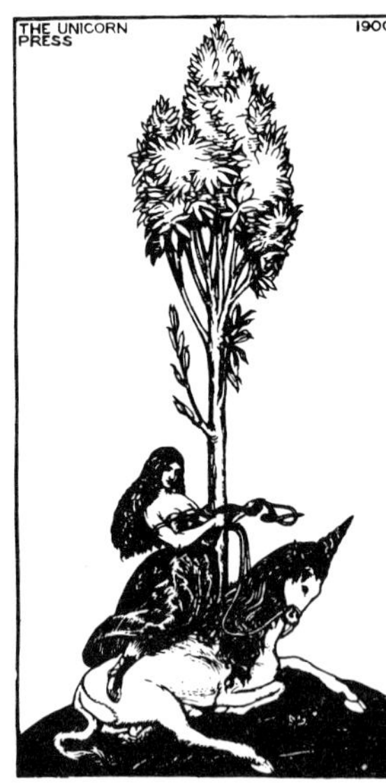

T. Sturge Moore: The Unicorn Impress

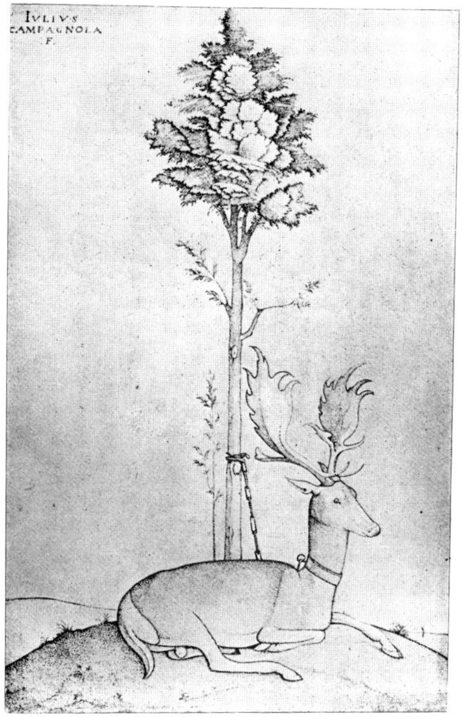

Giulio Campagnola:
The Captive Stag

who are not really distinctive enough to deserve individual notice. There is even Mary Sargant Florence, who in *The Crystal Ball* (Bell, 1894) produced one of the most altogether attractive books of the 1890s but seems to have done nothing else of note. But finally, a word must be spared for the artists whose work centred on Patrick Geddes's 'Northern Seasonal' *The Evergreen.* Initiated at Christmas 1894 as a publication of University Hall, Edinburgh, it was taken over and completely remodelled in the next year by Geddes, founder and moving spirit of an Edinburgh Arts and Crafts movement, and under his aegis four more numbers, each with the title of a season, emerged, 'Spring' and 'Autumn' in 1895, 'Summer' in 1896, and 'Winter' dated 1896-97. One design from 'Spring', 'Natura Naturans', by Robert Burns (1869-1941), has been frequently reproduced in books on art nouveau,[10] but really it gives a very misleading, and certainly all too encouraging, picture of *The Evergreen's* contents: for one thing it is not only the best design in any of the four issues, but it is virtually the only competent one, all the others, even those by the same artist, being distinguished mainly by the

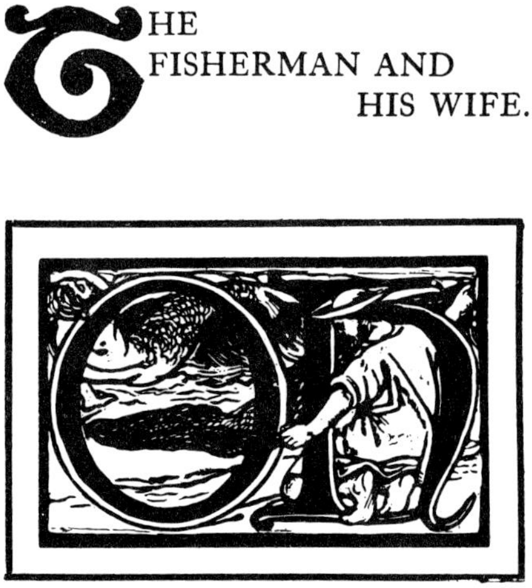

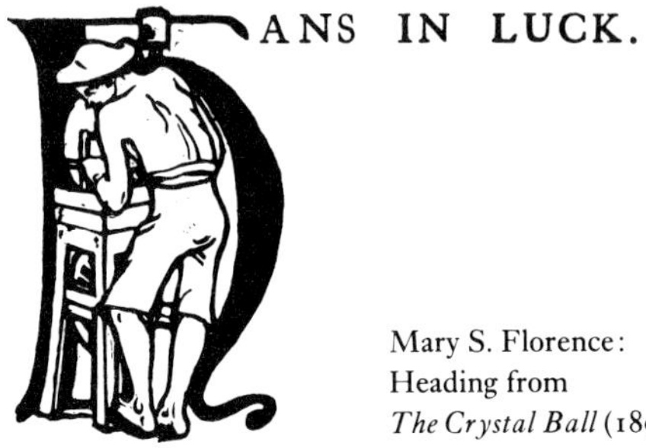

Mary S. Florence:
Heading from
The Crystal Ball (1894)

Mary S. Florence:
Decoration from
The Crystal Ball (1894)

coarseness of their conception and the amateurishness of their execution – and very few of the others, despite a certain amount of glum juggling with Celtic motifs, being even remotely art nouveau in feeling. It is all, as James Thorpe, unkindly but not unfairly puts it[11] 'rather dour and very Scotch'. This pervasive amateurishness is apparent also in the books of the best-known illustrator to appear in *The Evergreen*, W. B. Macdougall, whose once-famous versions of *The Book of Ruth* (Dent, 1896) and *The Blessed Damosel* (Duckworth, 1898) now convey little except a sadly deficient sense of form and a painfully limited repertoire of decorative motifs, though in *The Eerie Book* (J. Shiells, 1898) he does manage to exert at times a more effective self-discipline. ❧ A little better may be said of two designers often classified with this group, James J. Guthrie (1874-1952) and W. T. Horton (1864-1919). Guthrie's most characteristic work, a trifle reminiscent of Sturge Moore in its feeling for landscape and rock and tree-forms, is to be found in the four curious little books of texts and designs which make up the second series of his periodical *The Elf* (Old Bourne Press, 1900-02). Though perhaps here his decorations owe some of their delicate detail to the exquisite engraving of Clemence Housman, in general Guthrie was an all-round artist-craftsman, designing, en-

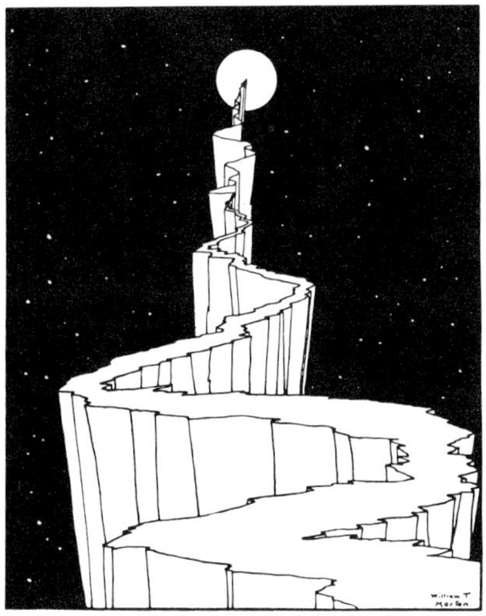

W. T. Horton: *A Book of Images* (1898)

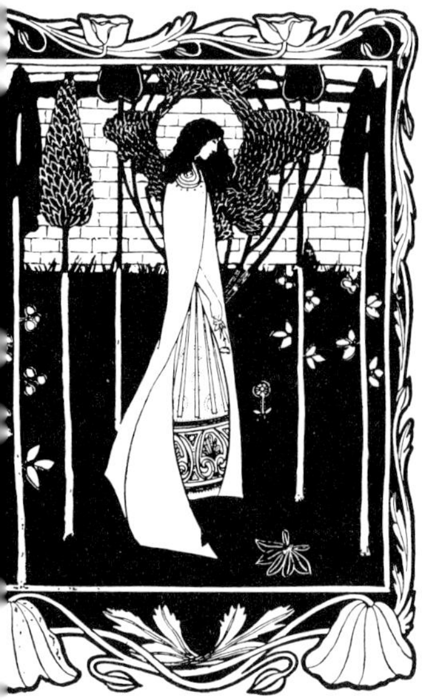

W. B. MacDougall: *Songs of Love and Death* by Margaret Armour (Dent, 1896) $7\frac{1}{2} \times 5\frac{1}{2}$ in.

graving and printing his own books and those of other authors at his Pear Tree Press, founded in 1899 (as well as devising some distinctive layouts for commercial publishers), inventing a 'proportional system of typographical composition', and experimenting with a kind of intaglio printing from elaborately worked plates finished off with colour applied by hand, differently in each copy, after the manner of Blake's illuminated books. He early evolved a highly personal style, a sort of folk-weave art nouveau with heavy emphasis on flowing, curling patterns of tree, cloud and water, and continued, with the aid of his sons, to produce recognisably Ninetyish illustrated books and booklets at his own press up to the end of the 1930s.[12] ❧ Horton was also a writer and amateur visionary, and also produced for a while a periodical largely written by himself, *Whispers – A Magazine for Surrey Folk* (1893). At about the same time he took up art; his strange symbolic designs were admired by Yeats, who introduced his first volume, *A Book of Images* (Unicorn Press, 1898), and even Beardsley, who included designs by him in four numbers of *The Savoy* (1896), admitted that he had 'sort of a kind of talent'.[13] Though impeded by severe technical limitations and even at best an extremely unequal artist, he could, when things happened to fall right – as they did most reliably with monstrous and

DIVINE DISCONTENT

By James Guthrie

Published by B. T. Batsford. London

There is a kinship between the first innocence and the last mastery

I. OF CONTENT

OUR praise of content is too idle. Among arduous days we set up this ideal of rest, our own desires far too tempestuous to let us be at such a haven, and circumstance too busy with our lives. So it is no foolish notion that contentment sets a limit upon meaner ambitions and gives room in the world for nobler. The man who beholds little of life believes there is no more. A child, still radiant with the trail of glory, adventures only upon the path of innocence, snug and content with food and warmth and sleep, securely shut from the hurt (which is knowledge) within his mother's arms. Maybe

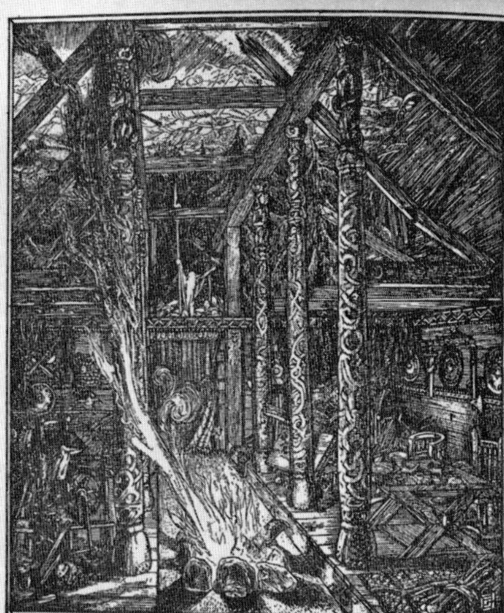

The Bill sings to Rannveig.

The
RIDING to LITHEND
By GORDON BOTTOMLEY

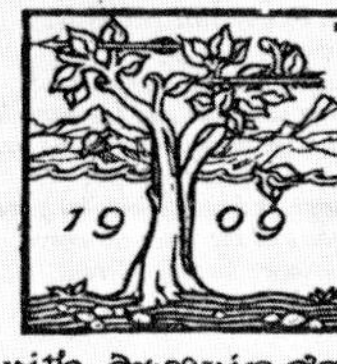

with drawings by
JAMES GUTHRIE

At the PEAR TREE PRESS, FLANSHAM, SUSSEX

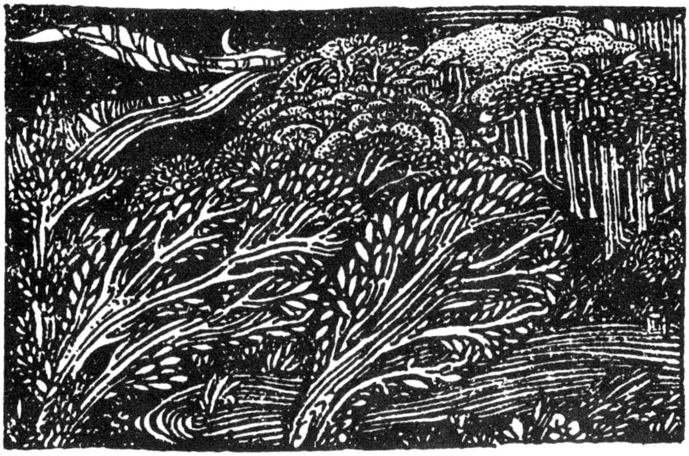

James Guthrie:
Trees by Harold Monro
(Poetry Bookshop, 1915)

sinister-grotesque subjects – achieve work of powerful suggestivity, not quite like that of anyone else. This occurs often enough in *A Book of Images*, his slightly nasty collection of nursery rhymes and coloured pictures *The Grig's Book* (Moffat and Paige, 1900), and his later volume of gnomic verses and symbolic pictures *The Way of a Soul* (Rider, published 1910, though most of the best designs seem to date from 1905-6) to make him an artist worth at least passing attention.[14]

James Guthrie:
Divine Discontent (Batsford, 1914)
Lettering by Percy J. Smith
$6\frac{3}{4} \times 4\frac{5}{8}$ in.

James Guthrie:
The Riding to Lithend (1909)
$8\frac{5}{8} \times 6\frac{3}{4}$ in.

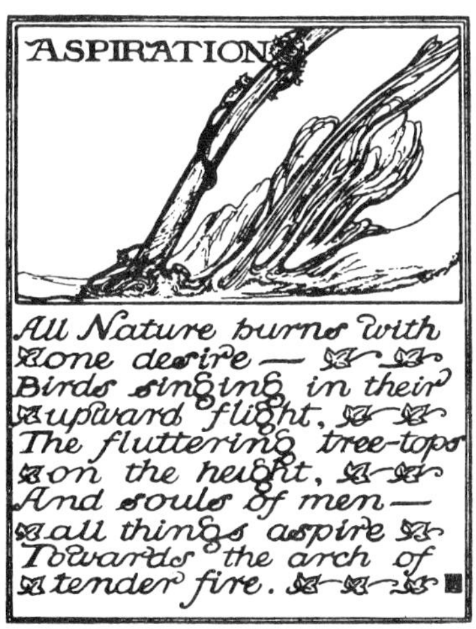

James Guthrie:
Page from *The Elf*
(Summer 1902) $6\frac{7}{8} \times 5\frac{1}{4}$ in.

Art Nouveau in the 1900s

In England – which is to say mainly in London – the 1890s were the period par excellence of the art nouveau book. By 1900 Beardsley was dead and the 'decadent' movement which he represented, fairly or unfairly, to the book-buying public had been in disgrace since the scandal surrounding Wilde's trial. Book designers and illustrators tended in the early 1900s to drift away into other forms of activity: Ricketts to oil painting and stage design, Housman to literature, Sturge Moore to poetry and criticism. At the beginning of 1904 Ricketts wound up the Vale Press and wrote its epitaph in his *Bibliography* of its books. The Boer War brought about a slump in book prices which hit the more expensive, exclusive type of book beautiful hard, and the major new private presses of the 1900s, Cobden-Sanderson's Doves Press (1900-16) and C. R. Ashbee's Essex House Press (1898-1910) continued the solid, healthy, respectable traditions of Morrisian Arts and Crafts rather than art nouveau, each of them in fact taking over craftsmen who had worked with Morris at Kelmscott; consequently both, as the decade wore on, came to seem more and more anachronistic and exert less and less influence on contemporary commercial book-design, existing instead in an ivory tower of their own. (It should be mentioned, though, that Ashbee was at the same time ready and eager to proselitize his ideas, par-

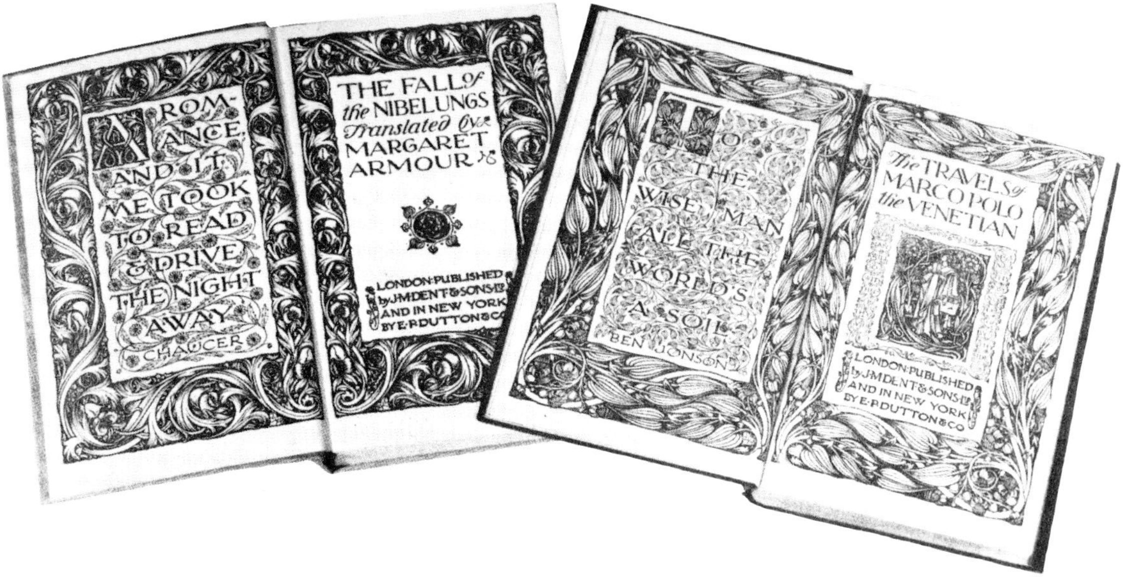

Reginald L. Knowles: The Everyman Library editions of *The Fall of the Nibelungs* (1908) and *The Travels of Marco Polo* (1908) $6\frac{3}{4} \times 4\frac{1}{8}$ in.

ticularly on architecture, in a series of excellent commercially produced, normally published books.) The most familiar examples of mass commercial book-production in these years, Dent's Everyman Library, with their elaborate floral borders at the title-opening and artistically decorated covers and endpapers, mostly the work of Reginald L. Knowles, harked straight back to Kelmscott, regarded by 1905, when the series was initiated, as the acme of safe good taste, and no doubt thought only slightly old-fashioned by most of the books' users when they were finally redesigned in 1935. ❧ Lucien Pissarro's Eragny Press, which had certain qualities in common with the Vale Press and began its life in 1894 in business association with Ricketts, admittedly continued to produce beautiful books with some art nouveau feel to them until 1914, but it remains outside the British tradition, not least because of its disturbing habit of publishing books in French, which limited its effectiveness in Britain, but also because Lucien Pissarro was by background (he was son of the Impressionist painter Camille Pissarro) and training (with Auguste Lepère, a dominating figure in the new French book illustration) much more French than British, and his

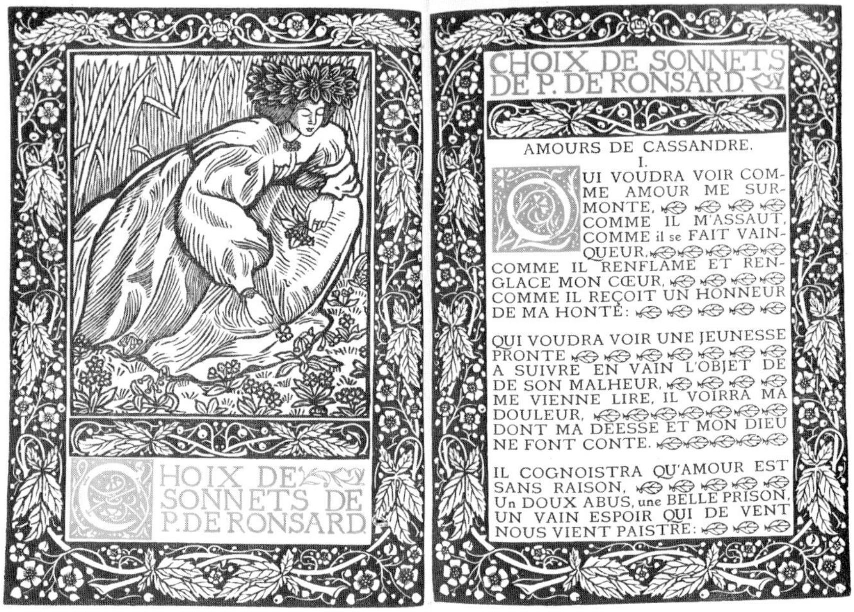
CHOIX DE SONNETS DE P. DE RONSARD

CHOIX DE SONNETS DE P. DE RONSARD

AMOURS DE CASSANDRE.

I.

QUI VOUDRA VOIR COMME AMOUR ME SURMONTE, COMME IL M'ASSAUT, COMME il se FAIT VAINQUEUR, COMME IL RENFLAME ET RENGLACE MON CŒUR, COMME IL REÇOIT UN HONNEUR DE MA HONTE:

QUI VOUDRA VOIR UNE JEUNESSE PRONTE A SUIVRE EN VAIN L'OBJET DE DE SON MALHEUR, ME VIENNE LIRE, IL VOIRRA MA DOULEUR, DONT MA DEESSE ET MON DIEU NE FONT CONTE.

IL COGNOISTRA QU'AMOUR EST SANS RAISON, Un DOUX ABUS, une BELLE PRISON, UN VAIN ESPOIR QUI DE VENT NOUS VIENT PAISTRE:

Lucien Pissarro: Eragny Press, *Choix de Sonnets de P. de Ronsard* (1902
red and black $8\frac{3}{8} \times 5\frac{3}{4}$ in.

experiments with three or four-colour wood-engravings were anomalous in a book-world moulded by the commanding tradition of English black-and-white illustration. ❧ But meanwhile something new was happening in Scotland. The first inklings of it south of the border were some exhibits in the London Arts and Crafts Exhibition of 1896 (which so shocked the Arts and Crafts Society, incidentally, that the designers were not invited to contribute again); in 1897 *The Studio*, as so often at this period, placed the seal of approval prominently on the new group in a two-part article by Gleeson White, 'Some Glasgow Designers and their Work'. The most notable figures among the Glasgow school at this period were 'The Four' – the architect Charles Rennie Mackintosh (1868 - 1928), the designer Herbert MacNair (1870 - 1953) and the Macdonald sisters Margaret (1865 - 1933) who married Mackintosh in 1900, and Frances (1874 - 1921) who married MacNair in 1899; all of them had in common, apart from their personal connections, the fact that they had studied at the Glasgow School of Art under the direction of Francis H. Newbery. To the Four may immediately be added Talwin Morris (1865-1911), an Englishman – the Macdonald sisters too were English, despite their name – who had no official connection with the Glasgow School of Art but lived and worked as Art Director of Blackie's publishing firm in Glasgow from 1893 and was a

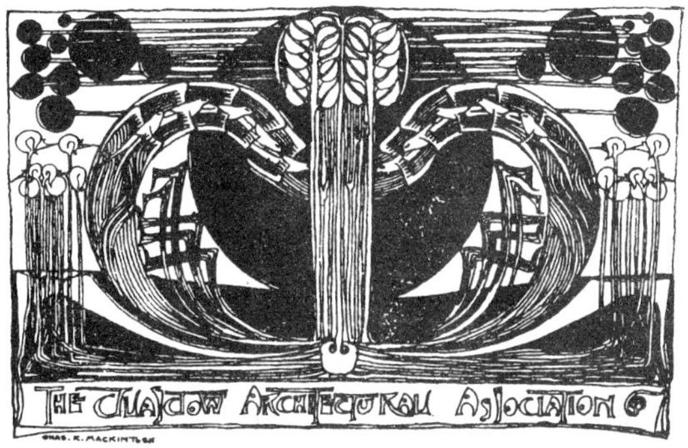

C. R. Mackintosh:
Conversazione programme, 1894

close personal associate of the Mackintoshes. Later came others, outstanding among whom are Jessie M. King (1878-1949) the illustrator and George Walton (1867-1933) the architect, as well as various lesser designers including Ann Macbeth (1875-1948), Katharine Cameron (1874-1965), Robert Traill Rose (1861-1942), and Norah Neilson Gray (1882-1931). When the Four and Talwin Morris became known outside Glasgow in 1896 they had already a fully formed style – a style which, in its broad outlines at least, they held in common. This is evident already in the six drawings – two each by MacNair, Margaret and Frances Macdonald – published in *The Yellow Book* Volume 10[1]: large, plain areas of undecorated paper, left white or evenly washed with light colour; small areas of tight-packed intricate detail punctuating the design; dominant vertical rhythms, and a tendency to vertical exaggeration in the forms; an emphasis on parallelism in design, with a constant reiteration of the same straight or slightly curved lines; a feeling of almost mathematical precision underlying the superficial fantasy; a taste for symmetry, set off by a characteristic habit of breaking the symmetry before it becomes too oppressive with occasional unpredictable cross-rhythms, particularly of wandering plant forms, *à la Japonaise*. Oh yes, and a passion for making patterns out of people, using the human figure as merely one more element, as susceptible as any other to formal distortion, in the building up of a nearly abstract decorative composition. ❧ Already, in fact, the characteristics of British art nouveau, or Continental late art nouveau. At this time the Four and Talwin Morris applied their style with equal ease and fluency to architecture, interior decoration, a variety of arts and crafts – embroidery, enamel, beaten brass and repoussé-work being particularly favoured by the Macdonalds, furniture design by MacNair – and of course various graphic arts, including pen-drawing, watercolour, illumination and poster design. Though Mackintosh designed some telling posters and was one of the first to bring together the principal elements of the style in his programme cover for a Glasgow Architectural Association *conversazione* (1894), he soon became entirely immersed in architecture and furniture design, and his actual book-work is confined to the 1920s, when he designed covers for Blackies to some popular science booklets and Henty stories for boys very much in Talwin Morris's, i.e., his own early, style. The Macdonald sisters and MacNair also became from quite early days involved in craftwork and decorative schemes to the virtual exclusion of graphic design – though around 1896-98 their art-studio in Glasgow produced a number of designs for book covers, book-illustrations etc., I have failed to trace any published book illustrated by them. Talwin Morris, on the other hand, was and remained primarily a book designer – and, moreover, a highly prolific designer of mass-produced books which circulated the country in millions during the years before the First World War. He therefore deserves some more detailed note

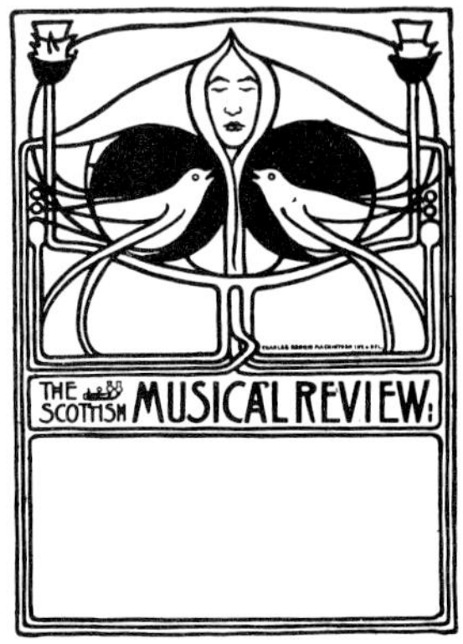

Charles Rennie Mackintosh: A Poster (1896). Compare with Talwin Morris's cover for *Jean Ingelow's Poems*

than the Four themselves, but before we come to examine his career it is worth looking quickly at the sources of the style which he shared with them and which he more than anyone else made a familiar part of the country's everyday life. The origins of the Glasgow style have been carefully charted by Professor Howarth in his pioneering book *Charles Rennie Mackintosh and the Modern Movement*, and I can do no better here than briefly summarize his findings. Beardsley, obviously, is a prime mover; if we look again at 'The Toilet of Salome' we can see at once many of the characteristics which went to form the Glasgow style. But the atmosphere of Beardsley's work is markedly different from that of the Four: though his morbidity has tended to be over-emphasized (really, on cool consideration, it is remarkable how healthy and unmorbid, almost jolly, most of his designs are, especially in comparison with the refined perversities of Ricketts) and the morbid element in the Four have been under-estimated, the misty Celtic-twilight fantasies of the Macdonald sisters, say, are radically unlike the hard sparkle of Beardsley at his best. If the form owes a lot to Beardsley, the emotional content owes much more to Burne-Jones, whose limp passivity and dreamy poeticism certainly had more to do with the collective fantasy of the so-called Celtic Twilight – as represented by the prose-poems of Fiona MacLeod, fey, feminine alter ego of the incisive art critic William Sharp – than any genuinely Celtic sources. These influences, though – of Burne-Jones, more remotely of Rossetti, and even perhaps to some extent of Beardsley – may well have come to Glasgow not only directly, but also at one remove, through the works of the Dutch painter Jan Toorop (1838-1928), or more exactly through the one work by Toorop the Four certainly knew in reproduction, his elaborate drawing 'The Three Brides', used as an illustration in the first number of *The Studio* (1893). Most of Toorop's

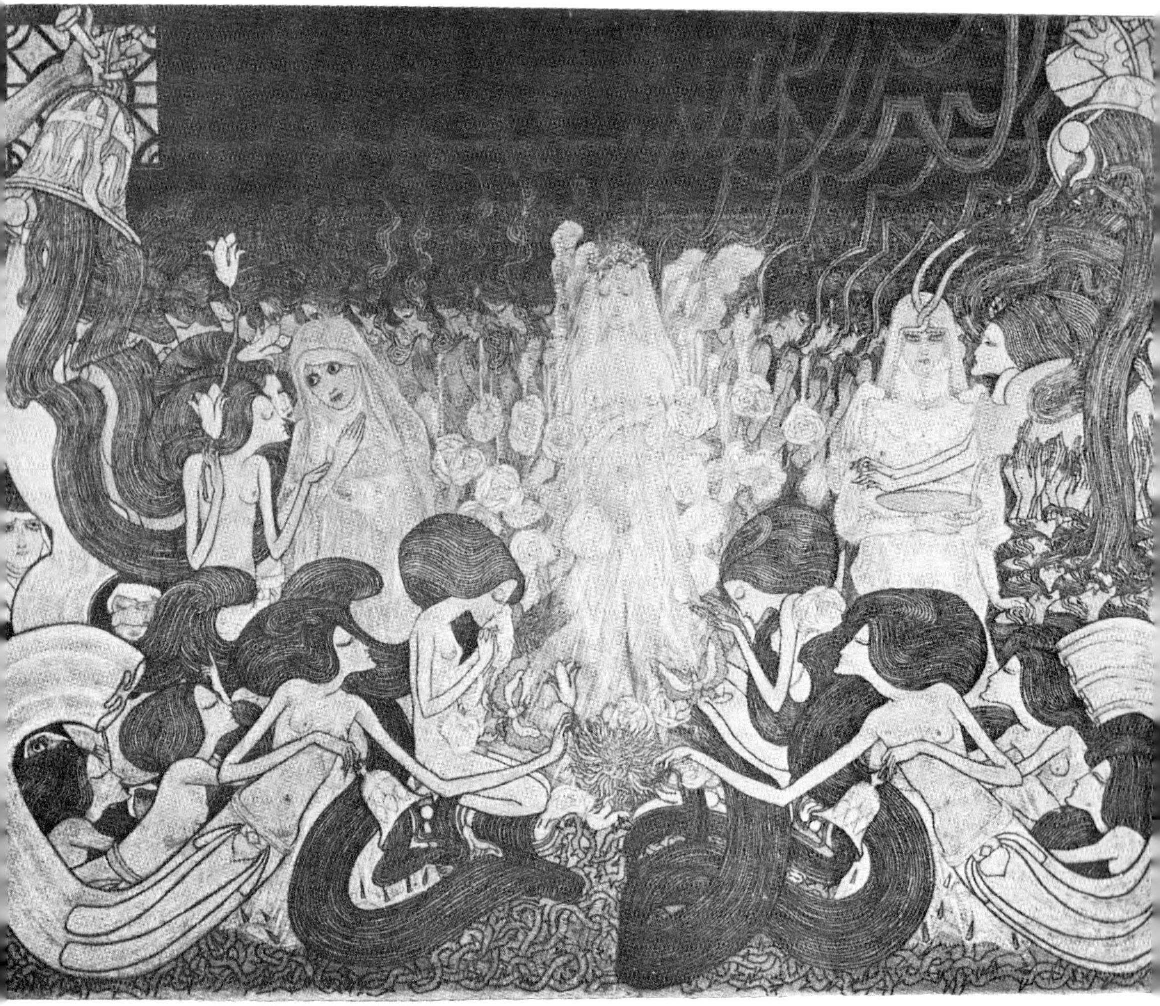

Jan Toorop: *The Three Brides*
(Kröller-Müller Museum, Otterlo)

affiliations were British: he had an English mother, an Irish wife, and between 1884 and 1889 spent as much time in London as in Holland, becoming well acquainted with the paintings of Burne-Jones, the designs of the Century Guild artists and probably, through them, with Blake. From these and from Beardsley, whose work he knew at least in 1893 and perhaps earlier, he adopted many motifs and turns of style which, subtly modified and combined in a novel manner in 'The Three Brides', proved powerfully influential on the Four: in this painting we find the missing link between the frieze-like figure-compositions of Rossetti and Burne-Jones and the figure-patterns of the Four, the weakness of some members of the Century Guild for designs in a series of roughly parallel vertical bands and the reiterated vertical patterning of the Four – not to mention the conventions in the representation of hair and of faces which the Four might have acquired through him or directly from Beardsley or both. ❧ Wherever the Glasgow style came from, exactly, Talwin Morris's is the earliest application of it in book design, and no doubt the most influential. He began his career articled to an architect uncle in Reading, then worked for a while in an architect's office in London. From the first, though, his main interest was in book design and illustration. In 1891 he took a post as assistant to H. M. Spielman, art editor of the new weekly *Black and White*, which gave a prominent place to illustrators as varied as Harry Furniss, Ricketts, G. F. Watts, George du Maurier, Hugh Thomson, Walter Crane and Lord Leighton during its first year alone. After some eighteen months in this job he applied (through an advertisement in *The Times*) for the post of Art Director to Blackies in Glasgow, was appointed and settled in Glasgow, where he rapidly came into contact with the Four. His work became known along with theirs; the first of Gleeson White's *Studio* articles (July 1897) was about Mackintosh and the Macdonalds; the second (September 1897) was devoted to MacNair and Morris. ❧ Unlike the Four, he seems to have found little obstacle to general acceptance of his work; not only was *The Studio* enthusiastic, frequently illustrating his designs in the later 1890s and 1900s, but, more important, his position at Blackies, an expanding popular publisher of no special pretensions, enabled him to bypass the difficult area of rigid middle-class, middle-brow, conventional taste and get straight through to a mass audience. For though ordinary popular books – novels, children's stories, encyclopaedias – may certainly be helped in their sales by a suitably appetizing exterior, this is seldom a decisive factor in whether they sell or not. If potential buyers of an expensive private-press book or de luxe illustrated

edition do not care for the style in which it is produced they will not buy it; potential buyers of an inexpensive book for reading, on the other hand, select almost exclusively by the contents, and are hardly conscious of the production-style as a positive factor in their choice at all. Though inevitably, considering his connections and the taste of the time, Talwin Morris did make designs for hand-tooled leather bindings executed by the Macdonalds and their associates, they are not an important part of his work; most of it, indeed, was at the other end of the publishing scale – designs for cheap printed cloth covers to cheap books, title-pages and end-papers which could be used over and over again with minor variations in various volumes of series, formularized layouts for innumerable sets of pocket anthologies, popular classics and encyclopaedias.
So enormous was his output that even today, more than half a century after his death and despite the ravages of two World Wars, it is practically impossible to look round a second-hand bookshop without coming across some example of his handiwork. Necessarily, to do it at all, he had to rely on a formula, but the nature of the formula is interesting. A moment's thought shows that of all possible decorative conventions the Glasgow devotion to

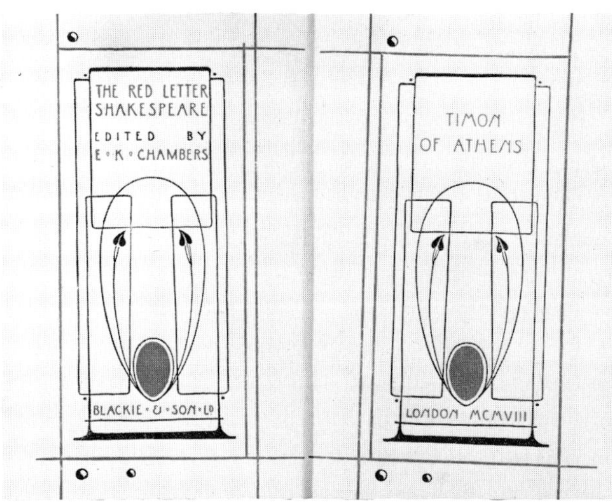

Talwin Morris: Red Letter Shakespeare (1908) $6\frac{1}{8} \times 3\frac{1}{2}$ in.

alwin Morris: Red letter series bindings.

Top (parchment boards): *Confessions of t. Augustine*, *Poems of Christina Rossetti* $6\frac{3}{8} \times 4$ in.; Centre: (suede) Keble's *The Christian Year* $6\frac{3}{8} \times 4\frac{3}{8}$ in.; Bottom (leatherette): *Poems by Jean Ingelow* (cloth) 6×4 in. De Quincey's *The Opium Eater* $6\frac{1}{8} \times 3\frac{7}{8}$ in.

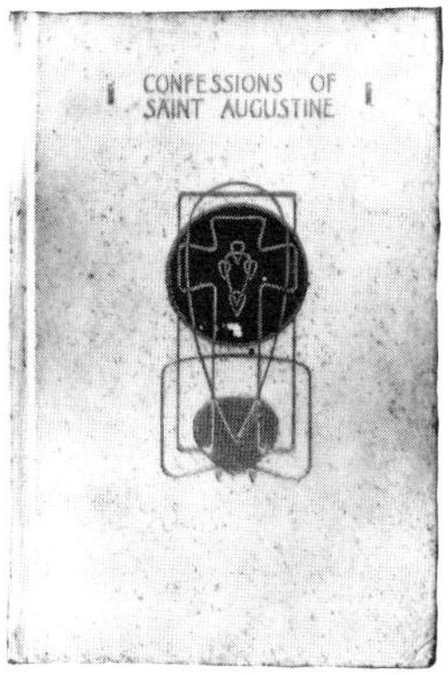

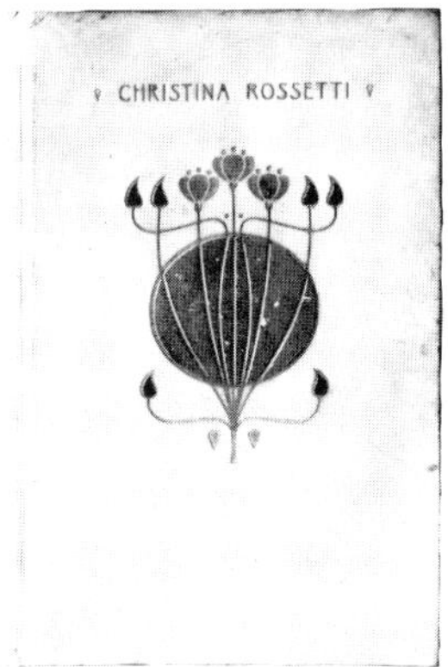

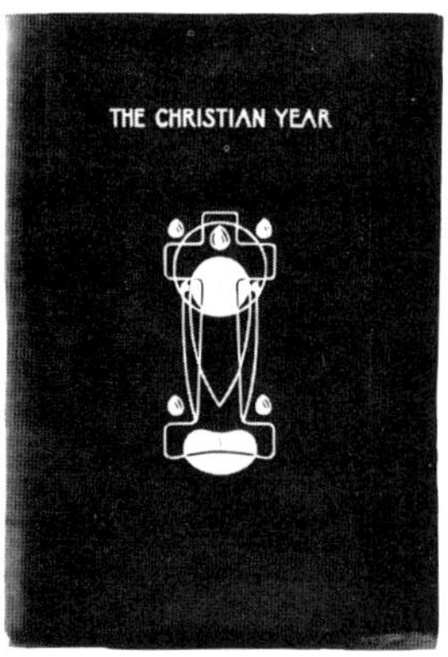

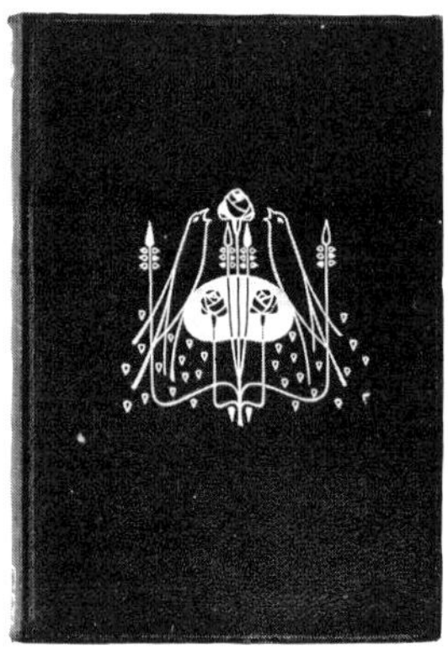

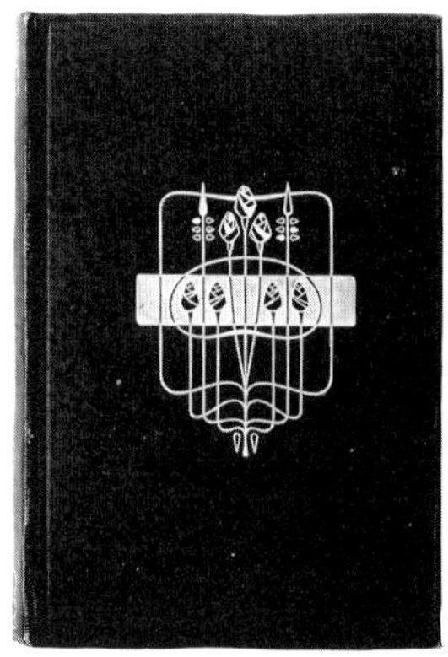

plain surfaces bounded by straight or slightly curved lines and arranged with geometrical precision in symmetrical patterns could hardly be better suited to the requirements of stamped or printed cloth covers. At their simplest they could be printed in black or colour on a plain-coloured cloth surface. They could be stamped in gold on leatherette or suede, or mass-produced parchment boards for the more expensive ranges. They could even be – and often were in the 1900s – gaily printed in several colours, with the basic outline in one and the intervening spaces flatly tinted in others. They were humble, practical, unnoticeable. They were abstract enough – after some of the early numbers of the

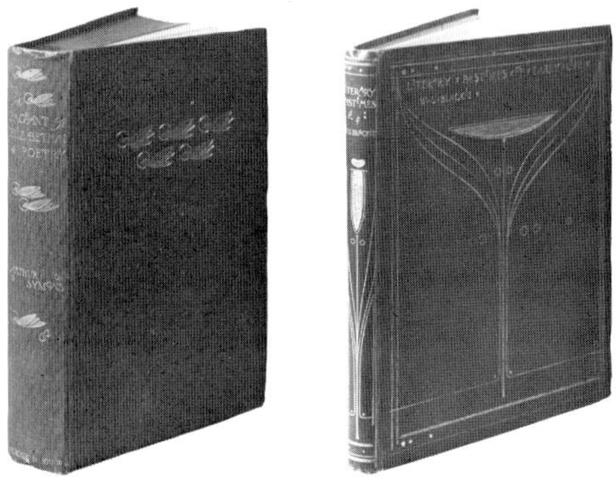

Talwin Morris:
Commercial cloth bindings.
A Pageant of Elizabethan Poetry, 7 x 5 in. *Literary Pastimes*, 8 x 6 in.

Red Letter series, Talwin Morris nearly always reduced representational elements to a minimum or banished them altogether – to offend no one, and could even be used without too much of a jolt as a frame for a brightly coloured pasted-on picture of Henty action or fairy-tale romance in quite an alien idiom, as often happened in Blackies children's books of the period. But just because of their easy acceptability for an indiscriminating public, or even a discriminating public in an area where their normal standards were relaxed, these designs of Talwin Morris probably had a more far-reaching effect in habituating the public at large to the conventions of art nouveau, and thus, by extension, to much in modern architecture and design, than any other single factor in this country. Talwin Morris was one of the great industrial designers of the 1900s, and deserves a small but honoured place in the history of twentieth-century taste. ❦ If he represents the first generation of the Glasgow School most adequately in book-production, the biggest and most important figure in the second generation is certainly Jessie M. King. She is one of those extraordinary individual artists who are in constant danger of being ignored or underestimated because their work leads nowhere directly and signifies nothing except itself – which, according to Hegelian organic views of artistic development, makes them at best suspect, at worst safely negligible.

It would be a thousand pities, though, if her art were to be neglected; being so much a matter of delicate nuances, of atmosphere, of extreme grace and femininity, it may never command the admiration of a majority, but for those susceptible to its magic it will always retain its unique resonance and bouquet. ❧ Jessie M. King was born in Glasgow in 1876, studied at the Glasgow School of Art, and won a travelling scholarship to France and Italy. In later life, when it was suggested that her style had been influenced by Beardsley (much direct influence seems unlikely, but an indirect influence via the Four is certainly present) she said that what really started her off was the Botticelli pen-and-ink drawings in the Uffizi.[2] On her return to Britain she began the great series of book-illustrations which were to occupy much of her time until the First World War, as well as providing mural decorations for a number of schools in Lanarkshire and designing jewellery to be made by School of Art trained craftsmen in Glasgow. At first her illustrations were the result of private commissions, one of the most popular crafts in Glasgow at the time being the extra-illustration and artistic binding of books for presentation or the delectation of prosperous art-fanciers.[3] The first published reference I can find to her is a note in *The Studio* in 1898[4] accompanying three designs by her for *The Light of Asia*; in these her style, though a trifle more crabbed and angular than it later becomes, appears to be already completely formed – it is an oddity of the Glasgow designers that they so often seem to spring into existence fully armed. She appears in *The Studio* again twice in 1899 and once in 1902 (in which year she won a Gold Medal at the Turin International Exhibition of Modern Decorative Art, where Fra Newbery and Margaret and C. R. Mackintosh were also honoured), before in Volume 26[5] she was accorded a whole article to herself, 'Miss Jessie M. King and her Work', by Walter R. Watson, with thirteen illustrations.[6] Also in 1902 she executed her first published series of book-illustrations, for an edition of George Buchanan's biblical drama *Jephtha* (Alex Gardner, Paisley). ❧ Between this and 1920 she published one children's book written as well as illustrated by herself (*Little White Town of Never Weary*, Harrap, 1917), six books of drawings, and some seventeen volumes illustrated and decorated by her, as well as between twenty and thirty books and booklets for which she designed only the cover. At first she was not too well-known, and for her first major commission by a London publisher, a series of twenty-five illustrations, decorative headings, etc., for Sebastian Evans's *High History of the Holy Grail* (Dent, 1903), a letter in the publisher's files from Sir Ernest Rhys to the artist offers her only fifteen guineas, apologising that it is not more. A commission from *The Studio* in the same year to design the magazine's complete Christmas Supplement, a sequence of texts and designs entitled *Seven Happy Days*, improved her standing as well as demonstrating her a complete mistress of colour, and in 1904 she produced what is perhaps all in all her finest book, William Morris's *The Defence of Guinevere* (John Lane). In this she had complete responsibility for illustrations, decoration and binding, and except for the fact that the full-page illustrations are all printed on a shiny art paper which does not sort too well with the rest of the book, the result is totally satisfactory, a haunting and tender evocation of a fragile medieval dream-world such as that conjured up by Maeterlinck's early plays. ❧ Shortly afterwards she began to work for two of the most enterprising publishers of their time, Gowan and Gray and T. N. Foulis, both Scottish and both now defunct. For these much of her best work was done. They both specialized in illustrated pocket-books and gift-books, with the accent naturally on attractive design, and even their smallest and cheapest envelope books (booklets, often

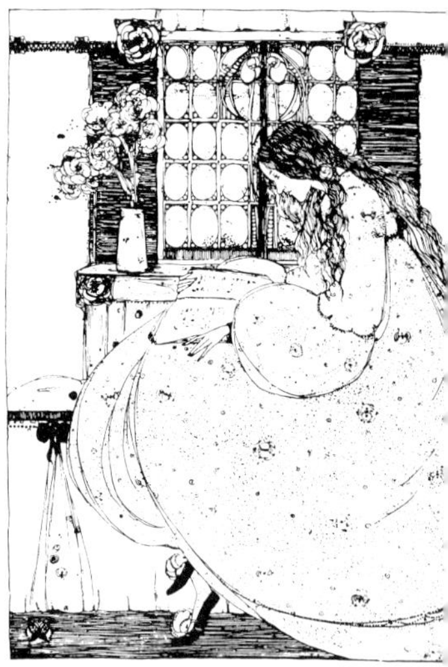

Jessie M. King: Illustration for Oliver Greg's *The Magic Grammar* (*The Studio*, 1902)

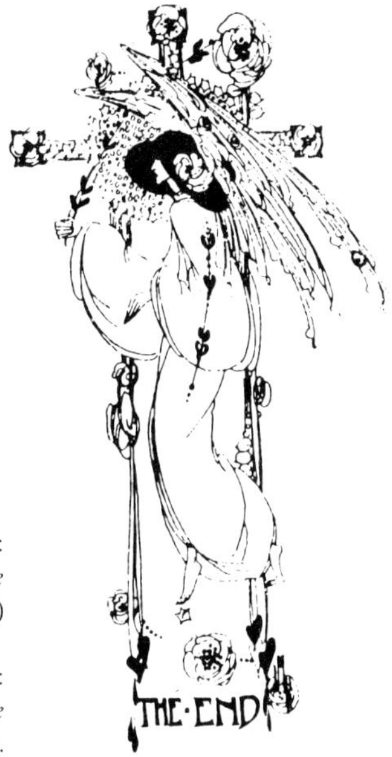

Jessie M. King:
The Defence of Guinevere
(1904)

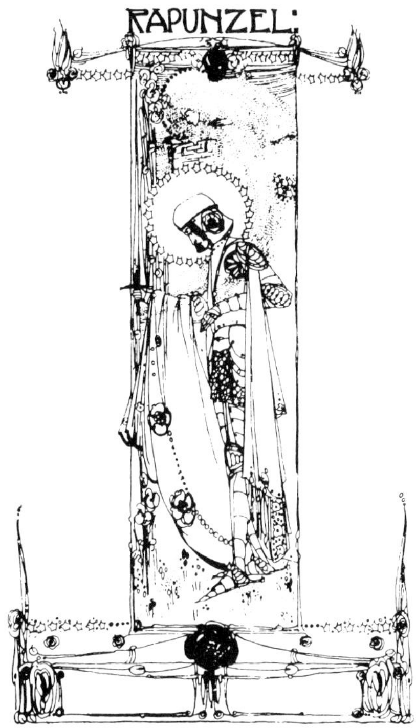

Jessie M. King:
The Defence of Guinevere
(1904) $7\frac{3}{8} \times 4\frac{3}{4}$ in.

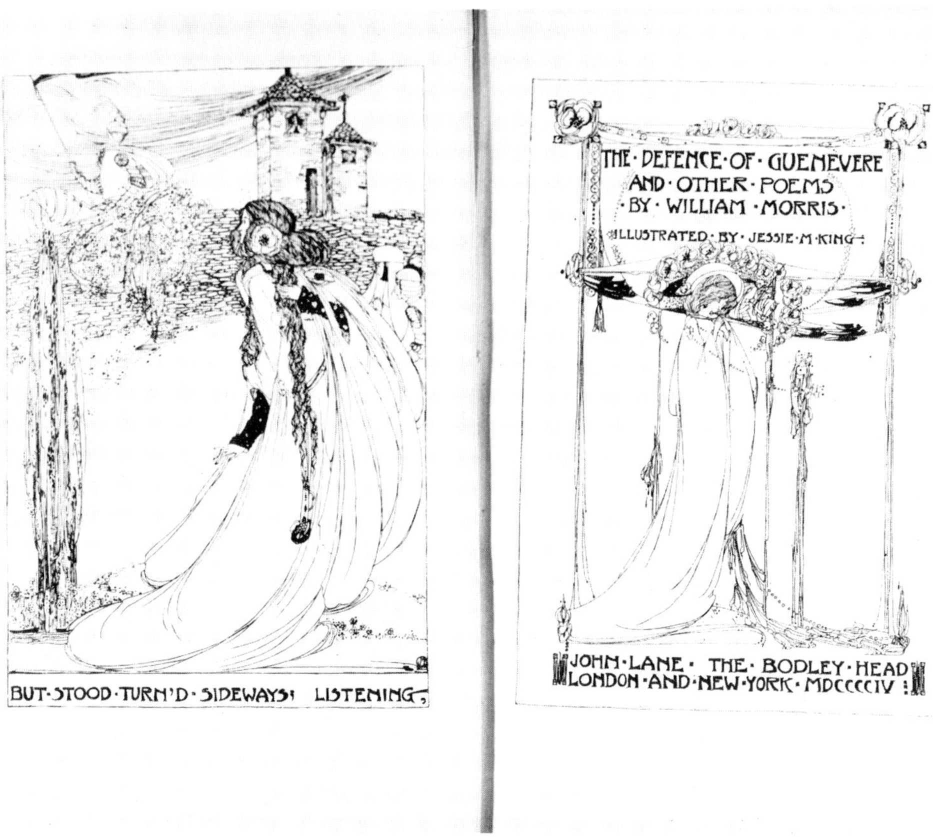

Jessie M. King: Title-opening of Morris's *The Defence of Guinevere* (1904)

paperbound, in the narrow upright format of Laurence Housman's *Goblin Market*, intended to be slipped into envelopes as small presents, something larger than a card but smaller than a formal gift) or sixpenny plays and nature-books were issued in decorated parchment bindings (often the work of Jessie M. King) as well as, probably, fancy-printed cloth, embossed suede and other finishes fashionable at the time. Moreover, the covers were frequently modified or replaced, depending on how fast a title was selling or just to make a change,[7] so that any one booklet is hardly ever found twice in exactly the same state. For Gowan and Gray she designed (from cover to cover) one of her most beautiful, severe works, the book of flower drawings *Budding Life* (1906), which are treated with a dramatic economy worthy of the best Japanese models, and another book of drawings, landscapes of Culross, called *Dwellings in an Old-World Town* (1909; reissued by Foulis in 1911), as well as one of her most ambitious but on the whole least personal works, the series of coloured landscapes for *The Book of Bridges/Ponts de Paris* (1911), text by E. Archambeau; for Foulis she made two more books of landscape drawings, *The Grey City of the North* (*Edinburgh*) (1910) and *The City of the West* (*Glasgow*) (1911) and some outstanding coloured illustrations for envelope books, the best to my taste being *Isabella, or The Pot of Basil* (1914). There are many more books from this rich period of her career, so that this account is in danger of becoming a mere list of titles. I must just mention, though, the *Comus* she illustrated for Routledge's Photogravure and Colour Series (1906), this being in photogravure and an immaculate example of designs perfectly suited to the somewhat unresponsive medium; the illustrations, tucked away in each case behind inappropriate and undistinguished title-openings by another hand, for the 'Golden Poet' selections of *Shelley* by Churton Collins and *Spenser* by W. B. Yeats (both

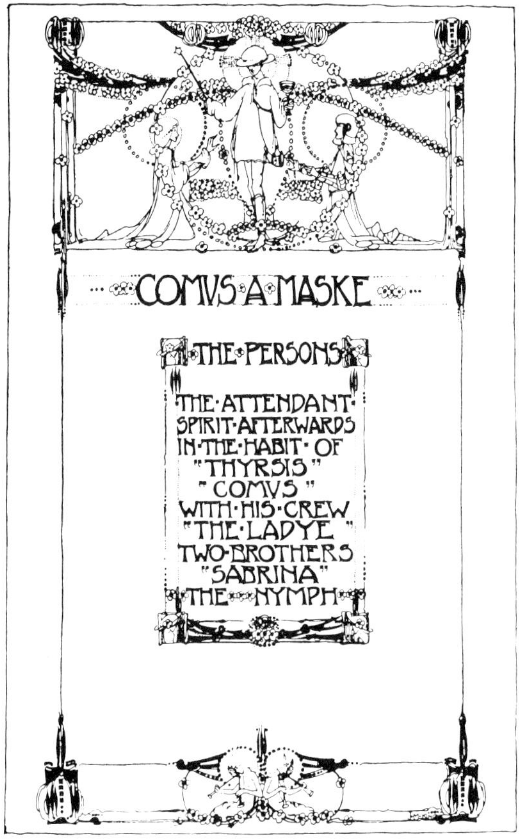

Jessie M. King:
Comus (1906) 8 × 5⅝ in.

Jack, 1908), in which excellent designs are spoilt by inadequate reproduction and a rather summary application of pink and gold in a primarily black-and-white context; and above all the sumptuous edition of Wilde's *A House of Pomegranates* she illustrated for Methuen in 1915. Of the sixteen full-page colour illustrations in this book – for which Jessie M. King also designed the covers, end papers, title-page and decorative initials throughout – it is difficult to speak too highly. In some of them – 'His Dream' of 'And to the City' for instance – there is a delicacy of draughtsmanship and a muted subtlety of colour-range which far surpasses anything in Rackham, to some of whose work there is perhaps a momentary resemblance; in others, particularly 'I had never seen anyone so pale', the colour is distributed with startling boldness, the central figure being set against the bare white expanse of wall and the tiny

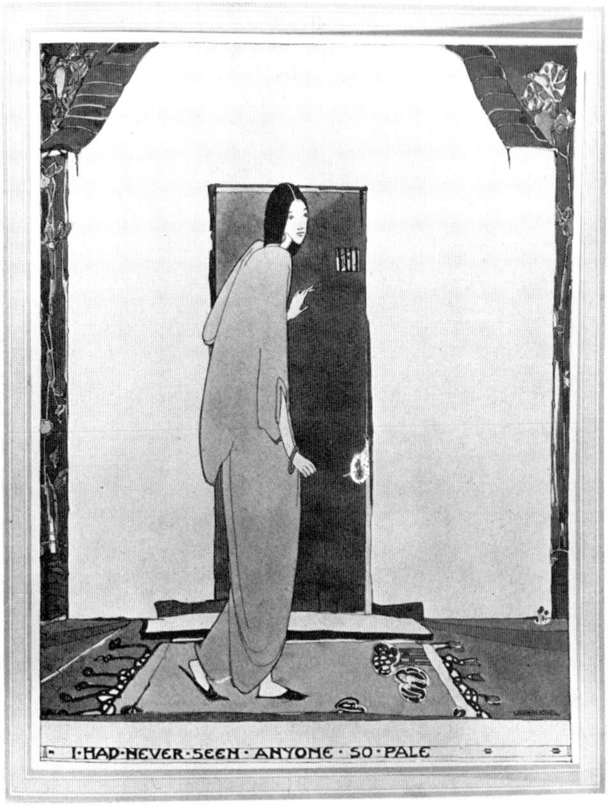

Jessie M. King: coloured illustration for Wilde's *A House of Pomegranates* (1915)

accent of colour at the peephole with the utmost nicety in a manner which at once recalls a favourite compositional gambit of the Four and points unmistakably forward to the 1920s of Mendelsohn and Corbusier. During and after the First World War Jessie M. King became interested in batik-work, a mode of colour-printing textiles which originated in the East Indies and which she explains amusingly in her illustrated book *How Cinderella Was Able to Go to the Ball* (Foulis, 1924). From this time on she devoted less and less of her time to book illustration, her principal works in this medium being two books of drawings, *Good King Wenceslas* (Studio, 1919) and *Kirkcudbright, a Royal Borough* (Gowan and Gray, 1934), the delicate coloured designs for Kipling's *L'Habitation Forcée* (Paris: René Kieffer, 1921), and the illustrations to a strange children's book, *The Enchanted Capital of Scotland* (Plaid Stationery of Scotland, Ltd, c. 1946). In these, in her batik work and in her drawings in

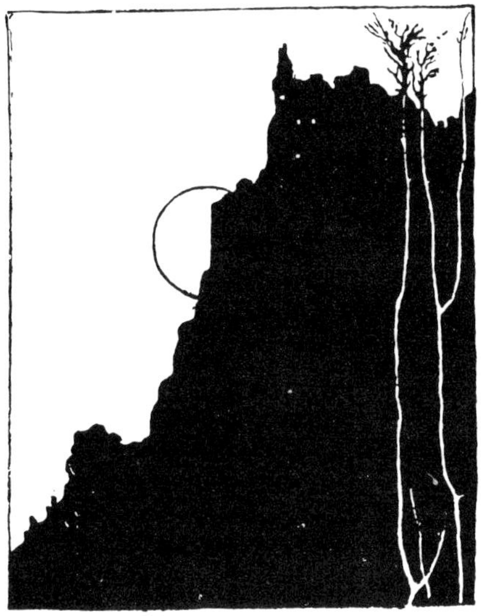

Katharine Cameron:
Rhymes of the Duchess May
(*c* 1914)

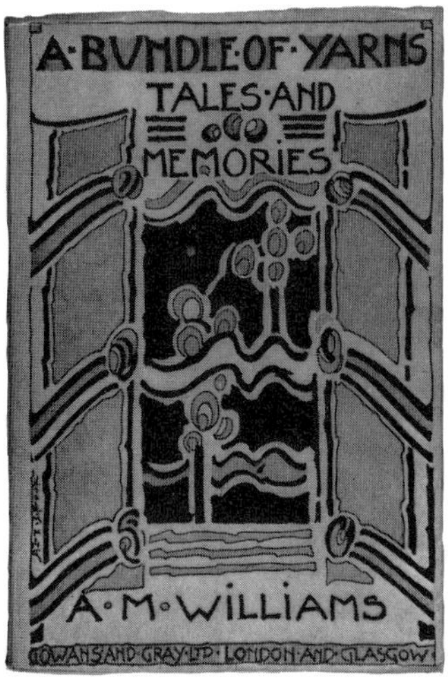

Jessie M. King:
Parchment cover for
A Bundle of Yarns (1930) 6 x 4 in.

coloured inks, two of which are reproduced with a note by her husband in *The Studio* in 1925,[8] her colour sense becomes still bolder and freer, taking on at times an almost Fauve brilliance – much as Mackintosh's did at the same time, starting with some fabric designs he and his wife made for Foxton's and Sefton's around 1920, though there seems to have been no connection between Jessie M. King and the Mackintoshes at this period. Some of Jessie M. King's later designs, such as the cover for A. M. Williams's *A Bundle of Yarns* (Gowan and Gray, 1930), even verge on the jazz-modern in idiom, helping to make explicit a line of descent which one may often suspect in 'modernistic' design of the late 1920s and early 1930s without ever quite being able to pin it down. After wandering for some years Jessie M. King and her husband finally settled down in her family home in Kircudbright, where she died, almost forgotten, in 1948. Nevertheless, the image she conjures up of pale ladies festooned in stars and attended by flights of birds, of wan haloed knights, lost in reverie and drifting through wispy landscapes of faint transfigured trees and insubstantial dream-castles of the mind, is not quite like anything else in art, and once entered, never wholly escaped from. What her vision lacks in variety, it makes up in imaginative intensity and in the sheer

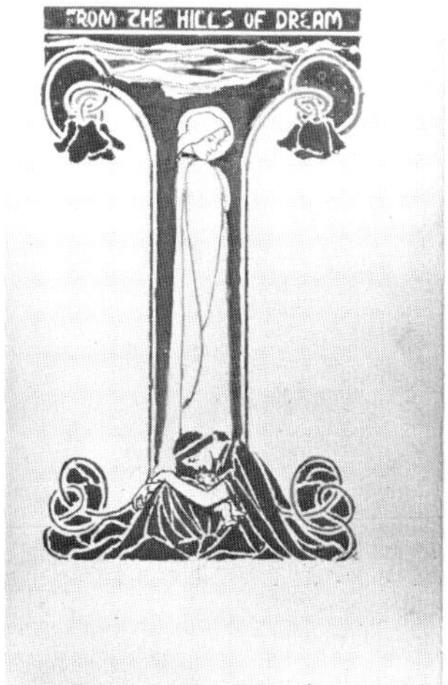

Robert Traill Rose:
Extra – illustration for Fiona MacLeod's
From the Hills of Dream (*c* 1897)

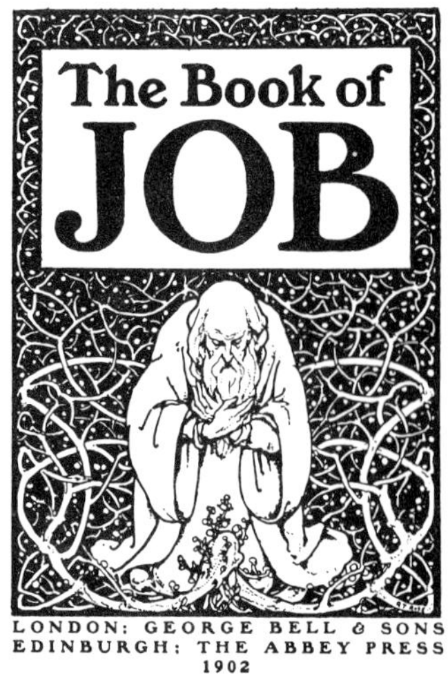

Robert Traill Rose:
Title-page to
The Book of Job (1902)
8½ × 7 in.

technical brilliance with which she marshals the furniture of her small but exquisite world: indeed, she has strong claims to be considered one of the most original and accomplished of all the art nouveau book-artists in Britain, and a worthy third in the triumvirate of greats along with Ricketts and Beardsley. ❧ The lesser figures among the Gowan and Gray/Foulis illustrators are very much lesser, and need not delay us long. The most interesting is Katharine Cameron, sister of the etcher D. Y. Cameron and wife of the art connoisseur Arthur Kay. According to her own account[9] her first and real love was landscape and flower-painting: she drifted into book-illustration around 1908 because she was asked to, went on illustrating as long as people went on asking her, and then returned happily to landscape and flower-painting with never a second thought, only keeping some of her books, which she never took seriously, on the insistence of her husband. This may well explain the curious split personality of her illustrative work. Her figure compositions are with rare exceptions – notably the beautiful 'Stella Maris' in *Legends and Stories of Italy* (Jack, 1909) – relatively impersonal, being mostly a pale, feminine version of Byam Shaw's historical style, with little of Shaw's rather vulgar panache or technical dexterity (*Rhymes of the Duchess*

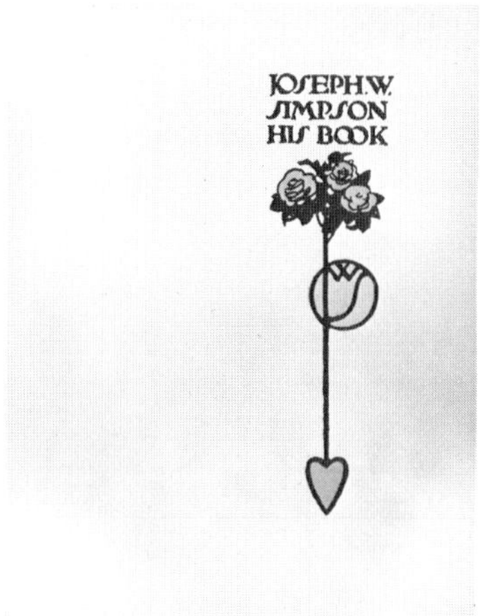

Joseph Simpson: Title-page of *Joseph W. Simpson. His Book* (Edinburgh: Otto Schulze, 1900), a collection of designs for bookplates $8\frac{3}{8} \times 6\frac{3}{8}$ in.

May, *The Lady of Shalott*, *Aucassin and Nicolette*, all Foulis, c. 1912). But when she is able to confine herself to landscape, as in Flora Grierson's *Haunting Edinburgh* (John Lane, 1929) or to flowers, as in Edward Thomas's anthology *The Flowers I Love* (T. C. and E. C. Jack, 1915) the results are as exquisite as anything the Glasgow School produced. Robert Traill Rose was an uneven artist with mystical aspirations and an unreliable colour sense, both of which may be seen in his illustrations to Newman's *The Dream of Gerontius* (Foulis, 1910). None of his published work in colour that I know of matches some of his tinted extra-illustrations, such as the title design in my copy of the first edition of Fiona MacLeod's *From the Hills of Dream* (Geddes, 1897); his black-and-white illustrations for *The Book of Job* (George Bell, 1902) unexpectedly show a far firmer sense of design, and make one regret that he did not deny himself colour more often. Ann Macbeth was a highly accomplished draughtsman, as some designs for costume drawn for *The Studio* show, but her work was mainly in embroidery, of which she and Mrs Newbery were the Glasgow School's outstanding mistresses, and therefore does not concern us. Norah Neilson Gray, a portrait painter and occasional illustrator, seems to be remembered by survivors of the Glaswegian art

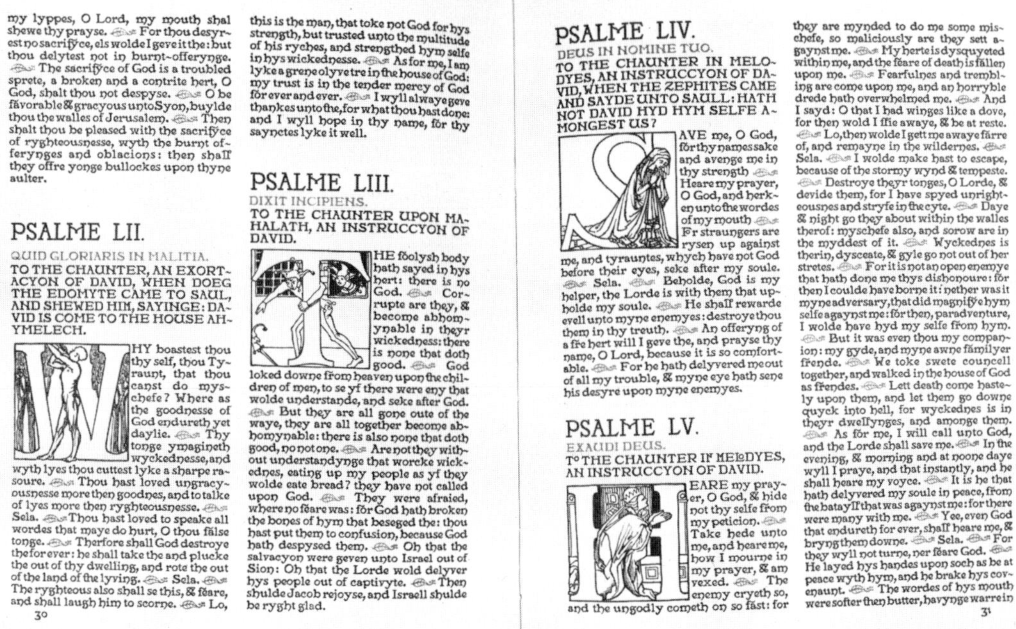
my lyppes, O Lord, my mouth shal shewe thy prayse. For thou desyrest no sacrifyce, els wolde I geve it the: but thou delytest not in burnt-offerynge. The sacrifyce of God is a troubled sprete, a broken and a contrite hert, O God, shalt thou not despyse. O be favorable & gracyous unto Syon, buylde thou the walles of Jerusalem. Then shalt thou be pleased with the sacrifyce of ryghteousnesse, wyth the burnt offerynges and oblacions: then shall they offre yonge bullockes upon thyne aulter.

PSALME LII.

QUID GLORIARIS IN MALITIA.

TO THE CHAUNTER, AN EXORTACYON OF DAVID, WHEN DOEG THE EDOMYTE CAME TO SAUL, AND SHEWED HIM, SAYINGE: DAVID IS COME TO THE HOUSE AHYMELECH.

WHY boastest thou thy self, thou Tyraunt, that thou canst do myschefe? Where as the goodnesse of God endureth yet daylie. Thy tonge ymagineth wyckednesse, and wyth lyes thou cuttest lyke a sharpe rasoure. Thou hast loved ungracyousnesse more then goodnes, and to talke of lyes more then ryghteousnesse. Sela. Thou hast loved to speake all wordes that maye do hurt, O thou false tonge. Therfore shall God destroye the for ever: he shall take the and plucke the out of thy dwelling, and rote the out of the land of the lyving. Sela. The ryghteous also shall se this, & feare, and shall laugh him to scorne. Lo,

30

this is the man, that toke not God for hys strength, but trusted unto the multitude of his ryches, and strengthed hym selfe in hys wickednesse. As for me, I am lyke a grene olyve tre in the house of God: my trust is in the tender mercy of God for ever and ever. I wyll alwaye geve thankes unto the, for what thou hast done: and I wyll hope in thy name, for thy saynctes lyke it well.

PSALME LIII.

DIXIT INCIPIENS.

TO THE CHAUNTER UPON MAHALATH, AN INSTRUCCYON OF DAVID.

THE foolysh body hath sayed in hys hert: there is no God. Corrupte are they, & become abhomynable in theyr wickedness: there is none that doth good. God loked downe from heaven upon the children of men, to se yf there were eny that wolde understande, and seke after God. But they are all gone oute of the waye, they are all together become abhomynable: there is also none that doth good, no not one. Are not they without understandynge that worcke wickednes, eating up my people as yf they wolde eate bread? they have not called upon God. They were afraied, where no feare was: for God hath broken the bones of hym that beseged the: thou hast put them to confusion, because God hath despysed them. Oh that the salvacyon were geven unto Israel out of Sion: Oh that the Lorde wold delyver hys people out of captivyte. Then shulde Jacob rejoyse, and Israell shulde be ryght glad.

PSALME LIV.

DEUS IN NOMINE TUO.

TO THE CHAUNTER IN MELODYES, AN INSTRUCCYON OF DAVID, WHEN THE ZEPHITES CAME AND SAYDE UNTO SAULL: HATH NOT DAVID HYD HYM SELFE AMONGEST US?

SAVE me, O God, for thy names sake and avenge me in thy strength. Heare my prayer, O God, and herken unto the wordes of my mouth. For straungers are rysen up against me, and tyrauntes, whych have not God before their eyes, seke after my soule. Sela. Beholde, God is my helper, the Lorde is with them that upholde my soule. He shall rewarde evell unto myne enemyes: destroye thou them in thy treuth. An offeryng of a fre hert will I geve the, and prayse thy name, O Lord, because it is so comfortable. For he hath delyvered me out of all my trouble, & myne eye hath sene his desyre upon myne enemyes.

PSALME LV.

EXAUDI DEUS.

TO THE CHAUNTER IN MELODYES, AN INSTRUCCYON OF DAVID.

HEARE my prayer, O God, & hide not thy selfe from my peticion. Take hede unto me, and heare me, how I mourne in my prayer, & am vexed. The enemy cryeth so, and the ungodly cometh on so fast: for they are mynded to do me some myschefe, so maliciously are they sett agaynst me. My herte is dysquyeted within me, and the feare of death is fallen upon me. Fearfulnes and tremblyng are come upon me, and an horryble drede hath overwhelmed me. And I sayd: O that I had winges like a dove, for then wold I fle awaye, & be at reste. Lo, then wolde I gett me awaye farre of, and remayne in the wildernes. Sela. I wolde make hast to escape, because of the stormy wynd & tempeste. Destroye theyr tonges, O Lorde, & devide them, for I have spyed unrighteousnes and stryfe in the cyte. Daye & night go they about within the walles therof: myschefe also, and sorow are in the myddest of it. Wyckednes is therin, dysceate, & gyle go not out of her stretes. For it is not an open enemye that hath done me thys dishonoure: for then I coulde have borne it: nether was it myne adversary, that did magnifye hym selfe agaynst me: for then, paradventure, I wolde have hyd my selfe from hym. But it was even thou my companion: my gyde, and myne awne familyer frende. We toke swete councell together, and walked in the house of God as frendes. Lett death come hastely upon them, and let them go downe quyck into hell, for wyckednes is in theyr dwellynges, and amonge them. As for me, I will call unto God, and the Lorde shall save me. In the evening, & morning and at noone daye wyll I praye, and that instantly, and he shall heare my voyce. It is he that hath delyvered my soule in peace, from the batayll that was agaynst me: for there were many with me. Yee, even God that endureth for ever, shall heare me, & bryng them downe. Sela. For they wyll not turne, ner feare God. He layed hys handes upon soch as be at peace wyth hym, and he brake hys covenaunt. The wordes of hys mouth were softer then butter, havynge warre in

31

C. R. Ashbee: Essex House *Psalter* (1902)
black and red $11\frac{5}{8}$ x 8 in.

world chiefly for her notorious inability to draw hands, which she always had to conceal as far as possible in her work. She endears herself chiefly as the inventor of the most sublimely inappropriate illustrations that long-suffering poem Wordsworth's *Ode on Intimations of Immortality* can ever have received (Dent, 1913): it must, surely, require genius of a sort to produce anything so superbly irrelevant as the pretty blond children with gossamer wings and ineffectual little hunting horns for 'The cateracts blow their trumpets from the steep' or the cute little rabbits bobbing among the saplings in 'Moving about in worlds not realised'. The 1900s in England need not detain us very long either. For the most part it is a period in commercial publishing of imposing illustrations interspersed with undecorated text. The private presses, in contrast, the Doves Press most severe among them, tend to cut down illustration or eliminate it altogether, seeking to produce their effects by the meticulous arrange-

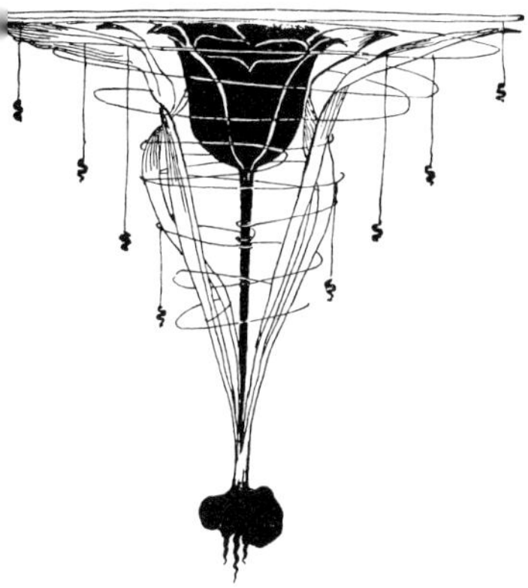

C. R. Ashbee: *Chapters in Workshop Reconstruction and Citizenship* (Guild of Handicraft, 1894)

ment of pure types instead, and only C. R. Ashbee's Essex House Press really continues to practice the Emery Walker ideal of a decorated book in which all the parts contribute naturally to an harmonious whole. Ashbee himself (1863-1924) is odd, unclassifiable figure; by temperament, training and conscious inclination he was an Arts and Crafts man, a devoted follower of Morris,[10] but he was also sensitive to the currents of taste active at the time, and much of his jewellery and metal work, for all its Arts and Crafts solidity, is distinctly art nouveau in feeling and in detail. The same is true of some of his books. The type he designed for his own use and employed in a number of them has a Morrisian flavour, being, like Morris's Golden, though far more alarmingly mannered, an attempt to impart a gothic flavour to a vaguely roman-based type.[11] The decorated initials and head and tailpieces hark back to the lusty early art nouveau of Mackmurdo, and the illustrations, when they occur, range in style from the Owen-Jonesish crispness and directness of the angels which decorate his poems *Echoes from the City of the Sun* (1905) to the highly mannered, condensed, clearly art nouveau vignettes at each initial in the Essex House *Psalter* (1902). The effect in the *Psalter* and the fine folio *Prayer Book of King Edward VII* (1903), printed in black and red, can be firm and magnificent; in books of poetry the high proportion of white lightens the effect; but in continuous prose, especially in smaller formats, like Ashbee's volume of lectures *American Sheaves and English Seed Corn* (1901) the result can easily be rather oppressive. ❧ Elsewhere the field belongs almost exclusively to the name illustrators, each with a following sufficient to make his work the centre of interest and chief selling-point of any book in which it appears. In fact, sometimes all pretence of producing a book in which reading plays any vital part is dropped, and we are given instead *Arthur Rackham's Book of Pictures*, *Edmund Dulac's Picture*

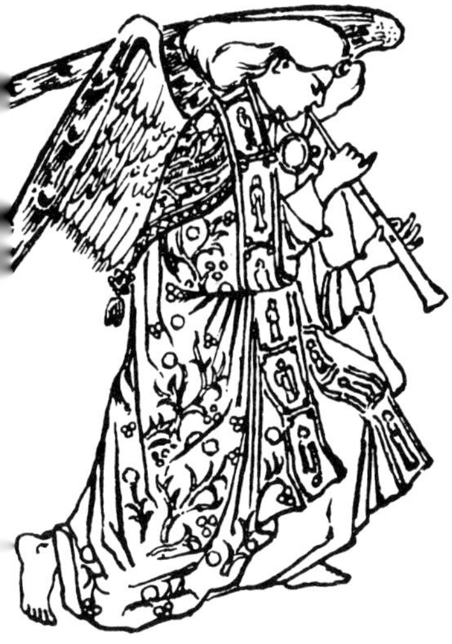

C. R. Ashbee: *Echoes from the City of the Sun* (1905)

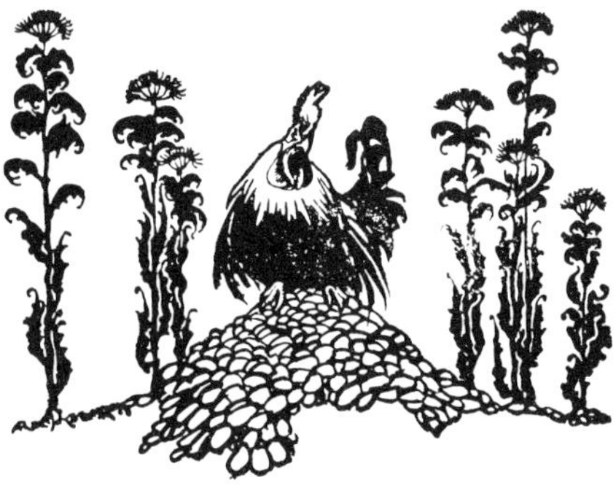

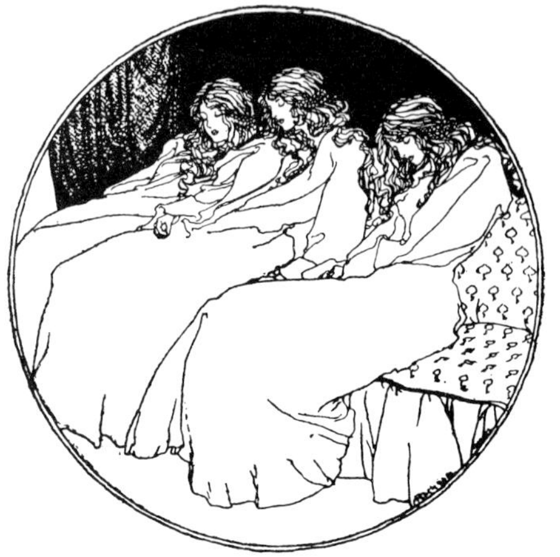

Arthur Rackham: *Grimm's Fairy Tales* (Freemantle, 1900)

Arthur Rackham: *Grimm's Fairy Tales* (Freemantle, 1900)

Book, etc. Hence the notion of any organic relationship between the illustrations and the rest of the book fades away and dies: the function of the book becomes simply to provide as convenient and unobtrusive a frame as possible for pictures which are conceived separately in total independence of it and then reverently incorporated. Not, it should be said, that such illustrations are necessarily bad in themselves; the designs of Arthur Rackham (1867 - 1939) for instance, the most famous of all such artists, have, though imaginatively lightweight and drastically limited in their range, a real skill and accomplishment within their chosen light fantastic register; Edmund J. Sullivan (1869 - 1933), more at home in black-and-white, excels in the sinister-grotesque; Edmund Dulac (1882 - 1953), another colourist, gives his fairy tale pictures an oriental richness; all bear the marks of art nouveau in the details of their forms and compositions, though none can be said to adhere to it wholeheartedly. ❧ More interesting on all counts are the little books of children's poems and stories Charles Robinson (1870 - 1937), most talented of the three Robinson brothers,[12] decorated for John Lane and others in the 1890s and 1900s – *A Child's Garden of Verses* (Lane, 1896); *Lullaby Land* (Lane, 1898), *Fireside Saints* (Blackie, 1904); these are quite unpretentious, have a genuine charm which stops just on the right side of sentimentality, and are, moreover, unlike most illustrated books of the time, really designed as books. Another illustrator

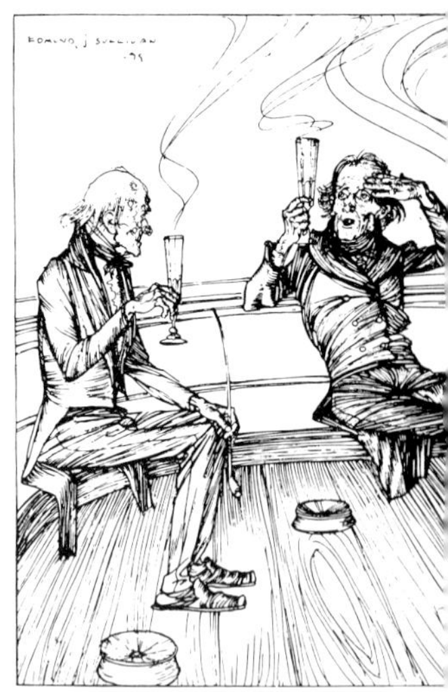

Edmund J. Sullivan: Tennyson's *A Dream of Fair Women* (Grant Richards, 1900)

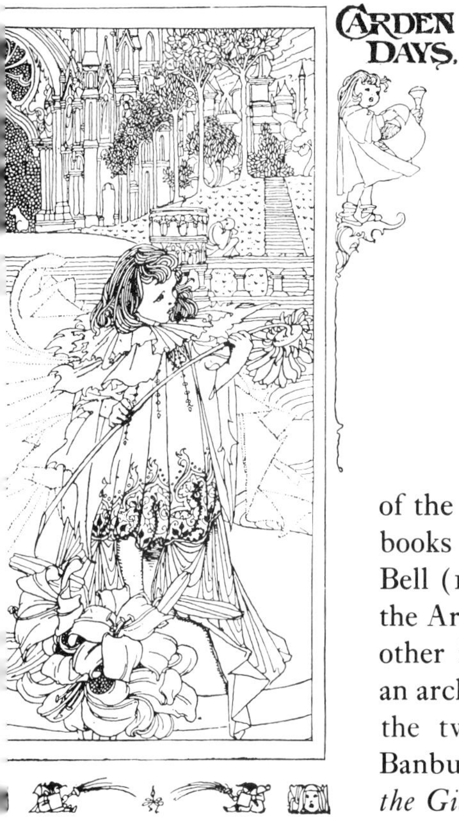

Charles Robinson:
Page from *A Child's Garden of Verses*
(1896) $6\frac{3}{4} \times 4\frac{1}{2}$ in.

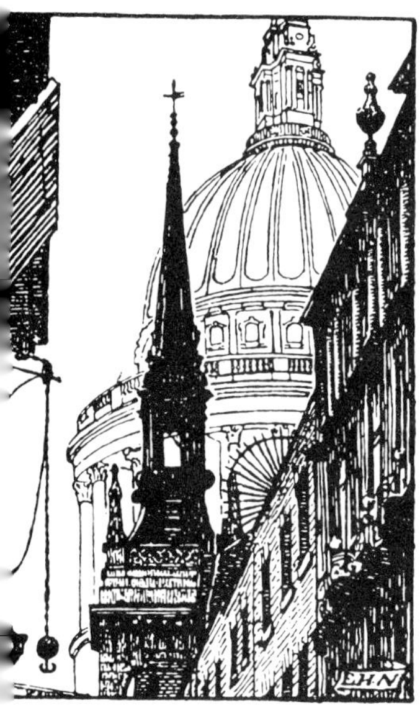

E. H. New: Drawing from
Life and Works of Sir Christopher Wren
(Essex House, 1903)

of the period who manages to make each of his best books into a coherent artistic whole is Robert Anning Bell (1863-1933). He began as a minor follower of the Arts and Crafts movement, serving, like so many other illustrators of the time, his apprenticeship in an architect's office. But his illustrative designs, from the two little volumes of fairy stories in Dent's Banbury Cross Series, *The Sleeping Beauty* and *Jack the Giant Killer* (both 1894) on, have a distinctive, and distinctly art nouveau, lightness and grace; while such later volumes as *Poems by John Keats* (Bell, 1897) and especially *The Tempest* (Freemantle, 1901) and *Poems by Percy Bysshe Shelley* (Bell, 1902) are among the best books of the era.[13] The 1900s were a great period for books on architecture in Britain, and many of them have claims to regard as art nouveau in their own right: M. H. Baillie Scott's *Houses and Gardens* (Newnes, 1906) shows him to have been, apart from the purely architectural merits of his designs, a most charming and accomplished art nouveau illustrator, and the architectural drawings of E. H. New, Ernest Godman, Walter H. Godfrey (all of whom worked closely with Ashbee at the Essex House Press), Inigo Thomas and others have a convention for rendering the essentials of their subjects as part of a spare decorative pattern which is intangibly but unmistakably art nouveau. A single, eccentric venture into the book beautiful, Gordon Bottomley's *The Gate of Smaragdus* (Unicorn Press/Elkin Mathews, 1904) deserves a glance;

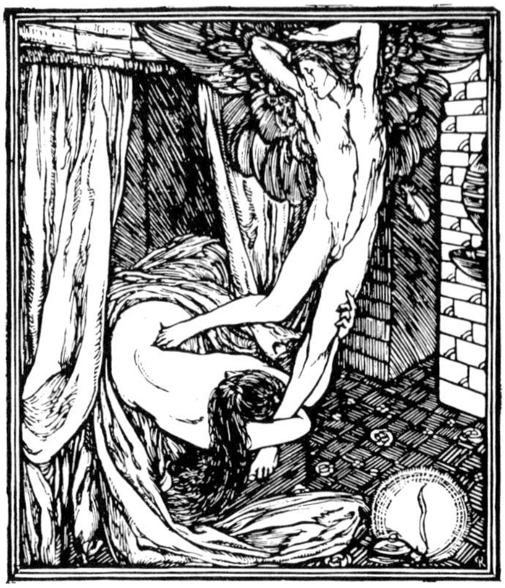

Charles Ricketts:
De Cupidinis et Psyches Amoribus
(Vale Press, 1901)

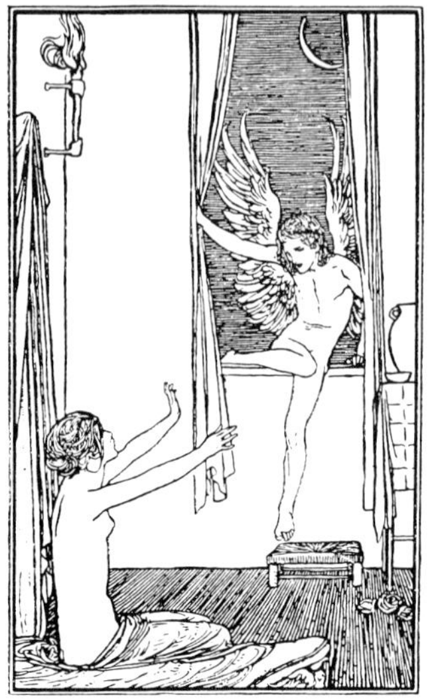

R. Anning Bell:
'A bright torch,
and a casement
ope at night,
To let the warm
love in', from
Poems by John Keats
(Bell, 1897) –
and interesting contrast
with the very similar,
apparently later
design by Ricketts

Robert Anning Bell: *Poems by Percy Bysshe Shelley* (1902) black and red $8\frac{1}{2} \times 5\frac{3}{8}$ in.

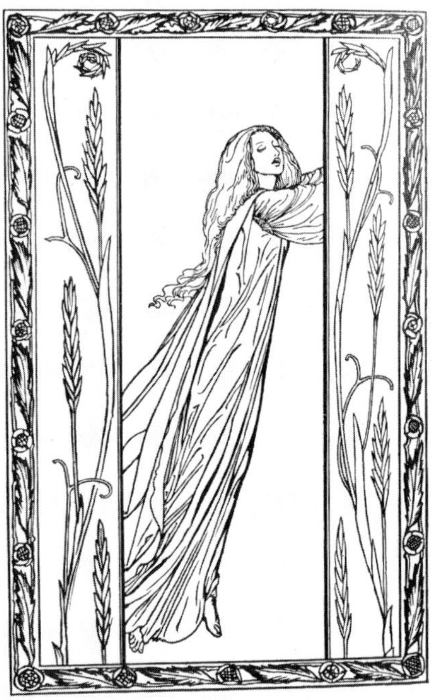

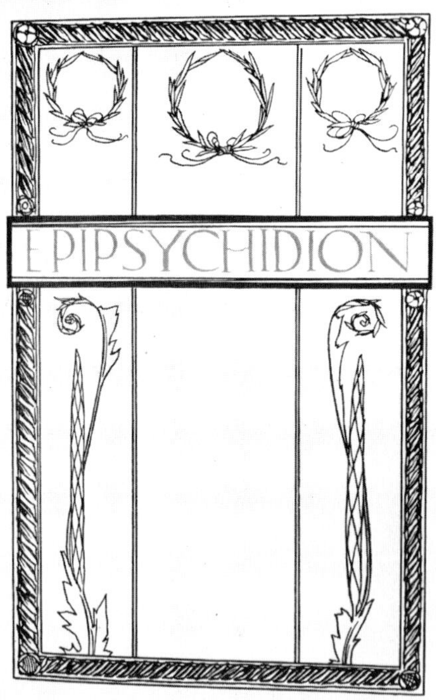

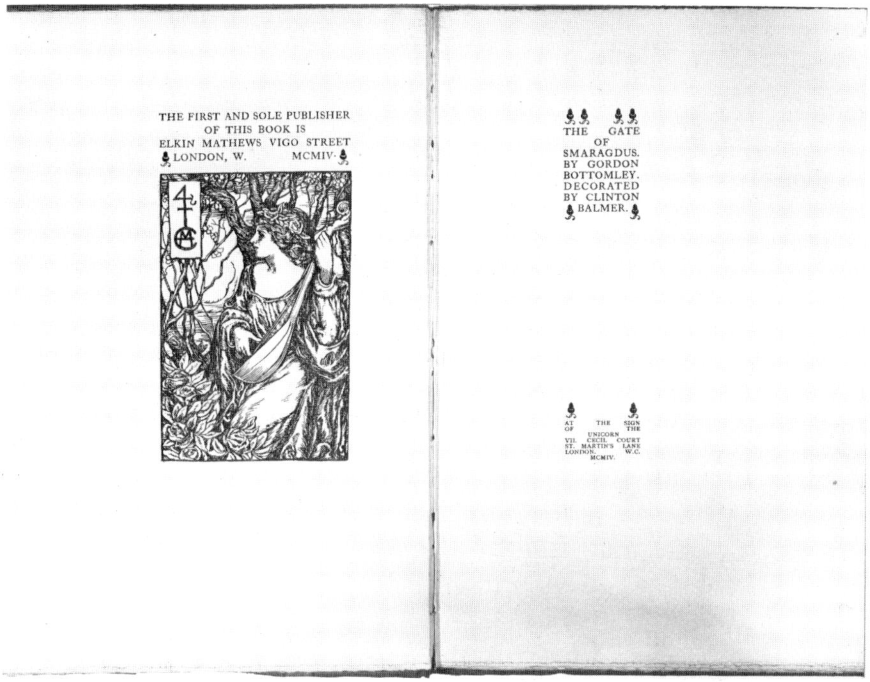
THE FIRST AND SOLE PUBLISHER
OF THIS BOOK IS
ELKIN MATHEWS VIGO STREET
LONDON, W. MCMIV.

THE GATE
OF
SMARAGDUS.
BY GORDON
BOTTOMLEY.
DECORATED
BY CLINTON
BALMER.

AT THE SIGN
OF THE
UNICORN
VII. CECIL COURT
ST. MARTIN'S LANE
LONDON. W.C.
MCMIV.

Gordon Bottomley: *The Gate of Smaragdus* (1904) $11\frac{1}{4} \times 7\frac{3}{8}$ in.

it was entirely designed by its author, a friend of Shannon and Ricketts, the text of the poems being in capitals throughout, after the manner of *The Sphinx*, illustrated by Clinton Balmer in a sub-Shannon style, and printed for Bottomley under his close supervision by local printers at Ulverston. Mention should perhaps also be made of S. H. Sime (1867 - 1941), a magazine illustrator of the Nineties with a sinister brand of humour who blossomed in the 1900s into a real if belated decadent with some very curious designs indeed, among the best the series for Lord Dunsany's *The Gods of Pegana* (Elkin Mathews, 1905) and several later books by the same author. There are, however, two other highly idiosyncratic figures on the English who really demand attention here, Edward Gordon Craig (b. 1872) and Claud Lovat Fraser (1890 - 1921). Craig is a protean figure who only occasionally touches on book-production, but he had strong and personal notions on the subject, and succeeded in stamping his own style and personality on all the magazines and most of the books with which he was

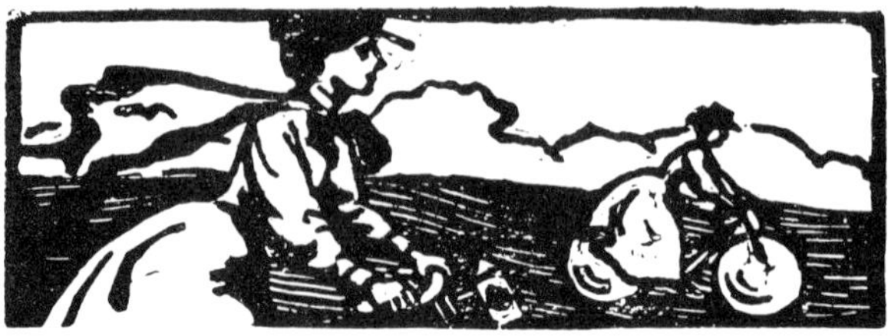

Louise Glazier:
Tailpiece from
A Book of Thirty Woodcuts
(Unicorn Press, 1903)

associated. He was obsessed with the idea of the book, its illustration, its page-layout, its paper, its binding, even its bookplate[14] as an 'architectural' composition, and experimented tirelessly with various formulas, some relatively restrained, some wildly outré, for dealing with the problems this posed. His first real appearance as a theorist and practical designer is in *The Page* (1898-1900), an illustrated magazine he edited, designed and wrote for, which ran to four numbers; it was deliberately crude and colourful, showing that Craig, like Lovat Fraser after him, had learnt from the penny-plain, tuppence-coloured broadside and the jolly, archaistic chapbooks published by Andrew Tuer some twenty-five years earlier. For the refined preciosity of much book-production in the Nineties it substituted a wilful crudeness and irregularity – which, were, of course, in their own way, equally precious. ❧ Craig's next magazine, *The Mask*, was longer-lived, the first number appearing in 1908 and the last as late as 1929. It was devoted exclusively to various aspects of the theatre, printed and published in Florence, but its circulation was mainly in Britain. The size and format varied from issue to issue, the first numbers being a large folio-size, though it later dwindled to a quarto (Craig's third magazine, *The Marionette*, 1918-19, was, in keeping with its title, minute, a tiny foolscap octavo). In *The Mask*, and in those of his books of the period over which he had any design control, particularly *On the Art of the Theatre* (Heinemann, 1911), he indulged to his heart's content his weakness for rich and quaint, and anyway obstrusive, effects – as well as occasionally his gift, acquired seemingly from Whistler, for simple, elegant and practical bindings. None of his books or magazines could be described as quiet; they are all

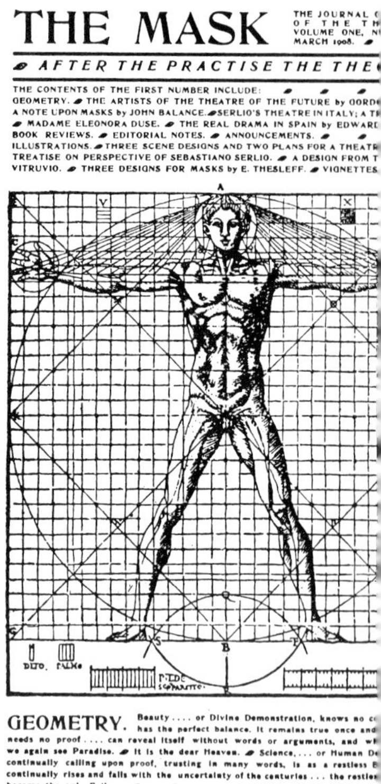
THE MASK
THE JOURNAL
OF THE
VOLUME ONE,
MARCH 1908.
AFTER THE PRACTISE THE
THE CONTENTS OF THE FIRST NUMBER INCLUDE:
GEOMETRY. THE ARTISTS OF THE THEATRE OF THE FUTURE by
A NOTE UPON MASKS by JOHN BALANCE. SERLIO'S THEATRE IN ITALY; A
MADAME ELEONORA DUSE. THE REAL DRAMA IN SPAIN by
BOOK REVIEWS. EDITORIAL NOTES. ANNOUNCEMENTS.
ILLUSTRATIONS. THREE SCENE DESIGNS AND TWO PLANS FOR A
TREATISE ON PERSPECTIVE OF SEBASTIANO SERLIO. A DESIGN FROM
VITRUVIO. THREE DESIGNS FOR MASKS by E. THESLEFF. VIGNETTES

GEOMETRY. Beauty .... or Divine Demonstration, knows no
has the perfect balance. It remains true once and
needs no proof .... can reveal itself without words or arguments, and
we again see Paradise. It is the dear Heaven. Science, ... or Human
continually calling upon proof, trusting in many words, is as a restless
continually rises and falls with the uncertainty of the centuries ...
become the only Evil.

Edward Gordon Craig:
First page of *The Mask*,
No. 1 (1908) 13 × 9 in.

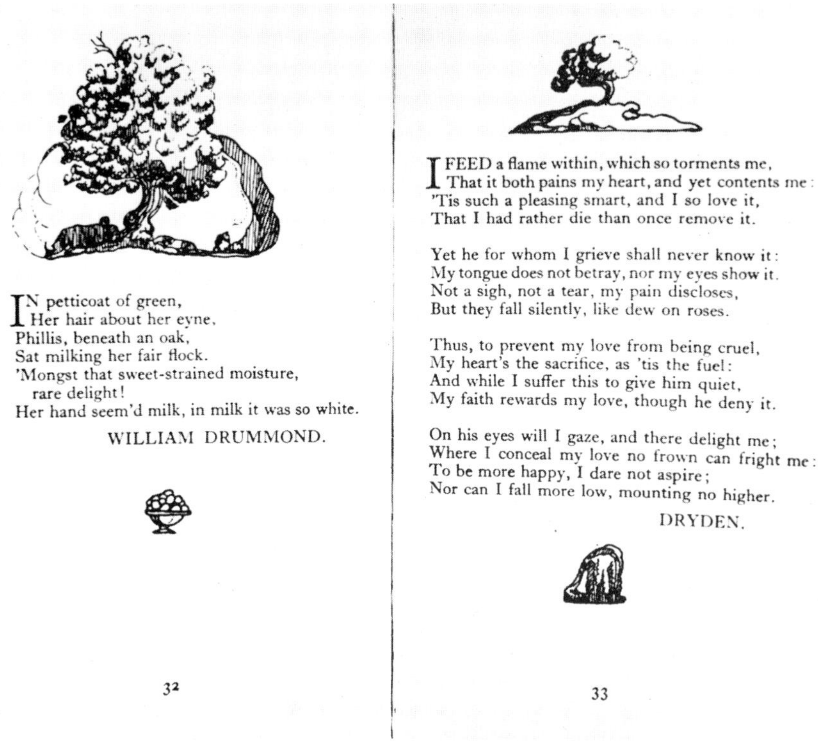

IN petticoat of green,
Her hair about her eyne,
Phillis, beneath an oak,
Sat milking her fair flock.
'Mongst that sweet-strained moisture,
rare delight!
Her hand seem'd milk, in milk it was so white.

WILLIAM DRUMMOND.

32

I FEED a flame within, which so torments me,
That it both pains my heart, and yet contents me:
'Tis such a pleasing smart, and I so love it,
That I had rather die than once remove it.

Yet he for whom I grieve shall never know it:
My tongue does not betray, nor my eyes show it.
Not a sigh, not a tear, my pain discloses,
But they fall silently, like dew on roses.

Thus, to prevent my love from being cruel,
My heart's the sacrifice, as 'tis the fuel:
And while I suffer this to give him quiet,
My faith rewards my love, though he deny it.

On his eyes will I gaze, and there delight me;
Where I conceal my love no frown can fright me:
To be more happy, I dare not aspire;
Nor can I fall more low, mounting no higher.

DRYDEN.

33

Claud Lovat Fraser: *The Lute of Love* (Selwyn and Blount, 1920) 6½ x 4 in.

highly wrought (even the magazines generally appeared in sumptuous limited de luxe editions as well as their more normal form) and elaborately patterned. Sometimes, indeed, excessively so: Craig approved of nice wide margins, but at this stage of his career abhorred white relief in the body of the text to such an extent that he liked to signal each paragraph with a small device instead of indenting and fill up the empty space at the ends of paragraphs with further devices and decorations. His designs were at the outset deliberately experimental, and caused some alarm among critics of the time,[15] but with the return of a taste for 'old-world' quaintness – one which both Lovat Fraser and Arthur Rackham, in their different ways, helped to satisfy – in the 1900s they became acceptable, and almost at length traditional. Especially since once Craig had created his style he stuck to it: *Index to the Story of My Days* (Hulton, 1957), designed by Edward Burrett under the author's supervision, must surely by any reckoning be the last direct issue of the Nineties book. Claud Lovat Fraser was also, far more deliberately, an exponent of quaintness. Where

Craig's eccentricities and irregularities were originally meant to shock, Lovat Fraser's were always meant to charm. He has been seen as an anti-art nouveau designer, and it has been said that 'Nothing . . . could be more marked than the difference between his books and those of such conscious beautifiers as William Morris, Walter Crane, Charles Ricketts and Lucien Pissarro. The essence of the Lovat Fraser books is that their design is absence of design, their charm integral rather than applied.'[16] In a sense this is true, but it is the habit of what at the time appear to be opposite aesthetic extremes to meet in retrospect, and what now strikes us about Lovat Fraser's 'Flying Fame' chapbooks and broadsides (1913 on) and Poetry Bookshop anthologies is the pronouncedly Ninetyish feel they have to them. True, it is the Nineties of the Beggarstaff Brothers (William Nicholson and James Pryde) and their posters, of the early woodcuts of Gordon Craig, but these too, in their frank acceptance of graphic design as essentially pattern in two dimensions, their taste for expressive irregularity over classical balance and formality, are part of the same movement of taste as art nouveau proper. Lovat Fraser is inescapably, almost by choice, a minor artist, a stylish prettifier; but through his books and his stage designs (especially those for Nigel Playfair's famous long-running revival of *The Beggar's Opera* in 1920) he has bequeathed us a view of the eighteenth century which still persists, despite some equally fanciful and picturesque attempts at relousing, and a style which is somehow none the less charming for all its evident determination to charm.

Epilogue

By the end of the 1914-18 war, the letter of art nouveau seemed to be dead, but its spirit lingered unaccountably on. At one level, the most obvious, there remained the work of fashionable illustrators in the art nouveau tradition or at least making prominent use of certain art nouveau conventions and tricks of style. Rackham and Dulac were at the height of their popularity between the wars, representing by this time the conservative, safe, approachable element in book-illustration – nothing advanced or incomprehensible about them. The final accolade of popular approval was granted to Rackham in the 1930s when Walt Disney explicitly acknowledged the close study he had made of Rackham's work before embarking on his first coloured 'Silly Symphonies' – a debt anyway easily recognizable in the background details of architecture and tree-forms – and tried to persuade Rackham to come and work on the designs of *Snow White and the Seven Dwarfs* (1937) for him in Hollywood, though Rackham declined on the grounds of age and ill health.[1]

Other illustrators of the time acknowledged in their work and in statements about it a debt to the Nineties. The mysterious cosmopolitan Alastair (Hans Henning Voight), of whom little seems to have been known, or at any rate little told, even by those who wrote most enthusiastically of his work,[2] continued throughout the 1920s to evolve a strange,

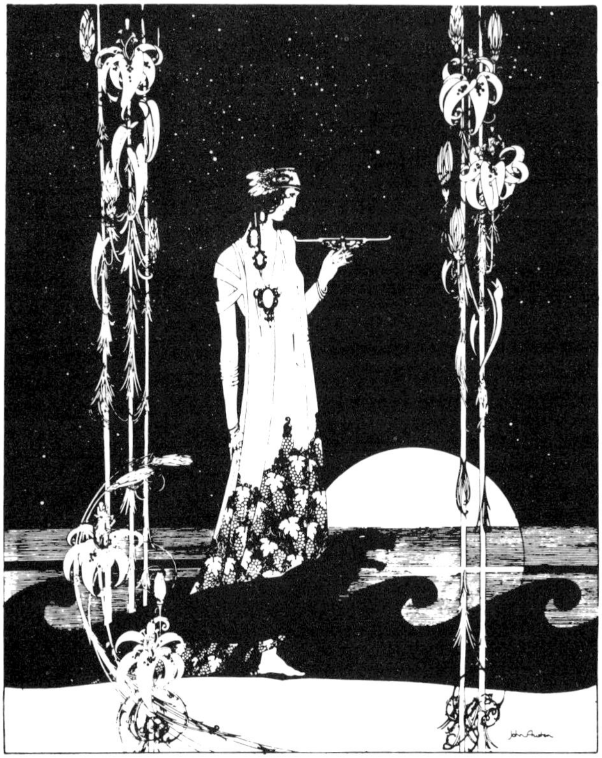

John Austen: 'Circe'
(*The Golden Hind*, 1923)

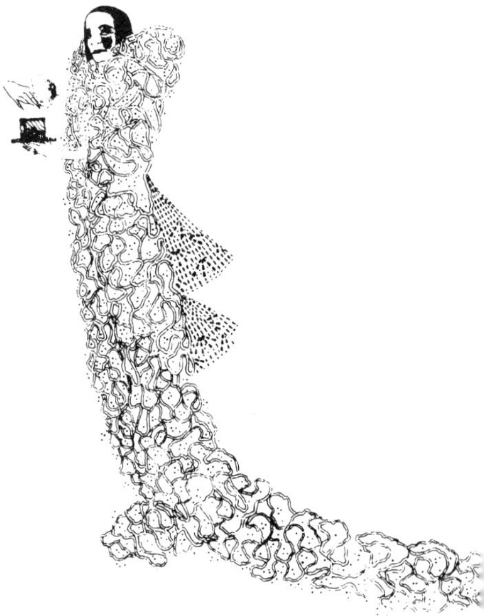

Alastair:
Erdgeist (*c* 1925)

perverse and, even taking into account its unmistakable debt to Beardsley, highly personal style of decoration which exudes from the pages of his later great series – *Salomé* (Paris: C. Crès, 1922), Wedekind's *Erdgeist* (Munich: Georg Müller, c. 1925), *Manon Lescaut* (John Lane, 1928) – the same powerful perfume of Nineties decadence as his extravagant earlier designs for *The Sphinx* (John Lane, 1920). A similar selection of influences produce far less agreeable (indeed, thoroughly disagreeable) results in the flashily ornate illustrated books of Willy Poganyi, another middle-European best known for his English-published work. John Austen (b. 1886) was in his early days an avowed disciple of Beardsley with a suitably art nouveau regard for 'human beings only as motives and material for decorative designs'.[3] Harry Clarke (1890-1931), particularly in his uniquely nasty illustrations for Poe's *Tales of Mystery and Imagination* (Harrap, 1919) is clearly subject more directly to the same influences. Mabel Lucie Attwell (1879-1964) continued well into the 1950s to decorate her faintly

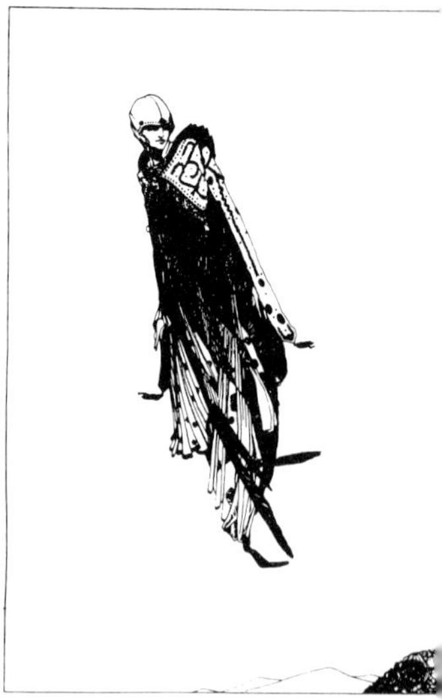

Harry Clarke: 'Out on the Wind of Time, Shining and Streaming', from *The Year's at the Spring* (Harrap, 1920)

W. A. Dwiggins: Cover (black and dark green on green paper) for *The Architect and the Industrial Arts* (1929) $8\frac{1}{2} \times 5\frac{1}{2}$ in.

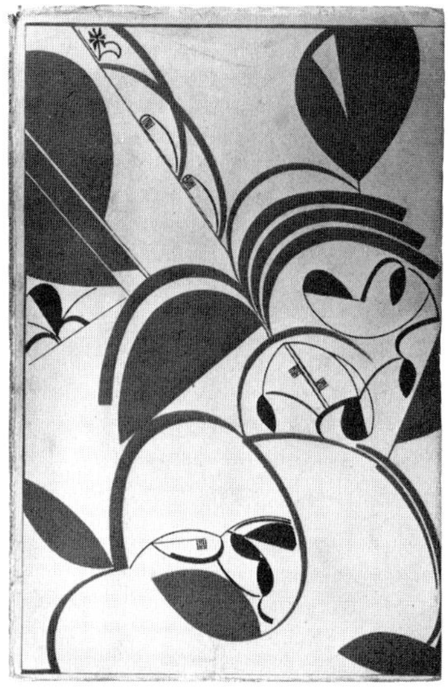

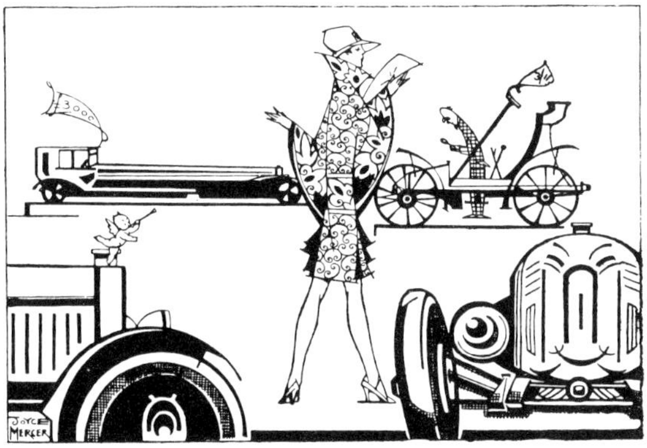

Joyce Mercer: 'You Will Not find Vanity Buying a Flash Car!', from *Vanity in Mayfair* (1929)

obscene world of childhood fantasy with art nouveau curves and caption her pictures in splodgy art nouveau lettering through scores of books, postcards and figured knick-knacks. And if one looks at W. A. Dwiggins's cover design and decorative devices for the catalogue of the New York Museum of Modern Art exhibition *The Architect and the Industrial Arts* (1929), or at Joyce Mercer's defiantly with-it illustrations for Oscar M. Sheridan's *Vanity in Mayfair* (Cecil Palmer, 1929) or the Collins Illustrated Pocket Classics edition of *Pinocchio* (1939), the close connection already remarked on between art nouveau and the short-lived 'jazz-modern' style of the late 1920s becomes unmistakable. But most important, beneath these superficial relations of largely unimportant artists with the decorative styles of the past, the whole approach to the art of the book which the art nouveau movement played such an important part in establishing lived on. Though in their types and overall designs the publications of the Nonesuch Press (founded 1923) are for the most part thoroughly classical, and Sir

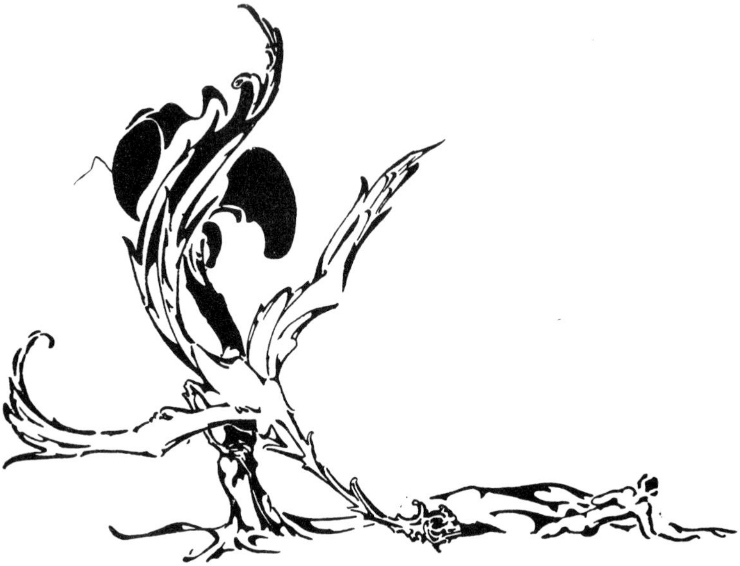

Peter Quennell:
Design for his own
Masques and Poems
(Golden Cockerel Press, 1922)

Francis Meynell would no doubt be very surprised to see himself classified as an art nouveau book designer, it is inconceivable that his books could be anything like what they are without, say, the example of Ricketts's Vale Press books in the relation of illustrations to text, and in his use of brightly patterned papers in the binding of quality books; or without Laurence Housman's experimentation with unusual formats – for though the formats of None-such Press books are seldom outré, they are certainly extraordinarily varied. ❧ With Eric Gill (1882-1940) the debt is even more pronounced: not only was he in his personal life and attitudes a thorough-going Morrisian Arts and Crafts man and social reformer, but in his book design and illustrations he shows every sign of having studied with the greatest care and attention the work of his predecessors in the 1890s, particularly, it seems to me, that of Ricketts.[4] Not only does his graphic style often bear clear marks of the influence of Ricketts – so much so, in fact, that some of Ricketts's later designs, like the bookplate for John Morgan, strike us at once, by a reversal of the proper time-sense, as Eric-Gillish – but as a book designer he shares several of Ricketts's foibles. Like Ricketts, he dislikes the traditional title-page and eliminates it wherever possible: the arrangement adopted in *Quia Amore*

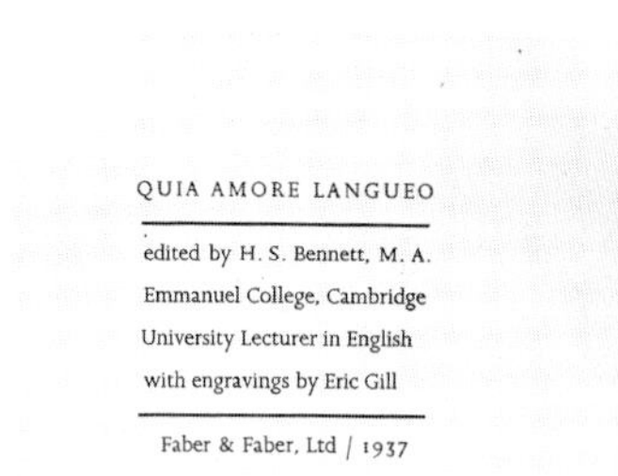
QUIA AMORE LANGUEO

edited by H. S. Bennett, M. A.
Emmanuel College, Cambridge
University Lecturer in English
with engravings by Eric Gill

Faber & Faber, Ltd / 1937

Eric Gill: Title-page for
Quia Amore Langueo
(1937) $5\frac{3}{4} \times 4\frac{3}{8}$ in.

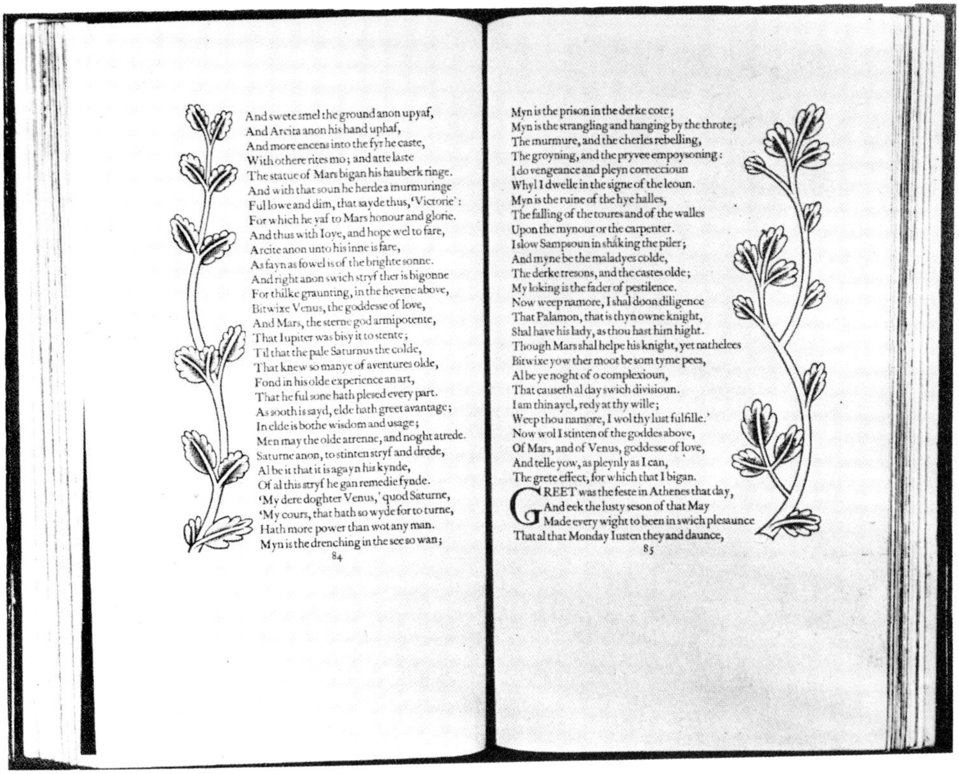

And swete smel the ground anon upyaf,
And Arcita anon his hand uphaf,
And more encens into the fyr he caste,
With othere rites mo; and atte laste
The statue of Mars bigan his hauberk ringe.
And with that soun he herde a murmuringe
Ful lowe and dim, that sayde thus, 'Victorie':
For which he yaf to Mars honour and glorie.
And thus with Ioye, and hope wel to fare,
Arcite anon unto his inne is fare,
As fayn as fowel is of the brighte sonne.
And right anon swich stryf ther is bigonne
For thilke graunting, in the hevene above,
Bitwixe Venus, the goddesse of love,
And Mars, the sterne god armipotente,
That Iupiter was bisy it to stente;
Til that the pale Saturnus the colde,
That knew so manye of aventures olde,
Fond in his olde experience an art,
That he ful sone hath plesed every part.
As sooth is sayd, elde hath greet avantage;
In elde is bothe wisdom and usage;
Men may the olde atrenne, and noght atrede.
Saturne anon, to stinten stryf and drede,
Al be it that it is agayn his kynde,
Of al this stryf he gan remedie fynde.
'My dere doghter Venus,' quod Saturne,
'My cours, that hath so wyde for to turne,
Hath more power than wot any man.
Myn is the drenching in the see so wan;

84

Myn is the prison in the derke cote;
Myn is the strangling and hanging by the throte;
The murmure, and the cherles rebelling,
The groyning, and the pryvee empoysoning:
I do vengeance and pleyn correccioun
Whyl I dwelle in the signe of the leoun.
Myn is the ruine of the hye halles,
The falling of the toures and of the walles
Upon the mynour or the carpenter.
I slow Sampsoun in shaking the piler;
And myne be the maladyes colde,
The derke tresons, and the castes olde;
My loking is the fader of pestilence.
Now weep namore, I shal doon diligence
That Palamon, that is thyn owne knight,
Shal have his lady, as thou hast him hight.
Though Mars shal helpe his knight, yet natheless
Bitwixe yow ther moot be som tyme pees,
Al be ye noght of o complexioun,
That causeth al day swich divisioun.
I am thin ayel, redy at thy wille;
Weep thou namore, I wol thy lust fulfille.'
Now wol I stinten of the goddes above,
Of Mars, and of Venus, goddesse of love,
And telle yow, as pleynly as I can,
The grete effect, for which that I bigan.
GREET was the feste in Athenes that day,
And eek the lusty seson of that May
Made every wight to been in swich plesaunce
That al that Monday Iusten they and daunce,

85

Eric Gill:
The Canterbury Tales
(Golden Cockerel Press, 1929)
$12\frac{1}{2} \times 7\frac{1}{2}$ in.

Langueo (Faber, 1937), for instance, closely follows the half-title/title-page form devised by Ricketts for a number of Vale Press books. Moreover, many of his most characteristic layouts, especially when the illustrations are conceived as an integral part of the page, as in the Golden Cockerel *Troilus and Criseyde* (1927) and *Canterbury Tales* (1929), have a distinct air of the Vale Press about them – thinned, modernised, streamlined (if one may use a word which Gill the anti-industrialist would have abhorred), but still evidently of the same family. Other characteristics of Gill's book design could be adduced – his approval of the 'natural' irregularity implied by leaving the right-hand edge of the type-body on each page unregistered; his distaste for intrusive white, which he satisfied in some of his books by running on the paragraphs and merely separating them by a small decorative paragraph device. But much of this is no more than to say that he was a child of his time, naturally formed by the aesthetic background of

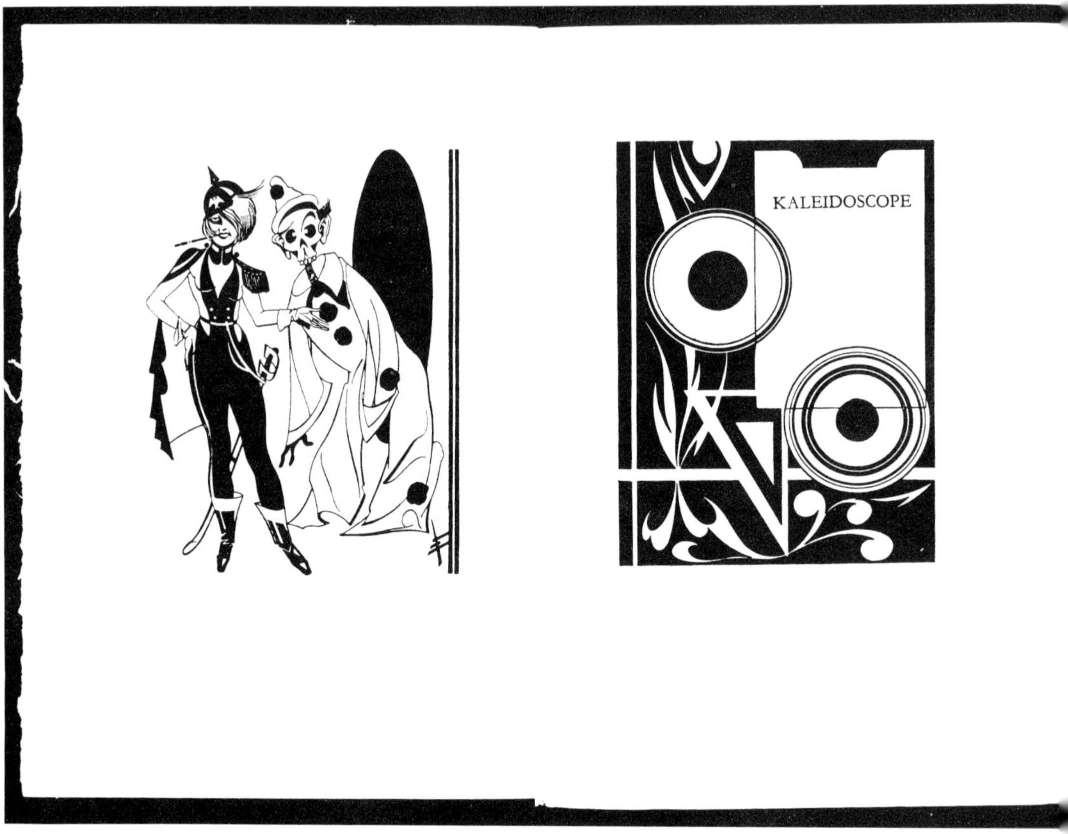

his youth and early manhood. So, indeed, one could say of all the great designers and typographers of the 1920s and 1930s: their roots are in art nouveau, while their branches reach out to embrace the whole of modern book design. If they could not have been without art nouveau, no more could the whole face of the book as we know it today.

Beresford Egan:
Opening of his own
But the Sinners Triumph
(Fortune Press, 1934) $7\frac{1}{2} \times 5$ in.

A Note on Types

It is perhaps curious that though Britain played such an important role in the revival of printing during the 1890s, British designers did little or nothing to evolve a species of types specifically suited to art nouveau illustration and layout. Maybe they shared the feeling expressed later by Eric Gill in his *Essay on Typography*, when he says 'Lettering is for us the Roman alphabet and the Roman alphabet is lettering'[1]; certainly except for Morris, who favoured gothic type (Chaucer and Troye) or at least roman given a strong gothic colouring (Golden), and Ashbee, who gave his Endeavour a similar gothic twist, all the great type designers of the era stuck firmly to roman, generally using an old-face convention as their starting point, and with only Ricketts's exotic half-uncial King's showing any real desire to experiment in another direction. The same is true of most of the Continental designers who followed in Britain's wake – Van de Velde (1865-1957), for example, who was first inspired in his book work by the example of Morris for the typography and of Cobden-Sanderson for the bindings, and doubted the possibility of a typographical renaissance similar to the British in France and the Low Countries, though later, in 1900-08, he designed and illustrated the great Cranach Press *Zarathustra* using a new type designed by G. Lemmen after the style of Lucien Pissarro. There was, indeed, little of significance anywhere in the world in the way of attempts to produce a workable art nouveau book type, though a number of German designers, raised in that country's dual tradition of gothic and roman book-types, tried their hand at it.[2] In Britain, as abroad, art nouveau lettering was mainly confined to decorative headings, title-pages and lettering on illustrative designs. None of the Continental art-nouveau display types seems to have been commonly used in Britain, if indeed most of them were used at all: when something of the kind was required, it was generally designed specially by the artist responsible for the design as a whole in order to fulfil the requirements of its particular situation, drawn freely with pen or brush, and reproduced by photo-engraving or some such process. Thus we have some excellent examples of the lettering of Beardsley, Ricketts (the only type-designer among them), Mackintosh and Jessie M. King. Possibly there is cause for regret that none of them attempted to design a formal art nouveau type-face, but I do not think so: the very idea seems somehow anomalous in a movement which sought above all to find form inherent in the formless rather than to impose on it a preconceived form from without.

in it the gathered crumbs of happiness of the con-fused and turbulent past." ¶ She led me up close to the house, and laid her shapely sun-browned hand and arm on the lichened wall as if to embrace it, and cried out: "O me! O me! How I love the earth, and the seasons, and weather, and all things that deal with it, & all that grows out of it, as this has done!" ¶ I could not answer her, or say a word.

William Morris: Golden

not see how these can be better spent than in making life cheerful & honourable for others and for ourselves; and the gain of good life to the country at large that would result from men seriously setting about the bettering of the decency of our big towns would be priceless, even if nothing specially good befell the arts in consequence: I do not know that it would; but I should begin to think

William Morris: Chaucer

I any the more: though it would indeed be hard if there were nothing else in the world, no wonders, no terrors, no unspeakable beauties. Yet when we think what a small part of the world's history, past, present, & to come, is this land we live in, and how much smaller still in the history

William Morris: Troye

nondum vetustatis injuria victas; et Protogenis rudimenta, cum ipsius naturæ veritate certantia, non sine quodam horrore tractavi. Jam vero Apellis, quam Græci monochromon appellant, etiam adoravi. Tanta enim subtilitate extremitates imaginum erant ad similitudinem præcisæ, ut crederes etiam animorum esse picturam. Hinc aquila ferebat, cœlo sublimis, deum. Illinc can-

Charles Ricketts: Vale

mihi non respondit: nec medici se inveniunt; profuit mihi tamen malicorium, et tæda ex aceto. Spero tamen jam ventrem pudorem sibi imponere; alioquin circa stomachum mihi sonat, putes taurum. Itaque, si quis vestrum voluerit suæ rei causa facere, non est quod illum pudeatur. Nemo nostrum solide natus est. Ego nullum puto tam magnum tormentum esse, quam continere. Hoc solum vetare ne Jovis potest. Rides, Fortunata! quæ soles me nocte desomnem facere. Nec tamen in triclinio ullum vetui facere

Charles Ricketts: Avon

Charles Ricketts: Kings

artes periissent, inter quas pictura ne minimum quidem sui vestigium reliquisset. Tum ille: Pecuniæ, inquit, cupiditas hæc tropica instituit. Verum, ut ad plastas convertar, Lysippum, statuæ unius lineamentis inhærentem, inopia exstinxit: et Myron, qui pæne hominum animas ferarumque ære comprehendit, non invenit heredem. At nos, vino

Lucien Pissarro: Brook

A BRIEF ACCOUNT OF THE ORIGIN OF THE ERAGNY PRESS.

MR. PISSARRO first learned to draw from his father, in the fields far from any art school. One day M. Lepère, the well-known engraver, showed him how his tools were held, & finding him interested, gave him two gravers and a scorper. Thus furnished with the means

C. R. Ashbee: Endeavour

Here, however, it is necessary perhaps to define a principle, or at least to offer a warning. Anything in the nature of what might be called the factory system as applied to industrial Art is harmful, & by the factory system I take as implied the method of organization, by which large bodies of men work under mechanical conditions with subdivision of labour. To extend this system to

Emery Walker and T. J. Cobden-Sanderson: Doves

the same time, is a more direct presentment of the same positive solution.

¶ These Books printed, as a first essay, the whole field of literature remains open to select from. To-day there is an immense reproduction in an admirable cheap form, of all Books which in any language have stood the test of time. But such reproduction is not a substitute for the more monumental production of

Notes

The Beginnings

1 *Life*, p. 362
2 *Life*, p. 364
3 *Life*, p. 363
4 See William Michael Rossetti's diaries, quoted Helen Rossetti Angeli, *Dante Gabriel Rossetti*, p. 246
5 *Ideas of Good and Evil*, p. 229
6 *Memorials* ii, 271
7 *Memorials* ii, 271
8 The essay is reprinted in his *Essays on Art*
9 *Essays on Art*, p. 195
10 e.g., Henry Wilson's piece in the *Architectural Review*, 1898, Volume 1, pp. 177-80, describing Burne-Jones's style, and particularly the type of beauty he favoured for his figures, as 'Celtic'
11 'Graphic Art' in Peter Selz and Mildred Constantine (editors): *Art Nouveau*, p. 28

The Victorian Book

1 p. 172
2 *The Quarto*, No. 1, pp. 33-7; *The Savoy* No. 1, pp. 112-24. In point of fact, Sandys first crops up in a relevant context as early as 1888, when the Century Guild *Hobby Horse*, Vol. III, published an illustrated article by J. M. Gray, 'Frederick Sandys and the Woodcut Designers of Thirty Years Ago'
3 *The Pageant*, pp. 253-67

4 p. 19

5 in *Toilers in Art*, edited by Henry C. Ewart, pp. 209-20. This curious volume seems to have been generally ignored, perhaps because it is clearly intended for the young and for self-educators. In addition to Swain's essay on Pinwell it includes Swain on Frederick Walker, Charles Henry Bennett and Frederick Eltze, and a short autobiography by Frederick Shields

6 In his *English Printed Books*, p. 30, Sir Francis Meynell oddly remarks that Lovat Fraser was apparently not aware of these forerunners, but Haldane Macfall in *The Book of Lovat* gives details of Lovat Fraser's knowledge of and enthusiasm for their work, and Holbrook Jackson in *The Printing of Books*, (essay dated 1923) p. 200 adds Charles Hindley's *Life and Times of James Catnach* (1878) and *The History of the Catnach Press* (1887) to the list of influences

7 *Life of James McNeill Whistler*, Revised edition, 1911, p. 291

8 *Fleuron VII*, p. 87

9 *The Artists of the 1890s*, p. 183

Arts and Crafts and Art Nouveau

1 *William Morris to Whistler*, p. 232

2 Sturge Moore: Introduction to *Charles Ricketts, R.A.*, p. 10

3 p. 105

4 No. I, pp. 13-17

5 pp. 156-8

6 *Decorative Illustration*, p. 162

7 v., e.g., Robert Schmutzler, *Art Nouveau*, p. 112

8 an artist, incidentally, whom Crane much admired, v. *Decorative Illustration*, pp. 154-5

Art Nouveau in the Nineties – (i) Charles Ricketts

1 Of the thirty-seven pictures in the book, fifteen were originally drawn by Shannon (plus, presumably, the version of 'The Vintage of Mitylene' included

in the prospectus but dropped from the finished volume), but they were all revised and redrawn on the wood by Ricketts to attain a unity of effect. Both Shannon and Ricketts worked on the actual cutting of the blocks

2 *The Fleuron VII*, p. 102

3 by Sir John Rothenstein, *The Artists of the 1890s*, p. 182

4 1886, pp. 159-60. On Blake's broadsheet *Little Tom the Sailor*, which was reproduced, Gilchrist (son of Alexander Gilchrist whose life of Blake Rossetti helped to complete) wrote 'What a marvellous sample of typewriting is the Ballad written out with a brush . . . While as legible as ordinary types, every letter has naive expression, capital letters flaunt capriciously down the page, each giving a defiant little kick of its own. With all the charm of decorative fitness the print answers directly its purpose as a broadsheet'

5 *Defence of the Revival of Printing*, p. 19

6 exemplified in his 'Note on Original Wood Engraving' (*The Pageant* 1897, pp. 253-66)

7 see his volume on *Albrecht Altdorfer* in the 'Little Engravings' series, and particularly his remarks on Ricketts in the introduction, p. 3

8 Rossetti, for instance, mistakenly believed that the designs in Ricketts's favourite Italian Renaissance book, the *Hypnerotomachia Poliphili*, were the work of Botticelli (Dunn, *Recollections of Dante Gabriel Rossetti*, p. 23)

9 The full-page designs for this volume, printed in very pale pinkish ink and almost indecipherable, are by Shannon; the cover, vignettes in the text and overall design by Ricketts

10 *Defence of the Revival of Printing*, p. 18

11 Ibid, pp. 20-1

12 *English Printed Books*, p. 33

13 Holbrook Jackson, *The Eighteen Nineties*, p. 267

14 *Defence of the Revival of Printing*, p. 30

15 Ibid, p. 31

16 quoted *The Eighteen Nineties*, p. 267

17 *The Eighteen Nineties*, p. 268

18 see his 1934 lecture 'The Typography of William Morris', *The Printing of Books*, pp. 175-85

19 instanced also by Schmutzler, *Art Nouveau*, p. 86

20 v. *Self-Portrait*, pp. 105-6

21 *Self-Portrait*, pp. 227-8

22 *Self-Portrait*, p. 111

23 p. 15

24 *Arts and Crafts Essays*, p. 132

Art Nouveau in the Nineties (ii) Aubrey Beardsley

1 Vincent O'Sullivan, who knew Smithers well, says of Smithers's Beardsley books (*Aspects of Wilde*, p. 116) 'the presentation of these books and of all his books was for the most part due to Smithers himself. Though he was surrounded by artists he did not seek their advice in such matters, or if he did, forgot it or found some excuse to follow his own way. The little edition of *The Rape of the Lock* . . . was, I am sure, an idea of Smithers himself without any primary suggestion from Beardsley, who seemed to be satisfied to rest on the other edition – the large edition. *The Savoy* also, very original as to presentation, he was mostly responsible for himself . . .

2 P. H. Muir in his essay 'Elkin Mathews in the "Nineties"' (*The Book Collector*, Spring 1952), notes that 'though there is no minimising of Beardsley's share in the physiognomy' of the Lane/Matthews books, the principal responsibility at this point for the layout of most not designed by Ricketts rests with Walter Blaikie, of the Edinburgh printers T. and A. Constable

3 see Aymer Vallance's 'Iconography' in Robert Ross's *Aubrey Beardsley*, for a comprehensive list

4 *Decorative Illustration*, p. 221

5 Ross, *Aubrey Beardsley*, p. 44, states that in fact Beardsley was designing in a 'Japanese' manner,

mainly as a result of his intensive studies of the Crivellis in the National Gallery, some time before a friend told him that his drawings resembled Kakemonos

6 At around this time we also find him, unexpectedly, asking Robert Ross urgently in an undated note for the loan of his set of Calvert's engravings (*Robert Ross, Friend of Friends*, p. 38)

7 Sir John Rothenstein, *The Artists of the 1890s*, p. 182

8 Ross: *Aubrey Beardsley*, p. 95

9 the original edition was, naturally, privately printed and strictly limited; the complete series is however reproduced in *Aubrey Beardsley: Drawings*, Berlin: Gerhardt Verlag, 1965

10 *Aubrey Beardsley*, p. 47

11 *The Eighteen Nineties*, p. 102

12 *The Artists of the 1890s*, p. 173

Art Nouveau in the Nineties –
(iii) Laurence Housman and some others

1 pp. 107-19

2 *The Venture*, for example, an annual he edited with Somerset Maugham, contained in its first number (1903) illustrations by Shannon, Ricketts, Sturge Moore, Reginald Savage and Lucien Pissarro, among others

3 *The Unexpected Years*, p. 159. After *Prunella* (Bullen, 1906) Housman did very little illustration; there are a few minor examples in a broader later style, such as those in his book of poems *The New Child's Guide to Knowledge* (Sidgwick and Jackson, 1912), and the tiny set-designs which punctuate his *Little Plays of St Francis* (Sidgwick and Jackson, 1921), *Followers of St Francis* (Sidgwick and Jackson, 1923), etc.

4 undated letter, c. 1954, to the author

5 v. *British Book Illustration Yesterday and Today*, pp. 138-9

6 v. *W. B. Yeats and T. Sturge Moore: Their Correspondence 1901-37*

7 Sturge Moore's enthusiasm for the serpentine designs of the *Songs of Innocence and Experience*, so influential on the early art nouveau of Mackmurdo and Heywood Sumner, was however somewhat tempered; in *Art and Life* (1910), p. 229, he explains disapprovingly how in Blake's paintings 'the forms of these plants growing like sea-anemones over the hills and valleys of his visionary world were suggested by the peculiar patterns the sticky oil paint raised upon the paper when the millboard was torn from it, and had nothing to do with the design as originally conceived'; and goes on to suggest that Blake's illuminated books have often been overestimated: 'A few pages reveal an instinctive sense of decorative propriety; the more part is rather curious than beautiful.'

8 'Little Engravings' *Albrecht Altdorfer*, Introduction, p. 3

9 a monograph on Campagnola, incidentally, was another of Moore's projects in 1902, v. the 'Little Engravings' *Albrecht Altdorfer*, Introduction, p. 3

10 e. g., Howarth, p. 231; Madson, p. 243; Schmutzler, p. 262

11 *English Illustration: The Nineties*, p. 195

12 There is a diverting note on Guthrie and his manner of working in *Poet and Painter*, the correspondence of Gordon Bottomley and Paul Nash, pp. 34-5

13 *Letters to Leonard Smithers*, p. 10

14 D. J. Gordon, *W. B. Yeats: Images of a Poet*, gives an interesting account of Horton and his relations with Yeats (pp. 101-3)

Art Nouveau in the 1900s

1 July 1896; eighteen months after Beardsley had been dismissed from the magazine

2 Mrs Mary Newbery Sturrock, in a letter to the author, May 1957

3 One of the books for which Jessie M. King designed and executed a decorated leather binding and a frontispiece on vellum was the edition of Zola's *Le Rêve* (Paris, 1892) with illustrations by Carlos Schwabe which in the opinion of Mrs Newbery exerted some influence on both Mackintosh and Jessie M. King

4 Volume 14, pp. 58-9

5 pp. 176-88

6 This article is the main source of information on her life and art to that date; for information about her later life and work I am indebted to letters and conversations with her daughter, Miss Merle E. Taylor, and with Mrs Newbery Sturrock, who knew her and her husband E. A. Taylor, the painter and furniture designer, well

7 information from Mr Douglas A. Foulis, in a letter to the author, September 1960

8 Volume 15, pp. 52-3

9 in conversation with the author, August 1960

10 see his book *An Endeavour towards the Teaching of J. Ruskin and W. Morris*

11 Stanley Morison (*Type Designs of the Past and Present*, p. 56) describes Endeavour sharply as the printing revival's most ignoble achievement

12 The others were T. H. Robinson and W. H. Robinson, the latter of whom later achieved a different fame as a cartoonist under the name of Heath Robinson. Both produced excellent illustrated books in the 1890s and 1900s, W. H.'s best perhaps the *Poems of Edgar Allan Poe* (Bell, 1900) and *The Works of Rabelais* (Navarre Society, 1913), T. H.'s *A Child's Book of Saints* (Dent, 1898)

13 Certain points of resemblance between Anning Bell's work and some of Ricketts's, particularly in the treatment of draped human figures, may be the result of direct influence from Ricketts on Bell, but more likely it derives from a shared devotion to the anonymous illustrations to the *Hypnerotomachia Poliphili* (Venice, 1499), described by

Ricketts in his *Defence*, p. 30, as the 'most vital of old Italian illustrated books'

14 see *Nothing, or The Bookplate*, p. 10

15 see Holbrook Jackson, *The Printing of Books*, pp. 132-3, for early reactions to *The Page*

16 Holbrook Jackson, *The Printing of Books*, p. 198

Epilogue

1 information from Mr Frank Tashlin, in conversation with the author, 1965

2 see Robert Ross, Introduction to *Forty-Three Drawings by Alastair*

3 *British Book Illustration Yesterday and Today*, p. 40

4 Gill certainly knew Ricketts's books well, and owned a number, including one of the ten vellum copies of Michael Field's *Julia Domna* (Vale Press, 1903) and two later books by Field with Ricketts cover designs, *Poems of Adoration* and *Mystic Trees*

A Note on Types

1 p. 24

2 For a useful brief outline of Continental work along these lines see Alan M. Fern, 'Graphic Design', in Peter Selz and Mildred Constantine (editors): *Art Nouveau*, especially pp. 38-45

Bibliography

This is not a comprehensive list of books on art nouveau and book design, but merely of some of the books which have been useful to me.

ABBOTT, CLAUDE ABBOTT, and BERTRAM, ANTHONY (eds): *Poet and Painter*. Being the Correspondence between Gordon Bottomley and Paul Nash, 1910-46. Oxford University Press. 1955

ANGELI, HELEN ROSSETTI: *Dante Gabriel Rossetti*. Hamish Hamilton. 1949

Arts and Crafts Essays by Members of the Arts and Crafts Exhibition Society. Rivington, Percival. 1893 (Longmans reprint, 1903)

ASHBEE, C. R.: *An Endeavour Towards the Teaching of John Ruskin and William Morris*. Essex House Press. 1901

The Private Press: A Study in Idealism. Essex House Press. 1909

BELLONZI, FORTUNATO: *Socialismo e romanticismo nell'arte moderna*. Rome: Salvatore Sciascia. 1959

BRIDGE, URSULA (ed): *W. B. Yeats and T. Sturge Moore*. Their Correspondence, 1901-37. Routledge and Kegan Paul. 1953

BURNE-JONES, GEORGINA: *Memorials of Edward Burne-Jones*. 2 vols. Macmillan. 1904

CASTLE, EGERTON: *English Book-Plates*. George Bell. 1892

CRAIG, EDWARD GORDON: *Nothing, or The Bookplate*. Chatto and Windus. 1924

Woodcuts and Some Words. Dent. 1924

CRANE, WALTER: *Of the Decorative Illustration of Books Old and New*. George Bell. 1896
William Morris to Whistler. George Bell. 1911
The Work of Walter Crane. Art Journal Easter Annual. 1898
An Artist's Reminiscences. Methuen. 1907
CROW, GERALD H.: *William Morris, Designer*. The Studio. 1934
DUNN, HENRY T.: *Recollections of Dante Gabriel Rossetti and His Circle*. Elkin Mathews. 1904
ELIZABETH MARIE, SISTER, I.H.M.: *Eric Gill, Twentieth Century Book Designer*. New York: The Scarecrow Press. 1962
EWART, HENRY C. (ed): *Toilers in Art*. Isbister. 1891
GIBSON, FRANK: *Charles Conder, His Life and Works*. John Lane. 1904
GILCHRIST, ALEXANDER: *Life of William Blake*. Macmillan. 1863, rev. 1880 (Everyman edition, ed. Ruthven Todd, Dent, 1942)
GILL, EVAN R.: *Bibliography of Eric Gill*. Cassell. 1953
GORDON, D. J., and others: *W. B. Yeats: Images of a Poet*. Manchester University Press. 1961
GRAY, BASIL: *The English Print*. A. and C. Black. 1937
GRAY, NICOLETTE: *Rossetti, Dante and Ourselves*. Faber. 1947
GWYNN, FREDERICK L.: *Sturge Moore and the Life of Art*. Richards Press. 1952
HOUSMAN, LAURENCE: *Arthur Boyd Houghton*. Kegan Paul. 1896
The Unexpected Years. Jonathan Cape. 1937
HOWARTH, THOMAS: *Charles Rennie Mackintosh and the Modern Movement*. Routledge and Kegan Paul. 1952
HUDSON, DEREK: *Arthur Rackham*. His Life and Work. Heinemann. 1960
INGPEN, ROGER: *William Thomas Horton*. A Selection of his Work, with a Biographical Sketch. Ingpen and Grant. 1927
JACKSON, HOLBROOK: *The Eighteen-Nineties*. Grant Richards. 1913 (Penguin edition, 1939)
The Printing of Books. Cassell. 1938

JAMES, PHILIP: *English Book Illustration, 1800-1900.* King Penguin. 1947
KEYNES, GEOFFREY: *William Pickering, Publisher.* The Fleuron. 1924
KONODY, P. G.: *The Art of Walter Crane.* George Bell. 1902
LEWIS, JOHN, and BRINKLEY, JOHN: *Graphic Design.* Routledge and Kegan Paul. 1954
MACFALL, HALDANE: *The Book of Lovat.* Dent. 1923
Aubrey Beardsley: The Man and His Work. John Lane. 1928
MCLEAN, RUARI: *Modern Book Design.* Faber. 1958
Victorian Book Design. Faber. 1963
MADSEN, STEPHEN TSCHUDI: *Sources of Art Nouveau.* New York: George Wittenborn. 1956
MEYNELL, FRANCIS: *English Printed Books.* Collins. 1946
MILLARD, CHRISTOPHER: *The Printed Work of Claud Lovat Fraser.* Henry Danielson. 1923
MOORE, T. STURGE: *Albrecht Altdorfer.* Little Engravings: Unicorn Press. 1902
A Brief Account of the Origin of the Eragny Press. Eragny Press. 1903
Art and Life. Methuen. 1910
Charles Ricketts, R.A. Cassell. 1933
MORISON, STANLEY: *Type Designs of Past and Present.* The Fleuron. 1926
MORRIS, MAY: *William Morris: Artist Writer Socialist.* 2 vols. Basil Blackwell. 1936
O'SULLIVAN, VINCENT: *Aspects of Wilde.* Constable. 193
PALGRAVE, FRANCIS TURNER: *Essays on Art.* Macmillan. 1866
PENNELL, JOSEPH: *Modern Illustration.* George Bell. 1895
PENNELL, JOSEPH and ELIZABETH ROBINS: *The Life of James McNeill Whistler.* 2 vols. Heinemann. 1908
PEVSNER, NIKOLAUS: *Pioneers of the Modern Movement from William Morris to Walter Gropius.* Faber. 1936. (Revised Penguin edition, *Pioneers of Modern Design,* 1960)
REID, FORREST: *Illustrators of the Sixties.* Faber. 1928

RHEIMS, MAURICE: *L'Art 1900*. Paris: Arts et Métiers Graphiques. 1965

RICHARDSON, DOROTHY: *John Austen and the Inseparables*. William Jackson. 1930

RICKETTS, CHARLES: *A Defence of the Revival of Printing*. Vale Press. 1899

Pages on Art. Constable. 1913

Recollections of Oscar Wilde. Nonesuch Press. 1932

Self Portrait. Letters and Journals edited by Cecil Lewis. Peter Davies. 1939

RICKETTS, CHARLES, and PISSARRO, LUCIEN: *De la Typographie et de l'Harmonie de la Page Imprimée. William Morris et son Influence sur les Arts et Métiers*. Vale Press. 1898

ROSE, MARY TWEEDIE STODART: *Alexander Rose and his grandson Robert Traill Rose*. Edinburgh: C. J. Cousland. 1953

ROSS, MARGERY (ed): *Robert Ross, Friend of Friends*. Jonathan Cape. 1952

ROTHENSTEIN, JOHN: *The Artists of the 1890s*. Routledge. 1928

The Life and Death of Conder. Dent. 1938

ROSS, ROBERT: *Aubrey Beardsley*. 1909

Forty-Three Drawings by Alastair. With a Note of Exclamation. John Lane. 1914

SCHMUTZLER, ROBERT: *Art Nouveau*. Thames and Hudson. 1964

SELZ, PETER, and CONSTANTINE, MILDRED (eds): *Art Nouveau*. Art and Design at the Turn of the Century. New York: The Museum of Modern Art. 1959

SKETCHLEY, R. E. D.: *English Book Illustration of To-Day*. Kegan Paul. 1903

SPARLING, H. HALLIDAY: *The Kelmscott Press and William Morris, Master-Craftsman*. Macmillan. 1924

Studio Special Numbers: *The Art of the Book*. Edited by Charles Holme. 1914

Modern Book Illustrators and Their Work. Edited by C. Geoffrey Holme and Ernest G. Halton. Text by M. C. Salaman. 1914

British Book Illustration Yesterday and Today.

Edited by Geoffrey Holme. Commentary by Malcolm C. Salaman. 1923

Modern Bookbindings and Their Designers. Winter 1899 - 1900

SULLIVAN, EDMUND J.: *The Art of Illustration.* Chapman and Hall. 1921

SYMONS, ARTHUR: *Aubrey Beardsley.* Unicorn Press. 1898

THORPE, JAMES: *English Illustration: The Nineties.* Faber. 1935

Edmund Sullivan. Art and Technics. 1948

VALLANCE, AYMER: *The Decorative Art of Sir Edward Burne-Jones, Baronet.* The Arts Journal. 1900

WALKER, R. A. (ed): *Letters from Aubrey Beardsley to Leonard Smithers.* The First Edition Club. 1937

WHEATLEY, HENRY B.: *Catalogue of the Loan Exhibition of Modern Illustration.* Victoria and Albert Museum. 1901

WHITE, GLEESON: *English Illustration. 'The Sixties': 1857-70.* Constable. 1897

WILLIAMSON, GEORGE C.: *George J. Pinwell and His Works.* George Bell. 1900

Murray Marks and His Friends. John Lane. 1919

YEATS, W. B.: *A Book of Images.* Drawn by William T. Horton and Introduced by W. B. Yeats. Unicorn Press. 1898

Ideas of Good and Evil. A. H. Bullen. 1903

Index